Girl of Steel

Girl of Steel

Essays on Television's Supergirl and Fourth-Wave Feminism

Edited by MELISSA WEHLER *and* TIM RAYBORN

McFarland & Company, Inc., Publishers
Jefferson, North Carolina

ALSO OF INTEREST BY TIM RAYBORN
AND FROM McFARLAND

Jessica Jones, Scarred Superhero: Essays on Gender, Trauma and Addiction in the Netflix Series, coedited with Abigail Keyes (2018)

A New English Music: Composers and Folk Traditions in England's Musical Renaissance from the Late 19th to the Mid–20th Century (2016)

Against the Friars: Antifraternalism in Medieval France and England (2014)

The Violent Pilgrimage: Christians, Muslims and Holy Conflicts, 850–1150 (2013)

ISBN (print) 978-1-4766-7201-4
ISBN (ebook) 978-1-4766-3937-6

LIBRARY OF CONGRESS AND BRITISH LIBRARY
CATALOGUING DATA ARE AVAILABLE

Library of Congress Control Number 2020009064

© 2020 Melissa Wehler and Tim Rayborn. All rights reserved

No part of this book may be reproduced or transmitted in any form or by any means, electronic or mechanical, including photocopying or recording, or by any information storage and retrieval system, without permission in writing from the publisher.

Front cover images © 2020 Shutterstock

Printed in the United States of America

McFarland & Company, Inc., Publishers
  Box 611, Jefferson, North Carolina 28640
    www.mcfarlandpub.com

In loving memory of my Girl of Steel,
Kathy Wehler—M.W.

Table of Contents

"Our Girl": An Introduction to Essays on the *Supergirl*
Television Series
   MELISSA WEHLER *and* TIM RAYBORN   1

Why Not Superwoman?
Constructing the Feminism of *Supergirl*

What to Do with *Supergirl*? Fairy Tale Tropes, Female Power
and Conflicted Feminist Discourse
   MARCIE PANUTSOS ROVAN   11

The Super "It" Girl: A New Brand for a Classic Icon
   MELISSA WEHLER   27

Lies, Damned Lies and Relationships: The Deceits and Secrets
That Plague the Couples of *Supergirl*, Season 2
   TIM RAYBORN   45

Supergirl and Lena Luthor: Constructing Public
and Private Personas
   JOHANNA CHURCH   65

Female Otherness and Intersectionality
in *Supergirl*

"Pull up your big-girl pants, and own your power": Feminist
Anger and the Working Woman in The CW's *Supergirl*
   JUSTIN WIGARD   85

Krypton's Rage: Contrasting the Emotions and Powers
of Supergirl in Television and the *New 52*
   NICHOLAS WILLIAM MOLL   102

"I embraced who I am and I don't want to stop":
Queering *Supergirl*
    JAIME CHRIS WEIDA   118

"It's real, you're real, and you deserve a full, happy life":
Supergirl's "Sanvers" as an Affirmation to Queer Tumblr
Fangirls Everywhere
    CHELSEA M. GIBBS   140

Supergirl's Sisterhoods: Feminism as a Family Affair

Sisterhood of Steel: The Powerful Bond That Is the Heart of The CW's *Supergirl*
    DONNA J. CROMEANS   161

"Women of power and the mothers who molded them":
Matriarchal Mentorship and Symbols of Sisterhood
in *Supergirl*
    COURTNEY LEE WEIDA   180

El Mayarah: The Danvers Sisters as Chosen Family
    SARAH J. PALM   199

About the Contributors   217

Index   219

"Our Girl"

An Introduction to Essays on the Supergirl Television Series

MELISSA WEHLER *and* TIM RAYBORN

Supergirl first flew onto our screens in October 2015, courtesy of Greg Berlanti's production company that had also brought the DC Comics *Arrow* and *The Flash* to The CW network. Created by producers Ali Adler and Andrew Kreisberg, it was set in a separate universe from the other DC series and initially kept apart, but the guest appearance by Barry Allen/The Flash in the first season hinted at more crossover potential between the three series in the future.[1] When CBS opted not to renew *Supergirl* for a second season, the series moved to The CW and has since become more integrated into the "multiverse" of Berlanti's other DC series.[2] Yet, despite being part of a multiverse, *Supergirl* immediately distinguished itself from the other DC series with its focus on women as the main characters. In addition to the lead, the series departed from its comic book source in creating a new character, Alex Danvers, the older, adoptive sister of Kara, otherwise known as Supergirl. For many viewers, the Danvers sisters' relationship became the core of the series. Many fan-favorite scenes occurred in the episodes with a quiet moment between the sisters on Kara's couch. The series also features other powerful female characters, including Cat Grant, media entrepreneur, Lena Luthor, business mogul, Lucy Lane, prosecutor turned DEO director, and Maggie Sawyer, no-nonsense police officer. These characters are often pitted against equally powerful female villains, such as Astra In-Ze, Livewire (also known as Leslie Willis), Silver Banshee (also known as Siobhan Smythe), and Indigo. There are also characters that operate in liminal spaces between heroism and villainy, such as M'gann M'orzz and Reign (Samantha Arias), that complicate any attempt to characterize the women of the series as a "good-bad" dichotomy.

2   Introduction

Core dynamics of the series changed somewhat in the second season, when the series adopted some of the tropes more familiar to The CW's programs. Kara and Alex, along with several other characters, found themselves enmeshed in romantic relationships. While this shift was applauded by some, others saw the change in focus as a drift away from the original themes of sisterhood and family in the first season. However, it did allow for the series to explore emotional storylines in more detail, including one of the most praised character arcs of the series: the coming-out of Alex Danvers, which earned a GLAAD award nomination. The diverse pantheon of female characters allows the series to explore different conversations about the female experience, as many of these characters represent a complex, realistic portrayal of intersectional fourth-wave feminism. Thus, as a series frequently devoted to women's issues and featuring prominent female characters as leads, a book studying these themes is timely.

Supergirl *Revised*

Supergirl premiered in 2015, seven years after the beginning of fourth-wave feminism.[3] Fourth-wave feminism has been defined by its use of the internet as the mechanism for its messaging as well as how it uses that mechanism to create a "call-out" culture "in which sexism or misogyny can be 'called out' and challenged. This culture is indicative of the continuing influence of the third wave, with its focus on micropolitics and challenging sexism and misogyny insofar as they appear in everyday rhetoric, advertising, film, television and literature, the media, and so on."[4] Using online platforms, fourth-wave feminism has been largely defined by its "calling out" of rape culture, toxic masculinity, and exclusionary identity politics.[5] As an emerging movement and object of academic study, the fourth wave is still actively being defined, and this collection of essays contributes to this scholarly conversation.[6]

The most notable engagement with contemporary feminism in the series is that no single character embodies a feminist "ideal"—an idea challenged by third-wave feminism and exploded by conversations about the urgency of intersectionality and inclusion in the fourth wave. Rather, each character represents certain attributes of the contemporary feminist conversation. Kara, Lena, Lucy, and Alex, for instance, demand that the characters and the audience view millennial feminists and feminism as legitimate benefactors of third-wave feminism. Their feminism relies on self-creation—self-confidence, self-actualization, and self-care—that they leverage to enact institutional and societal change. Viewers watch these characters continuously struggle, succeed, and fail in their self-creation in ways that are realistic, relatable, and representative of the audience's own experiences. Other characters, such as Cat Grant, Astra, and Reign, consistently disrupt clear narratives about what it means to be a feminist and refuse easy categorization. Often, these characters affirm a traditional feminist perspective one moment only to upend it later in the episode. The series refuses to take a clear stance on its characters' feminism demonstrates a keen understanding of how the conversation about feminism is now one about the plurality and intersection of *feminisms* rather than about one "right" kind of feminism.

Critics of the series could accuse it of equivocating when it comes to these discussions, but its unashamed embrace of progressive politics and themes—again to the delight of some and to the annoyance of others—would refute such an accusation. Thinly veiled references to real-world events are common, with some being more subtle than others. The series announces its feminist ethos by titling the second episode "Stronger Together," the slogan for Hillary Clinton's presidential campaign and the motto of the House of El. Moreover, the final two episodes of the second season were titled "Resist" and "Nevertheless, She Persisted," two phrases that have become feminist mottos and rallying cries for those opposed to the policies of the Trump administration.[7] These decisions knowingly insert the series into conversations about women's roles in culture, society, and politics. Moreover, the characters themselves do not shy away from taking political positions. Cat Grant, for instance, talks about supporting Hillary Clinton in her failed 2008 bid for the Democratic presidential nomination and "tolerating" right-leaning Fox News correspondent Bill O'Reilly.[8] She also wants to know if President Olivia Marsdin is "still a Democrat" after finding out she was an alien, implying that she cared more about Marsden's political affiliation than her alien identity.[9] Obviously, none of these individual moments make the series or its characters inherently feminist; however, taken together, they do demonstrate that the series thoughtfully and purposefully engages in these discussions, and they do so without being beholden to any dogma about the "right" way to engage in feminist discourse.

Super Girls from the Margins to the Mainstream

It is important to remember that the *Supergirl* series does not exist in a media vacuum, but rather within a context of other superhero and female superhero media that is also highly engaged in fourth-wave feminist discussions. *Supergirl* debuted at a time when female superhero characters, stories, and franchises were moving from the periphery into the mainstream. *Marvel's Jessica Jones* (2015) debuted to critical acclaim one month after *Supergirl*.

4 Introduction

Wonder Woman (2017) set several box office records at the time of its release and is set for a sequel; additionally, the female characters of *Black Panther* (2018) quickly became audience favorites. While these characters and stories differ in their tone, context, and style, they all variously assert their identity as a feminist project, rather than as a project simply featuring female characters. Critics have accused these works of being feminist (feminism being a negative descriptor in this context), of pandering to feminist audiences, of being too overtly feminist, of not being feminist, and of not being feminist enough. Actors, directors, and writers alike have been called on to explain and justify their approaches to female superhero characters and have been measured against the invisible yardstick of so-called "real" feminism.[10]

In this collection, we address the problem of monolithic feminism by mirroring diverse feminisms represented in the series. As such, we focus on the ways the series interprets, engages, and presents topics related to the female experience, including family, friends, and romance. Authors deploy theories and approaches from fourth-wave feminism in their explication of the series, supplemented by theories and approaches from diverse fields of academic inquiry, including feminism and gender theory, queer studies and theory, fan studies, and media and film studies. We limit our discussion to the first two seasons of the series, allowing authors in some cases to compare and contrast the approach that the *Supergirl* writers and showrunners have taken on two different networks. By limiting the scope to these themes and seasons, the authors in the collection are able to grapple with the conflicted and conflicting role of women in the superhero genre and engage in the emerging scholarship of fourth-wave feminism. Given this limited scope, Supergirl's rich history as a character, and *Supergirl*'s own complex mythos, it would be difficult for any essay collection to thoroughly analyze all aspects of the series. Our work opens up avenues for additional critical study on, for instance, the way the series engages with other social, political, and cultural conversations, including race, immigration, and incarceration.

Section and Essay Summaries

The essays in this collection have been arranged to contextualize the series in popular culture discussions and academic conversations. The first four essays analyze the ways the series engages with conversations about feminism and about crafting female identities. Marcie Panutsos Rovan, in "What to Do with Supergirl? Fairy Tale Tropes, Female Power and Conflicted Feminist Discourse," explores the conflicted feminist discourse surrounding *Supergirl* to argue that the series addresses the cultural need for a wider range of powerful female characters. She examines the ways critics argue over whether the series is too overtly feminist or not feminist enough; whether the hero is too feminine or not feminine enough; whether her story arc is too similar to or too different from that of a male superhero. Rather than suggesting an inherent weakness with the series, this essay argues that these critics represent a larger conflict within feminist discourse and a lack of consensus on our expectations for strong female characters.

In "The Super 'It' Girl: A New Brand for a Classic Icon," Melissa Wehler draws on conversations in media and gender studies to examine the dual function of media in the *Supergirl* series. She argues that the writers of the series engage with the legacy of Supergirl past and the expectations of Supergirl present. The essay explores how Supergirl is "branded" by Cat Grant, yet simultaneously rebranded and reclaimed by the *Supergirl* writers as a complex, 21st-century feminist icon.

The next two essays in this section examine the ways relationships are constructed in the series. Tim Rayborn, in "Lies, Damned Lies and Relationships: The Deceits and Secrets That Plague the Couples of *Supergirl*, Season 2," examines the four couples of the second season, noting how and why each uses lies and the keeping of secrets from one another and the consequences of those deceptions. He looks at theories of lying in interpersonal relationships and elsewhere, noting that there are larger secrets and deceptions at work in the series (Supergirl's secret identity, the DEO's existence) overshadowing the characters' lives.

Finally, Johanna Church, in "Supergirl and Lena Luthor: Constructing Public and Private Personas," explores the use of masquerade and identity in the series, using Kara and Lena as case studies. The essay analyzes Kara's and Lena's public and private personas and how these personas mimic social expectations about powerful women.

The subsequent four essays explore how the series engages with discussions of otherness in fourth-wave feminist discourse. The first two essays in this section explore the ways Supergirl is "othered" by her powers in the series. In "'Pull up your big-girl pants, and own your power': Feminist Anger and the Working Woman in The CW's *Supergirl*," Justin Wigard explores issues of anger as they manifest within Supergirl through a critical feminist lens, defining anger as an instrument of political and social change for working women in The CW television series. He looks to pivotal instances of anger and analyzes their ramifications in terms of whether anger constructively or detrimentally impacts feminist politics.

Next, Nicholas William Moll argues in "Krypton's Rage: Contrasting the Emotions and Powers of Supergirl in Television and the *New 52*" that the connection of superpowers and emotion is consistently presented as central to Supergirl's characterization in both the series and the comic books. Moll argues that Supergirl's emotions are alternatively cast as strengths and flaws in both the series and the comic books. The essay draws on media and franchise theories to explore the use of characters from the expanded DC Universe as a source of contrast with Kara in both forms of media as well as an examination of emotion as the keystone character trait in adapting *Supergirl* to television.

The next two essays analyze otherness by examining *Supergirl*'s impact on queer audiences and queer studies. Jaime Chris Weida asserts in "'I embraced who I am and I don't want to stop': Queering *Supergirl*" that *Supergirl* "queers" traditional superhero tropes and narratives. The series reverses the "male superhero/female sidekick or assistant" trope, repeatedly showing women in positions of power and passes the Bechdel Test. This essay proposes that *Supergirl* not only adds queer visibility to the superhero genre but also offers a much-needed opportunity to queer the entire genre as a whole.

In "'It's real, you're real, and you deserve a full, happy life': *Supergirl*'s 'Sanvers' as an Affirmation to Queer Tumblr Fangirls Everywhere," Chelsea M. Gibbs considers the Alex/Maggie relationship by looking at the history of LGBTQ and coming-out storylines on television and by examining the ways that *Supergirl* has sidestepped the most frustrating tropes. Further, the essay explores how this series and others place fandom and fan works into a new framework, as previous considerations (from Henry Jenkins and his followers) have represented fan works as "correcting" the flaws of sexist, racist, and/or homophobic treatments.

The collection concludes with three essays on how families and familial bonds craft the show's feminist narratives. In "Sisterhood of Steel: The Powerful Bond That Is the Heart of The CW's *Supergirl*," Donna J. Cromeans examines the evolution and power of the unique sisterhood between Kara and Alex Danvers. The essay looks at the elements of sisterhood that depicts the sibling hierarchy, the older protective sister, the bond of adoptive siblings, cases of sibling rivalry and squabbles, sibling self-sacrifice, and sibling relationship development. The essay also focuses on the growth and differences of the sisterhood in the first and second seasons and how near-catastrophic events help both women grow, making them stronger not only as sisters but as women as well.

Courtney Lee Weida, in "'Women of power and the mothers who molded them': Matriarchal Mentorship and Symbols of Sisterhood in *Supergirl*," contextualizes *Supergirl* as a collection of valuable narratives and symbolism centered on women's ethics of heroism and care, including comparisons to related feminist superhero tropes, with analysis centering on the wider inner circle of Kara's female family members and mentors who are privy to her three identities as Zor-El, Danvers, and Supergirl.

Finally, Sarah J. Palm, in "El Mayarah: The Danvers Sisters as Chosen Family," explores how and why Kara and Alex come to identify as sisters, dropping the qualifier of "adopted" entirely. In doing so, they enact "sisterhood"—and by extension, "family"—as a choice. The series consciously presents this "chosen family" as more meaningful than biological family through the use of language, action, and even musical motifs. Ultimately, the essay argues that the relationship between Alex and Kara taps into a greater cultural shift towards a broader understanding of "family" and an acceptance of the idea that true family is not simply determined by biology.

In the ever-growing collection of superhero television series, *Supergirl* remains unique. Viewers watch a female hero with almost godlike powers face the same struggles as the non-superpowered characters on the series. As a child, Kara Zor-El is discouraged from using her superhero abilities while she watches her cousin, Superman, applauded for using his. In the workplace, Kara Danvers learns about gender inequities through her boss, Cat Grant, who reminds her that women play by different rules than men.[11] As Supergirl, she works tirelessly to be taken seriously by National City's mercurial citizens, who are quick to point out when they believe she has fallen short of her th Kryptonian legacy.[12] Supergirl does not face these issues alone; rather, she navigates them alongside and with the assistance of dozens of strong female characters, who are heroes in their own rights. Cat Grant and Lena Luthor demonstrate the difficulties of being female entrepreneurs in male-dominated industries, living in a liminal space that they have had to create for themselves.

On a planet full of actual aliens, Alex Danvers and Maggie Sawyer's queer identities are the most alienating of all, and they struggle to overcome commonplace discriminations of contemporary society. These characters actively defy social narratives about what it means to be powerful women, and while they are set in a fictional world, their struggles are all too real to the viewers of the series, especially the female viewers. The women of *Supergirl*, like their real-life counterparts, are not always successful in their unique battles, but they demonstrate the importance of always fighting for truth, justice, inclusivity, and equal rights—the American way.

Notes

1. *Supergirl*, "World's Finest," season 1, episode 18, directed by Nick Gomez, story by Greg Berlanti, teleplay by Andrew Kreisberg and Michael Grassi, aired March 28, 2016, on CBS.
2. In late 2016 and 2017, The CW aired crossover events with characters from all of The CW DC shows teaming up to face common threats.
3. The dates of fourth-wave feminism range from 2008 to 2013. Fourth-wave feminism, as a concept, was already being discussed in feminist circles as a phenomenon happening in digital spaces. Jessica Valenti, founder and editor of the blog Feministing noted in 2009 that "third-wave feminists" were "20 years older" than the feminists of her generation and that "Maybe the fourth wave is online." By 2013, several books containing "fourth-wave" in the title have been published. Jessica Valenti, "Fourth-Wave Feminism," interview by Deborah

Solomon, *New York Times*, November 13, 2009, www.nytimes.com/2017/08/25/movies/patty-jenkins-james-cameron-wonder-woman-film.html.
    4. Ealasaid Munro, "Feminism: A Fourth Wave?," *Political Insight* 4 (2013): 22–25.
    5. Kira Cochrane, in her foundation book on fourth-wave feminism, identifies four areas of fourth-wave feminism that include rape culture, online feminism, humor, and intersectionality and inclusion.
    6. This collection adds to conversations by other fourth-wave feminist scholars, including Prudence Chamberlain's discussion of fourth-wave feminism, Nicola River's discussion of postfeminism(s), and Laura Bates' seminal work on everyday sexism.
    7. "Resist" became a popular protest chant and online campaign in the wake of the election of President Donald Trump. The hashtag, #Resist, began appearing following his 2016 victory. "Resist" was adopted by many on the progressive left as a way to galvanize protests and organize groups to disrupt the Trump administration's agenda. "Nevertheless, She Persisted" refers to a rebuke made by Senate Majority Leader Mitch McConnell who used the phrase to rebuke Senator Elizabeth Warren's objections to the conformation of Jeff Sessions as U.S. Attorney General. The phrase was immediately adopted by fourth-wave feminists as a protest against what they felt was the silencing of women under the Trump administration.
    8. These episodes are respectively, *Supergirl*, "Livewire," season 1, episode 5, directed by Kevin Tancharoen, story by Roberto Aguirre-Sacasa and Caitlin Parrish, aired March 28, 2016, on CBS and *Supergirl*, "Resist," season 2, episode 21, directed by Millicent Shelton, story by Jessica Queller and Derek Simon, aired May 15, 2017, on The CW.
    9. *Supergirl*, "Resist," season 2, episode 21.
    10. An important example of this phenomenon is when Patty Jenkins, director of the *Wonder Woman* film, took to Twitter to defend the film's feminism against attacks by another director, James Cameron. In an interview with *The Guardian*, Cameron stated, "All of the self-congratulatory back-patting Hollywood's been doing over Wonder Woman has been so misguided [....] She's an objectified icon, and it's just male Hollywood doing the same old thing." Jenkins responded that "James Cameron's inability to understand what Wonder Woman is, or stands for, to women all over the world is unsurprising as, though he is a great filmmaker, he is not a woman [....] There is no right and wrong powerful kind of woman." Andrew R. Chow, "Is 'Wonder Woman' Feminist? James Cameron's Comments Draw a Rebuke," *New York Times*, August, 25, 2017, www.nytimes.com/2017/08/25/movies/patty-jenkins-james-cameron-wonder-woman-film.html.
    11. *Supergirl*, "Falling," season 1, episode 16, directed by Larry Teng, written by Robert Rovner and Jessica Queller, aired March 14, 2016, on CBS.
    12. *Supergirl*, "Human for a Day," season 1, episode 7, directed by Larry Teng, written by Yahlin Chang and Ted Sullivan, aired December 7, 2015, on CBS.

Selected Bibliography

Bates, Laura. *Everyday Sexism*. London: Simon & Schuster, 2014.
Chamberlain, Prudence. *The Feminist Fourth Wave: Affective Temporality*. London: Palgrave Macmillan, 2017.
Chow, Andrew R. "Is 'Wonder Woman' Feminist? James Cameron's Comments Draw a Rebuke." *New York Times*. August 25, 2017. www.nytimes.com/2017/08/25/movies/patty-jenkins-james-cameron-wonder-woman-film.html.
Cochrane, Kira. *All the Rebel Women: The Rise of the Fourth Wave of Feminism*. London: Guardian Books, 2013.
Munro, Ealasai. "Feminism: A Fourth Wave?" *Political Insight* 4 (2013): 22–25.
Rivers, Nicola. *Postfeminism(s) and the Arrival of the Fourth Wave*. London: Palgrave Macmillan, 2017.
Valenti, Jessica. "Fourth-Wave Feminism." By Deborah Solomon. *New York Times*. November 13, 2009, https://www.nytimes.com/2009/11/15/magazine/15fob-q4-t.html.

Why Not Superwoman?
Constructing the Feminism
of *Supergirl*

What to Do with *Supergirl*?
Fairy Tale Tropes, Female Power and Conflicted Feminist Discourse

Marcie Panutsos Rovan

When *Supergirl* premiered in October 2015, I made the mistake of reading reviews rather than checking it out for myself. What I heard was overwhelmingly negative. Though I do not remember the specific criticisms, they all seemed to center on the show's problematic relationship with feminism—the idea that the series was trying too hard to be feminist and failing in the attempt. Coupled with my own objections to calling a twenty-something superheroine a "girl," this was enough to deter me from watching. Consequently, I was surprised when a friend and scholar I admire recommended the series and praised its engagement with gender politics. Intrigued, I decided to watch. Sitting down to view the first episode with a critical eye, I was prepared to affirm my original prejudgment. I was confused about why Kal-El was sent to Earth to survive, but Kara was sent to "protect" and nurture her baby cousin. I was irritated that a female Kryptonian would be told to repress her powers because her male cousin had the protection of the planet covered and "Earth didn't need another hero." I was insulted by Cat Grant's ludicrous explanation of how calling a millennial woman a "girl" was somehow empowering. I was prepared to write the series off, along with so many early critics. But, as the series progressed, it challenged me to reassess. Each new episode delivered new and admirable representations of female power and the challenges that come with it.

The criticism of *Supergirl*, though, did not seem to reflect this evolution in the show's gender ideology. Critics still complained (and still complain today) that the series is either too overtly feminist or not feminist enough, that the heroine is too feminine or not feminine enough, and that her story arc is too similar to or too different from that of a male superhero. At first glance, *Supergirl* seems to provide a compelling symbol of female empowerment, the "girl power" Cat Grant suggests in defending the name. Our heroine is strong, fast (faster even than her male counterpart), and virtually invincible. Despite this fact, she must repeatedly prove her worth to others throughout the first season. Engaging directly with issues of gender discrimination, the series engages in conversations of interest to feminist scholarship: collaborative female leadership, the impossibility of "having it all," the need for powerful women to repress their emotions, and the sacrifices and choices that women must make to be successful. Yet a quick Google search of "Supergirl and feminism" produces a host of articles and editorials that take the series to task for failing to promote the *right* kind of feminist ethos.

This ongoing barrage of criticism is the price paid for being one of the first contemporary shows to feature a superheroine. When representation is limited, we expect our token heroine to be all things to all people. Given the many conflicted discourses surrounding contemporary feminism, such expectation puts our heroine in a bind. If critics cannot agree on what they want from a heroine, how can they expect a series to deliver? The result is a critical discourse that focuses on the perceived problems of this representation, a discourse that is often contradictory. By entering into this discourse and analyzing the many criticisms of *Supergirl*, we can better understand the challenges of breaking stereotypes to create a space where a powerful woman can be whatever she chooses to be. My project here is not to determine whether *Supergirl* or Supergirl is feminist according to any particular strain of feminist theory. Rather, I seek to unpack the feminist discourse that permeates popular and critical responses to the series and illustrate the challenges of creating complex superheroines in a culture that lacks adequate representation of (super)powerful females.

The debate around *Supergirl* demonstrates a problem of interpretation. What do we as a culture make of a female superhero who does not fit into our binary expectations? *Supergirl* self-consciously reflects on gender biases by calling attention to the ways in which Kara's gender sets her apart from her male cousin. Kara's foster family (and especially her foster father) coerced her into repressing her powers and parts of her identity. Her earliest heroic actions were met with suspicion and hostility. She was labeled Super*girl* against her wishes and without her opinion or consent. Despite her heroism, she must constantly battle for the public's trust, amid media scrutiny that is colored by sexism. Kara has an origin story that is very different from her male cousin's, and her gender is a major factor in those differences. Citizens of National City expect immediate perfection from her and doubt her abilities; she is not afforded the same learning curve that Superman had. Even in the twenty-first century, it seems the public is not quite ready for a female superhero. Unsurprisingly, this problem extends beyond the world of the series to its public perception. This continued criticism represents the larger conflicts within feminist discourse and a lack of consensus on our expectations for strong female characters. By bringing these debates into focus and refusing to conform to any one set of expectations for powerful women, the series addresses the cultural need for a wider range of powerful female characters.

Supergirl criticism generally falls into two categories: complaints that the feminism in the series is overdramatic and complaints the show's feminism is seriously flawed or disingenuous. These critics sometimes use the same scene, conversation, or component of the series to make diametrically opposing claims. In the first category, critics complain that *Supergirl*'s self-conscious engagement in feminist discourse detracts from the storyline and becomes obtrusive. In the second category, criticisms range from pointing out the flaws in the show's feminist ethos to accusing it of "faux-feminism" or even of being actively "anti-feminist." A close examination of some of these critiques reveals more about the critics than the series and highlights the ways in which female representation is a cultural minefield.

In the first camp, critics argue that the feminism of the series is too heavy-handed and focuses too much on "buzz words" and slogans at the expense of plot. Alisha Grauso notes anecdotally that she knows many men who claim "the show has turned them off by 'pandering' so hard to women and young girls," declaring "they're right" that the series "spends too much time justifying her femaleness and the feminine in general."[1] Grauso argues that "the ham-fisted reminders of [girl power] forced into almost every episode are not only unnecessary, but more than a little patronizing to a female audience that doesn't need TV writers to justify them being on equal footing with boys and men."[2] Sarah Long also bemoans the way *Supergirl* "blatantly waves stereotypical feminist phrases in people's faces."[3] Others, like Lindsay Kornick, complain about the show's "liberal agenda" and its "questionable and obviously feminist setup" in scenes that suggest Kara is more powerful than Kal-El.[4] Laura Harcourt classifies the series as "unabashedly feminist."[5] She asserts that it "doesn't try to hide its liberal, feminist agenda" and that it "stop[s] barely short, at times, of Kara screaming 'FEMINISM!' whilst punching some hapless villain sunwards."[6] Jaromir Francois similarly accuses the series of "forc[ing] feminism down the viewer's throat" in its first season.[7] Jessica Goldstein argues that "The show is so defensive about 'girl'... that it overcompensates at every turn."[8] For these critics, the series is too concerned with seeming feminist to engage in genuine feminist discourse.

Beyond this self-consciousness, others argue that the series promotes a distorted or misguided vision of feminism, arguing argue that *Supergirl*'s feminist preoccupation is actually detrimental and sometimes insulting to women. Kaitlin Thomas points to Kara's "incredulity" that Cat Grant is both a powerful CEO and a mother as evidence that the show's insistence on pointing out its own feminism can actually be harmful.[9] Thomas argues that powerful female characters like Cat hold more sway when an audience sees this as a normal without the series calling attention to how unusual it is. Even those who defend the show's feminism, like Derek Stauffer, acknowledge that "*Supergirl* doesn't have much of a deft hand exploring these issues. It is very black and white."[10] For many critics, *Supergirl*'s engagement in feminist discourse is so substantial and problematic that it can no longer truly be considered feminist.

In the "faux feminism" camp, critics like Angelica Jade Bastién cite the "surface level white feminism" as one of its biggest failings, arguing that much of the writing "seems like [the series is] patting itself on the back for even existing."[11] Bastién cites a lack of women of color, an insensitive joke about homosexuality with respect to Kara's "coming out" as *Supergirl*, and the reliance on "the feminist-lite message of 'girl-power'" as evidence that the series fails to engage meaningfully in the larger feminist discourse.[12] Cate Young agrees that *Supergirl*'s feminism "exists largely at a very superficial level" and notes its "glaring omission of women of color."[13] Several critics point to the lack of diverse female perspectives as a critical problem for the show's feminist credibility. These critics suggest that the show's dedication to feminism is superficial at best, evidenced by this lack of diversity both in racial representation and in acknowledgment of diverse viewpoints.

The "Supergirl" labeling conversation is a major point of contention for critics who argue that the series oversimplifies or misrepresents feminism. When Kara objects to the branding of "Supergirl," her boss, Cat Grant takes offense to her accusation that the label is "antifeminist" because it is calling the hero "something less than she is."[14] Cat responds that she herself is the hero for "brand[ing]" Supergirl and argues that there is nothing wrong with "girl" because "I'm a girl. And your boss. And powerful and rich and hot and smart."[15] She then suggests that if Kara has a problem with the name, then "isn't the real problem *you*?"[16] Several critiques focus on this awkward justification of the Supergirl moniker as evidence of the show's "faux feminism." Bastién falsely characterizes it as "some wonderful fake, white feminist tripe that encapsulates whats [sic] wrong with men writing ham-fisted feminist tales,"[17] overlooking the fact that the teleplay for the pilot episode was written by a woman, Ali Adler. Chelsea Donaldson similarly accuses the series of "mansplain[ing]" feminism.[18] Goldstein offers a more sophisticated critique of this conversation, noting that "the show's internal defense of the name 'Supergirl' does not make sense and invites more criticism than it effectively refutes," because calling a woman a girl is "infantilizing," Cat's explanation is "empirically ridiculous," as she herself would likely be insulted if someone referred to her as a girl.[19] She extends this critique of an admittedly awkward moment in the pilot to a critique of the show's feminism writ large, demonstrating how the series repeatedly misses the mark for genuine discourse. Nicholas Yanes sees this as a problem of "struggling to adapt the feminism of the 2010s to a concept from the 1950s/60s" and argues that this "unsuccessful attempt to justify the name" is emblematic of a larger problem in the show's failure to establish Supergirl as an equal to Superman.[20] While the justification within the series is admittedly problematic, dismissing the entire series based on the words of a single character seems just as absurd as Cat's explanation. Cat Grant may at times be a "bad feminist" as these critics suggest. Both her naming of Supergirl and her first interview, in which she immediately asks the heroine about her "plans to start a family,"[21] are uncomfortable moments for many feminist critics. But the problems with a single character do not necessarily undermine the entire show's feminist ethos.

The uncomfortable labeling of Supergirl is a frequent subject for challenging the feminist ethos of the series, but it is only a starting point for many critics who take the series to task for its "faux feminism." Another frequent cause for complaint is the show's emphasis on Kara's love life. Some critics claim that Kara's romantic entanglements somehow make her less of a hero. Bastién argues that *Supergirl* is far too concerned with the protagonist's relationships. Donaldson laments the show's emphasis on Kara's relationships, suggesting, "her strength is quickly diminished by the fact that her two male co-workers and teammates (James and Winn) are hopelessly in love with her for no apparent reason."[22] Donaldson also objects to the "woman vs. woman" competition and jealousy found in Kara's relationship with James' ex-girlfriend, Lucy, overlooking the way these two women form a friendship and later a collaboration through the DEO. Donaldson asserts that "the majority of the season is … wrapped up in love-triangle bullshit," claiming that this romantic intrigue is "the central motivation to her character" and "takes precedent over the plot."[23] This critique does not seem to be supported by a critical viewing of the series or by comparison to other superhero shows. The first season of *The Flash* is arguably far more focused on Barry Allen's love life and love triangles than *Supergirl* is focused on Kara's, yet criticism of that series rarely considers the hero's feelings for Iris as a weakness in his storyline. Critics are apparently less concerned about a love-struck male hero than a female one.

Despite the fact that these critics seem to be preoccupied with the gender dynamics of *Supergirl*, many of them ironically claim that the writers spend too much attention on Kara's gender. Grauso, for instance, states, "it doesn't *matter* that Kara is a girl; it's irrelevant to her being a superhero."[24] Francois objects to the "unnecessary drawing of attention to the inequality of gender" within the series.[25] Long calls the series to task for its failure to "illustrate that female lead characters don't have to be any different than male lead characters,"[26] and one commenter on that article advises that the writers should "write a script for a man and then change all of the pronouns from 'he' to 'she'" if they truly want to create a "feminist TV show."[27] Notably, this is what the writers have set out to do. In an interview, Greg Berlanti stated that the writers operate from the principle of "what would our code be if it were a dude, and let it be the same, and let the audience figure out for themselves what they think the difference is."[28] Matt Zoller Seitz acknowledges this principle in his review, noting that "the deliberate echoing of the original 1978 *Superman: The Movie* … [seems] like the show is flat-out saying, 'Here is, literally, the story of Superman—but with a woman' and calling out the audience for resisting such a recasting."[29] For critics like Grauso and Long, however, the writers fail in this attempt to neutralize gender differences. To these critics, the writers spend too much time reminding us that Kara is a woman.

Even on this question of how much attention the series should or does pay to the heroine's gender, feminist critics cannot agree. Celina Durgin counters Grauso's claims about the show's overemphasis on gender difference by suggesting that the real problem is the show's lack of acknowledgment of gender differences. Durgin criticizes *Supergirl*'s "questionable core assumption: that feminism necessarily entails women filling traditionally masculine roles in exactly the same way."[30] She points to the parallels between Supergirl and Superman to argue that having the same powers, abilities, and physical strength as her male cousin takes something away from Kara's femininity. Instead, Durgin would like to see Supergirl embody a "life-giving, nurturing, maternal strength that glorifies the womanliness of women, even when they're forced by circumstance to fight with fists."[31] She argues that having Supergirl fight like Superman is "deeply sexist."[32] To these critics, the series does not spend enough time reminding us that Kara is a woman. In other words, *Supergirl* demonstrates the wrong kind of feminism for Durgin and other critics as it fails to embody their individual ideals of female strength and power.

Beyond this infighting within various schools of pop-culture feminism about the myriad shortcomings that make the series fail in its feminist goals, several anti-feminist groups have lauded the series. Such critics have extended critiques of the show's feminist ethos to claim that *Supergirl* is consciously fighting back against feminism. Self-proclaimed "Men's Rights Activist" August Løvenskiolds claims, "*Supergirl* aims to drive a kryptonite dagger into the heart of feminism," based on a few key factors: Supergirl's original mission objective (she was sent to Earth to protect and care for her baby cousin), Cat Grant's dismissal of objections to the "Supergirl" moniker, Kara's preoccupation with dating, Supergirl's non-sexualized costume, and some blatant misrepresentations of both the series and feminism.[33] Løvenskiolds argues that Cat Grant "gives zero credit to feminism" for her success, despite Cat's frequent acknowledgments and critiques of the patriarchal system that limits female power and expression. He further insists that feminists are all about self-promotion; therefore, Kara is anti-feminist because she helps others.[34] Karen Townsend similarly praises the series for "pushing back on feminist labels of women."[35] In both instances, the series is "anti-feminist" because it does not fit the critic's overly simplified view of what feminism looks like. Thus, these ironic praises of the series can be attributed to the same category as critiques of its "faux feminism"; in all instances of "faux feminist" critiques, the series does not fit the critic's definition or view of feminist programming.

Fans and critics alike seem deeply troubled by the idea that *Supergirl* fails to live up to their expectations for what a superheroine should be. This media and fan criticism is exemplified in the microcosm of the series itself, through the media portrayals of Supergirl. When Kara challenges Cat's overly critical coverage of Supergirl by comparing the superheroine's missteps to Superman's early career, Cat declares that "Every woman worth her salt knows that she has to work twice as hard as a man to be thought of as half as good."[36] This statement serves as justification for the general belief that Supergirl, as a female, must be better even than the well-established male hero or face harsher scrutiny. The same notion seems to color criticism of the series. Grauso asserts that because Supergirl is "the first super-powered female character to topline her own show," the show "owes us to be better."[37] Bastién declares, "It's 2015, you don't get kudos for just showing up, for making a woman your leading character in a genre that seems intent on sidelining us. That's the bare minimum."[38] While her point is fair, her declaration reflects a larger cultural problem. In a genre where female representation is lacking, those who attempt to add female characters and voices undergo special scrutiny. Criticisms of *Supergirl* are just as unfair as media criticism of Supergirl the hero. Both the audience and the citizens of National City expect more from her because she is a woman. Supergirl is expected to be a perfect embodiment of female strength and power; a feminist icon behind all the varied strands of feminist thinkers can rally. In short, we expect her to "have it all."

The criticism of *Supergirl*—that it is not feminist, too feminist, or faux feminist—reflects the mainstream attitudes about feminism exposed by these pop-culture critics, namely that to be a feminist hero means to "have to all." Twenty-first-century feminists are very familiar with (and generally critical of) the concept of "having it all" in terms of the expectations placed upon real-life women. We have come to recognize the problems with this expectation, acknowledging that it foists an undue burden on women to be all things to all people. It creates an unrealistic and unattainable expectation for perfection. This concept, which is falsely attributed to second-wave feminism, actually originated in marketing and became popularized in the wake of Helen Gurley Brown's 1982 book of the same title.[39] Yet it is a phrase that has come to symbolize the "false promise of feminism."[40] As a culture, we are largely in agreement that women cannot "have it all" or be all things to all people. The mere suggestion that we can or should is bristling. Yet in considering representations of powerful women in popular culture, we seem to forget this basic principle. Critics expect the heroine to be the representational embodiment of several conflicting strains of feminist discourse. She must be powerful and strong and able to hold her own with any man. She should not be too powerful or "masculine." She must reject "femininity" and show that she is no different from a male hero. She must retain her femininity and the powers and leadership abilities that many see as uniquely feminine. She must not rely on others for help, as this is a sign of weakness. She must be willing to work collaboratively with others—and especially other women—as this is a sign of feminine strength. She must seek nonviolent approaches to conflict resolution. She must be willing and able to kick ass just like a man. The expectations are daunting and mutually exclusive.

Part of the struggle of contradictory expectations can be traced to our earliest literary experiences of gender. In her seminal 1972 essay, "'Some Day My Prince Will Come': Female Acculturation through the Fairy Tale," Marcia Lieberman explores the ways that fairy tale tropes shape cultural expectations for gender role behavior. Stereotypes about female power and gender norms are ingrained in us from a young age. In these stories, we learn that sisters compete for the love and marriage of desirable suitors, that a girl's beauty is her most valuable asset, that passivity and docility are intrinsic qualities in "good" female characters, and that successful marriage is the ultimate reward for beauty and good behavior.[41] Competition between females is central to many of these stories, and one of the competing females is clearly superior to the others in terms of both appearance and temperament. More to the point, these stories establish a dichotomy of female characters.[42]

Fairy tales condition children to expect female characters to fit into neat binary categories: "good" females are beautiful, submissive, passive, kind, weak, and demure; "bad" females are powerful, ambitious, aggressive, and often lascivious. Consequently, powerful females are seen as unfeminine.[43] These stereotypes are subtly reinforced through subsequent cultural representations. While there is some variety, the general principle tends to hold: weak characters are feminine and beautiful, powerful characters are masculine.[44] To be powerful, women must sacrifice femininity (or exchange it for a more sexualized version). Because of this pervasive cultural myth, we expect strong female characters to be strong in all things, as evidenced by some of the "faux feminist" critiques leveled at *Supergirl*. They are not permitted moments of weakness or frivolity; they should not be emotional or overly sensitive; they must work alone; and they should avoid romantic entanglements. In response to these stereotypes, there is a conscious movement within feminism to elevate an alternative kind of female power. Such criticism explores gender difference as an asset and looks at how female leadership differs from male leadership for the better. This branch of feminism dates back at least as far as the early suffrage movement, where women argued that female voters would be a moralizing influence on the political sphere.

No female character could possibly represent the ideal of every strain of feminist thought and trying to create such a character would result in an unrealistic, unrelatable, inconsistent depiction. Nevertheless, female characters, like female leaders in the real world "tend to be held to higher standards than their male counterparts."[45] In an article for *The Atlantic*, Sharmilla Ganesan explores the similarities among female world leaders and argues that one of the biggest commonalities is the need to overcome "the suspicion that they can't be good leaders simply because" of their gender. Discussing the "higher standards"[46] that these female leaders are held to, Ganesan argues that part of the problem is the awareness "that you are representing all women."[47] When there is a scarcity of representation, those who defy the odds become representative of their group. The same holds true in fiction as it does in life. Since Supergirl is one of the few superheroines in television and film, she is held to a higher standard, expected to stand in for women, or feminism, writ large. This expectation calls to mind Berlanti's motivating belief that "there's a dearth of female heroes across film and TV," and this absence places an extra burden on shows that try to fill the void.[48]

This is an unrealistic expectation. We cannot and should not demand that a single character stands as a model of female power for half the population of the world. Karra Shimabukuro highlights the problems of this representative mentality by drawing a parallel to male heroes: "We don't require our male actors to stand in as representative of their gender, so why do we expect this of our female characters?"[49] Expecting a character to epitomize female power basically demands an essentialist view of what that power entails. Attempting to reduce all-powerful women to a specific set of characteristics would be just as harmful as the blatant stereotyping that occurs in fairy tales. Women are diverse, and female power manifests in many different ways. As Shimabukuro notes, "We have to let go of our concept that feminist figures have to look or act in a certain way."[50] Supergirl should not be dismissed as a failed feminist hero simply because she does not fit the mold that individual feminists have constructed of their ideal heroine.

The perceived problem with *Supergirl* is that it represents both sides (and therefore neither side) of the binary regarding "feminine" versus "masculine" strength. Kara is beautiful, caring, and sensitive. She seeks out nonviolent methods of conflict resolution and emphasizes collaboration through her work with the DEO and the support of her friends and sister. She loves, cries, and feels. She is (initially) quite passive in her personal life and career. She even worries about what to wear on dates. At the same time, she kicks ass, demonstrating that she is stronger even than Superman. She is ambitious and competitive. She gets angry. She puts her duty to Earth above the man she loves. She represses her own emotions when necessary to do what needs to be done. Kara does not fit into the traditional dichotomy, and critics do not know what to do with a multi-dimensional female superhero.

Even some critics of the series acknowledge that "Kara Danvers is a complex being" rather than "the typical 'strong woman' trope."[51] Donaldson observes, "She's not brooding or angry…. She isn't ashamed of crying and she learns how to utilize her anger to her advantage. She feels things, and embraces her feelings, but also struggles with letting other people carry the load."[52] Others note, "Kara is relatable in her 'human' form" because she is both "awkward nerdy and silly" and also "strong, intelligent, fearless, and confident."[53] Harcourt criticizes the show's overt feminism primarily because it overshadows the multidimensional qualities of Kara's heroism, noting, "Kara solves her problems just as often with self-reflection, negotiation, and kindness as she does with violence."[54] *Supergirl* is not perfect; she is a flawed, multi-faceted character. However, these imperfections do not make her less of a hero and should not make her any less of a feminist role model.

The creation of this new contemporary Supergirl reflects a conscious desire to adapt the comic book heroine into a feminist role model for a new generation. In his study of comic book heroines, Mike Madrid describes the original 1960s Supergirl as "the ideal teenager of her day: pretty, perky, courageous, and obedient … with her good manners and selfless heroism."[55] This description could as easily apply to most fairy tale heroines. Supergirl was clearly on the "good girl" side of the gender binary, placing her in a surprisingly passive role for a superheroine. The larger problem with the original story arch is Supergirl's role in relationship to Superman. The series establishes "a parental status quo"[56] wherein a teenaged Supergirl remains hidden from the world until Superman deems her ready for action. She acts as "the obedient and dutiful daughter who does what she is told and stays out of sight."[57] Madrid further notes that "Superman is often shown as a harsh authoritarian parent"[58] who maintains control over the teen girl's powers, while she serves as a dedicated helpmate and "the ideal submissive daughter."[59] Supergirl's "adventures often focused less on adventure, and more on a quest to find love,"[60] as was true of most comic book heroines in the 1960s. As her character progressed, Supergirl "was never allowed to grow up into Superwoman," despite graduating college in the 1970s before reverting back to a teenager in the 1980s.[61] Not until the twenty-first-century television reincarnation does Supergirl demonstrate any impulse towards independence.

The television series corrects much of the inherent sexism of the original story and of the early history of comic book heroines in general. This Supergirl is an adult woman with a career and a measure of independence.

Although her powers are initially controlled by her adoptive family, who have taught her to repress them at all costs, her story begins with the decision to reject that lifestyle of repression and embrace who she is. Countering her sister's admonitions, she declares, "I didn't travel 2000 light years to be an assistant."[62] Although her Kara Danvers alter-ego is still very much a "good girl," her new identity allows her an opportunity to redefine who she is. She is still Superman's younger/older cousin, as in the original story, but she decides to find her own path to heroism. Rejecting James Olsen's suggestion of calling on Superman for help, she declares, "I'm not Superman's cousin, I'm Supergirl, and if I'm going to be defined, it's going to be by my victories and my losses—no one else's."[63] Far from serving as Superman's submissive helpmate, this Supergirl is a badass in her own right, capable of defeating villains who bested her cousin and demonstrating strength and speed superior to the Man of Steel. While romance still plays a part in her story (as it does in Superman's, Spiderman's, The Arrow's, The Flash's, and most other male comic book heroes' stories), that romance is subordinate to the main plot. Her actions and decisions fly in the face of earlier comic books' assumptions "that women don't have that same dedication to the noble cause, because their need for love is often of equal or greater importance than their quest for justice"[64] Her decision to sacrifice her relationship with Mon-El in order to save Earth demonstrates that Supergirl's primary objective is to protect the Earth at all costs, even at the cost of her own happiness.

Beyond the character of Supergirl herself, the series demonstrates a commitment to feminist issues in its development of villainesses and supporting characters. Rejecting the fairy tale gender dichotomy, the series features a plethora of powerful women, both "good" and "evil." Alex Danvers, Lena Luthor, Maggie Sawyer, and Cat Grant are all at the top of their respective fields and demonstrate a commitment to protecting the citizens of National City that rivals Supergirl's. On the other side, the series presents several formidable villainesses, such as Livewire, Astra, Silver Banshee, and Lillian Luthor. Each of these characters exists along a spectrum of behavior; they are not stereotypes but multidimensional characters with complex motives. The writers use this cast of powerful female characters to explore a wide range of female relationships that include mentorship, familial conflicts, rivalries, collaborations, friendships, and romance. Along the way, they are able to engage in an overt discourse of feminism and examine the impact of gender bias on the perception of these powerful women.

Supergirl's conscious emphasis on feminist rhetoric may seem a bit heavy-handed at times, but the critical responses highlighted throughout this essay demonstrate the need for these discussions to persist. Some critics cringe at allusions to the "Ask Her More" campaign[65] or questions like "How Does She Do It?"—yet these are accurate representations of the questions powerful women are asked. We are living in a world where Olympic gold medalist Katinka Hosszu obliterated a world record in swimming and a commentator credited her husband and coach as "the guy responsible" for the win,[66] while other female Olympic medalists, like Corey Cogdell, were not even mentioned by name but referred to as "the wife of" their husbands by news agencies.[67] This is a world where female actors are repeatedly asked about their diet or beauty tips while men are asked about their process or ideas, where a presidential candidate was supported with slogans like "Trump that Bitch" and "Life's a Bitch; Don't Vote for One." It might seem cliché to have a character comment that "Every woman worth her salt knows that we have to work twice as hard as a man to be thought of as half as good,"[68] but it is also the lived reality of many women in power. With that in mind, it is liberating to see a series with a media conglomerate at its core calling persistent gender biases into question, even obliquely.

Admittedly, the treatment of sexism in the series as seen it its pilot lacks finesse. Yet as the series progresses, its engagement with gender bias becomes more nuanced. In "Stronger Together," Kara explains her willingness to work with others to achieve her goals—a quality that differentiates her from her male cousin—by noting that "accepting help from people is not a shame; it's an honor."[69] In "Red Faced," Kara and Cat have a meaningful conversation about the politics of female power and the need for women to repress emotions. Where men's outbursts may be seen as a demonstration of power and force, a woman behaving in the same way would be committing "professional and cultural suicide."[70] Cat acknowledges that this double standard is unfair but counsels her protégé to accept it and to adapt her behavior accordingly. Later episodes deal with the struggles of balancing a career with personal obligations, including motherhood, family, and romance. We also see women collaborating in difficult work environments, struggling to distance themselves from others, especially men, and recovering their reputation after scandal. The series addresses many of the struggles that women face and depicts a variety of female characters and relationships.

Supergirl helps bring conversations about gender representation to the forefront by providing viewers with a heroine who is not perfect, but is instead flawed, multifaceted, and deeply human (despite her alien origins). The series avoids stereotyping female characters and offers examples of different paths to and representations of female power. Despite this fact, the series is still continually lambasted for not depicting the 'right' kind of feminist hero. Rather than suggesting an inherent weakness within the series, such pop-culture critics highlight the problem of expecting a single character to represent an entire spectrum of powerful women. Failing to acknowledge the many other representations of female power provided by supporting characters, pop-culture critics focus on the ways in which *Supergirl* fails to meet their standards for feminist heroines. This does not mean that *Supergirl* is not feminist, too feminist, or faux feminist. It means that she is a complex character rather than an ideal. The fact that the same debate followed the film adaptation of *Wonder Woman* two years after *Supergirl*'s premiere and then again for the film adaptation of *Captain Marvel* four years after *Supergirl* is further evidence that our culture desperately needs more powerful female characters represented in its media. Once female heroes are no longer tokens, asked to represent their entire gender, perhaps we will stop demanding perfection from our heroines and start celebrating them for being as multidimensional and flawed as their viewers.

NOTES

1. Alisha Grauso, "How *Supergirl*'s Feminism Misses the Point," *Film School Rejects*, February 4, 2016, https://filmschoolrejects.com/how-supergirls-feminism-misses-the-point-9f13020c691b.
2. Grauso, "How *Supergirl*'s Feminism Misses the Point."
3. Sarah Long, "How *Supergirl* Is Disappointing Its Feminist Fans," *SheKnows*, November 9, 2015, http://www.sheknows.com/entertainment/articles/1102071/supergirl-season-1-episode-3.
4. Lindsay Kornick, "CW's *Supergirl* Uses Superpowers to Further Liberal Agenda in Finale," *MRC NewsBusters* (blog), May 22, 2017, http://www.newsbusters.org/blogs/culture/lindsay-kornick/2017/05/22/cw-supergirls-superpowers-further-liberal-agenda-finale.
5. Laura Harcourt, "*Supergirl*'s Biggest Problem Is a Man, but There's Still Hope," *Screener*, October 9, 2016, http://screenertv.com/television/supergirl-dc-comics-dark-secret-eddie-berganza.
6. Harcourt, "*Supergirl*'s Biggest Problem."
7. Jaromir Francois, "*Supergirl* Season Two: Feminism in the Right Direction," *Comicsverse*, October 24, 2016, https://comicsverse.com/supergirl-season-two-feminism-in-the-right-direction.
8. Jessica Goldstein, "A *Supergirl* Investigation: 'Shouldn't She Be Called Superwoman?,'" *ThinkProgress*, October 27, 2015, https://thinkprogress.org/a-supergirl-investigation-shouldn-t-she-be-called-superwoman-a35aa5cc81be/.
9. Kaitlin Thomas, "*Supergirl* 'How Does She Do It?' Review: Why Are We Still Doing This in 2015?," TV.com, November 24, 2015, http://www.tv.com/news/supergirl-how-does-she-do-it-review-why-are-we-still-doing-this-in-2015-144777387456.
10. Derek Stauffer, "Is '*Supergirl*' Getting Too Political?," *Buddy TV*, May 16, 2017, http://www.buddytv.com/articles/supergirl/is-supergirl-getting-too-polit-64716.aspx.
11. Angelica Jade Bastién, "Showing Up Isn't Enough: Thoughts on the '*Supergirl*' Pilot and Its Faux-Feminism," *Madwomen and Muses* (blog), May 22, 2015, https://madwomenandmuses.tumblr.com/post/119617816648/showing-up-isnt-enough-thoughts-on-the.
12. Bastién, "Showing Up Isn't Enough."
13. Cate Young, "Exploring Supergirl's Flimsy Feminism," *Cate Young* (blog), February 29, 2016, https://www.cate-young.com/battymamzelle/2016/02/Supergirls-Flimsy-Feminism-And-The-Erasure-Of-WoC-In-Popular-Feminist-Narratives.html.
14. *Supergirl*, "Pilot," season 1, episode 1, directed by Glen Winter, story by Greg Berlanti, Ali Adler, and Andrew Kreisberg, teleplay by Ali Adler, aired October 26, 2015, on CBS.
15. *Supergirl*, "Pilot," season 1, episode 1.
16. *Supergirl*, "Pilot," season 1, episode 1.
17. Bastién, "Showing Up Isn't Enough."
18. Goldstein, "A *Supergirl* Investigation."
19. Goldstein, "A *Supergirl* Investigation."
20. Nicholas Yanes, "Why CBS Would Be Right to Cancel *Supergirl*: A Ratings and

Narrative Analysis," *Sequart*, March 31, 2016, http://sequart.org/magazine/63190/why-cbs-would-be-right-to-cancel-supergirl-a-ratings-and-narrative-analysis/.
    21. *Supergirl*, "Pilot," season 1, episode 1.
    22. Chelsea Donaldson, "Let Feminism Be Smart: A Criticism of Supergirl, and Why Media Needs to Be Better," *Medium*, October 13, 2016, https://medium.com/@cdisquick/let-feminism-be-smart-a-criticism-of-supergirl-and-why-media-needs-to-be-better-7b420a002a4c.
    23. Chelsea Donaldson, "Let Feminism Be Smart."
    24. Grauso, "How *Supergirl*'s Feminism Misses the Point."
    25. Francois, "*Supergirl* Season Two."
    26. Long, "How *Supergirl* Is Disappointing."
    27. "Alex" quoted in Long, "How *Supergirl* Is Disappointing."
    28. Alyssa Rosenberg, "*Supergirl*'s Creators Lean Into Their Show's Feminism," *Washington Post*, October 26, 2015, https://www.washingtonpost.com/news/act-four/wp/2015/10/26/supergirls-creators-lean-into-their-shows-feminism/?utm_term=.d14f0bc9b37b.
    29. Matt Zoller Seitz. "*Supergirl* Is a Smart, Feminist Series (and That's Why Some People Won't Watch It)," *Vulture*, October 23, 2015, http://www.vulture.com/2015/10/supergirl-review-feminist-series.html.
    30. Celina Durgin, "What *Supergirl*'s Feminist Cheerleaders Get Wrong About Female Strength," *National Review*, October 31, 2015, https://conservativenews247.com/news/201785_what_supergirls_feminist_cheerleaders_get_wrong_about_female_strength.
    31. Durgin, "What *Supergirl*'s Feminist Cheerleaders Get Wrong."
    32. Durgin, "What *Supergirl*'s Feminist Cheerleaders Get Wrong."
    33. August Løvenskiolds, "CBS's *Supergirl*: In Your Face with Antifeminism," *A Voice for Men*, October 28, 2015, https://www.avoiceformen.com/mega-featured/cbss-supergirl-in-your-face-with-antifeminism/.
    34. Løvenskiolds, "CBS's *Supergirl*."
    35. Karen Townsend, "Why CBS's *Supergirl* Is Anti-Feminist, Family-Friendly Viewing," *MRC News Busters* (blog), October 27, 2015, https://www.newsbusters.org/blogs/culture/karen-townsend/2015/10/27/why-cbs-supergirl-anti-feminist-family-friendly-viewing.
    36. *Supergirl*, "Stronger Together," season 1, episode 2, directed by Glen Winter, story by Greg Berlanti and Andrew Kreisberg, teleplay by Andrew Kreisberg and Ali Adler, aired November 2, 2015, on CBS.
    37. Grauso, "How *Supergirl*'s Feminism Misses the Point."
    38. Bastién, "Showing Up Isn't Enough."
    39. Jennifer Szali, "The Complicated Origins of 'Having It All,'" *New York Times Magazine*, January 2, 2015, https://www.nytimes.com/2015/01/04/magazine/the-complicated-origins-of-having-it-all.html?mcubz=1.
    40. Szali, "The Complicated Origins of 'Having It All.'"
    41. Marcia Lieberman, "'Some day my prince will come': Female Acculturation Through the Fairy Tale," *College English* 34, no. 3 (1972): 384–387.
    42. Lieberman, "'Some day my prince will come,'" 393.
    43. Lieberman, "'Some day my prince will come,'" 391–393.
    44. Lieberman, "'Some day my prince will come,'" 391–393.
    45. Sharmilla Ganesan, "What Do Women Leaders Have in Common?," *The Atlantic*, August 17, 2016, https://www.theatlantic.com/business/archive/2016/08/what-do-women-leaders-have-in-common/492656.
    46. Ganesan, "Women Leaders."
    47. Agnes Igoye quoted in Ganesan, "Women Leaders."
    48. Greg Berlanti quoted in Rosenberg, "*Supergirl's* Creators Lean Into."
    49. Karra Shimabukuro, "*Supergirl*: Not the Feminist Superhero People Want," *Sequarti*, November 29, 2015, http://sequart.org/magazine/61464/supergirl-not-the-feminist-super hero-people-want.
    50. Shimabukuro, "Not the Feminist Superhero."
    51. Donaldson, "Let Feminism Be Smart."
    52. Donaldson, "Let Feminism Be Smart."

53. Danielle, "Holding Out for a Hero: A Feminist Take on *Supergirl*," *The Radical Notion*, April 5, 2016, http://www.theradicalnotion.com/holding-out-for-a-hero-a-feminist-take-on-supergirl/.
54. Harcourt, "*Supergirl's* Biggest Problem."
55. Mike Madrid, *Supergirls* (Minneapolis: Exterminating Angel Press, 2016), 83.
56. Madrid, *Supergirls*, 86.
57. Madrid, *Supergirls*, 87.
58. Madrid, *Supergirls*, 89.
59. Madrid, *Supergirls*, 92.
60. Madrid, *Supergirls*, 90.
61. Madrid, *Supergirls*, 95–96.
62. *Supergirl*, "Pilot," season 1, episode 1.
63. *Supergirl*, "Fight or Flight," season 1, episode 3, directed by Dermott Downs, written by Michael Grassi and Rachel Shukert, aired November 9, 2015, on CBS.
64. Madrid, *Supergirls*, 61.
65. The "Ask Her More" campaign challenges sexism in reporting by calling on media outlets to ask women about their achievements rather than their appearance.
66. David Bauder, "Katinka Hosszu's Husband 'Responsible' for Gold Medal Win," *Huff-Post*, August 7, 2016, http://www.huffingtonpost.ca/2016/08/07/katinka-hosszu-husband_n_11378688.html.
67. Chicago Tribute (@chicagotribune), "Wife of a Bears' Lineman Wins a Bronze Medal Today in Rio," Twitter, August 7, 2016, https://twitter.com/chicagotribune/status/762401317050605568?lang=en.
68. *Supergirl*, "Stronger Together," season 1, episode 2.
69. *Supergirl*, "Stronger Together," season 1, episode 2.
70. *Supergirl*, "Red Faced," season 1, episode 6, directed by Jesse Warn, written by Michael Grassi and Rachel Shukert, aired November 30, 2015, on CBS.

Selected Bibliography

Bastién, Angelica Jade. "Showing Up Isn't Enough: Thoughts on the *Supergirl* Pilot and Its Faux-Feminism." *Madwomen and Muses* (blog), May 22, 2015. http://madwomenandmuses.com/post/119617816648/showing-up-isnt-enough-thoughts-on-the-supergirl-pilot-and-its-faux-feminism.

Danielle. "Holding Out for a Hero: A Feminist Take on *Supergirl*." *The Radical Notion*, April 5, 2016. http://www.theradicalnotion.com/holding-out-for-a-hero-a-feminist-take-on-supergirl.

Donaldson, Chelsea. "Let Feminism Be Smart: A Criticism of *Supergirl*, and Why Media Needs to Be Better." *Medium*, October 13, 2016. https://medium.com/@cdisquick/let-feminism-be-smart-a-criticism-of-supergirl-and-why-media-needs-to-be-better-7b420a002a4c.

Durgin, Celina. "What *Supergirl*'s Feminist Cheerleaders Get Wrong About Female Strength." *National Review*, October 31, 2015. https://conservativenews247.com/news/201785_what_supergirls_feminist_cheerleaders_get_wrong_about_female_strength.

Francois, Jaromir. "*Supergirl* Season Two: Feminism in the Right Direction." *Comicsverse*, October 24, 2016. https://comicsverse.com/supergirl-season-two-feminism-in-the-right-direction.

Ganesan, Sharmilla. "What Do Women Leaders Have in Common?" *The Atlantic*, August 17, 2016. https://www.theatlantic.com/business/archive/2016/08/what-do-women-leaders-have-in-common/492656.

Goldstein, Jessica. "A *Supergirl* Investigation: 'Shouldn't She Be Called Superwoman?'" *Think Progress*, October 27, 2015. https://thinkprogress.org/a-supergirl-investigation-shouldnt-she-be-called-superwoman-a35aa5cc81be.

Grauso, Alisha. "How *Supergirl*'s Feminism Misses the Point." *Film School Rejects*, February 4, 2016. https://filmschoolrejects.com/how-supergirls-feminism-misses-the-point-9f13020c691b.

Harcourt, Laura. "*Supergirl*'s Biggest Problem Is a Man, but There's Still Hope." *Screener*, October 9, 2016. http://screenertv.com/television/supergirl-dc-comics-dark-secret-eddie-berganza.

Kornick, Lindsay. "CW's *Supergirl* Uses Superpowers to Further Liberal Agenda in Finale." *MRC NewsBusters* (blog), May 22, 2017. https://www.newsbusters.org/blogs/culture/lindsay-kornick/2017/05/22/cw-supergirls-superpowers-further-liberal-agenda-finale.

Lieberman, Marcia. "'Some Day My Prince Will Come': Female Acculturation Through the Fairy Tale," *College English* 34, no. 3 (1972): 383–395. http://jstor.org/stable/375142.

Long, Sarah. "How *Supergirl* Is Disappointing Its Feminist Fans." *SheKnows*, November 9, 2015. http://www.sheknows.com/entertainment/articles/1102071/supergirl-season-1-episode-3.

Løvenskiolds, August. "CBS's *Supergirl*: In Your Face with Antifeminism." *A Voice for Men*, October 28, 2015. https://www.avoiceformen.com/mega-featured/cbss-supergirl-in-your-face-with-antifeminism.

Madrid, Mike. *Supergirls*. Minneapolis: Exterminating Angel Press, 2016.

Rosenberg, Alyssa. "*Supergirl*'s Creators Lean into Their Show's Feminism." *Washington Post*, October 26, 2015. https://www.washingtonpost.com/news/act-four/wp/2015/10/26/supergirls-creators-lean-into-their-shows-feminism/?utm_term=.d14f0bc9b37b.

Seitz, Matt Zoller. "*Supergirl* Is a Smart, Feminist Series (and That's Why Some People Won't Watch It)," *Vulture*, October 23, 2015. http://www.vulture.com/2015/10/supergirl-review-feminist-series.html.

Shimabukuro, Karra. "*Supergirl*: Not the Feminist Superhero People Want." *Sequarti*, November 29, 2015. http://sequart.org/magazine/61464/supergirl-not-the-feminist-superhero-people-want.

Stauffer, Derek. "Is '*Supergirl*' Getting Too Political?" *Buddy TV*, May 16, 2017. http://www.buddytv.com/articles/supergirl/is-supergirl-getting-too-polit-64716.aspx.

Szali, Jennifer. "The Complicated Origins of 'Having It All." *New York Times Magazine*, January 2, 2015. https://www.nytimes.com/2015/01/04/magazine/the-complicated-origins-of-having-it-all.html?mcubz=1.

Thomas, Kaitlin. "*Supergirl* 'How Does She Do It?' Review: Why Are We Still Doing This in 2015?" TV.com, November 24, 2015. http://www.tv.com/news/supergirl-how-does-she-do-it-review-why-are-we-still-doing-this-in-2015-144777387456.

Townsend, Karen. "Why CBS's *Supergirl* Is Anti-Feminist, Family-Friendly Viewing." *MRC NewsBusters* (blog), October 27, 2015. https://www.newsbusters.org/blogs/culture/karen-townsend/2015/10/27/why-cbs-supergirl-anti-feminist-family-friendly-viewing.

Young, Cate. "Exploring *Supergirl*'s Flimsy Feminism." *Cate Young* (blog), February 29, 2016. https://www.cate-young.com/battymamzelle/2016/02/Supergirls-Flimsy-Feminism-And-The-Erasure-Of-WoC-In-Popular-Feminist-Narratives.html.

The Super "It" Girl

A New Brand for a Classic Icon

Melissa Wehler

Kara Danvers, upon hearing that her boss, Cat Grant, has nicknamed the new superhero in town "Supergirl," stammers a question that has long-challenged fans and scholars alike: "A female superhero. Shouldn't she be called Superwoman?"[1] Kara defends her indictment of the name with a familiar line of criticism: "If we call her 'Supergirl,' something less than what she is, doesn't that make us guilty of being anti-feminist?"[2] Unruffled, Cat replies, "And what do you think is so bad about 'Girl'? [...] I'm a girl. And your boss, and powerful, and rich and hot and smart. So if you perceive 'Supergirl' as anything less than excellent, isn't the real problem you?"[3] Though perhaps a little heavy-handed, this exchange establishes the show's approach to managing the socio-cultural legacy of *Supergirl* as both the subject and object of pop-culture critique. The exchange also recognizes the historical criticisms of the character of Supergirl as a lesser Superman—Kara's own "something less" argument—while simultaneously rewriting them. Cat's sharp defense speaks past the Kara Danvers in the scene directly to the audience: this Supergirl is not "something less," and if you think so, the real problem is *you*.

Drawing on conversations in media and gender studies, this essay examines the dual function of media in the *Supergirl*. First, I argue that media depictions in the series help shape Supergirl as the "excellent" hero of National City: altruistic, sincere, and powerful. These media interjections also challenge Supergirl by holding her accountable to the public and evaluating her powers in terms of the common good. Second, I argue that show's media also serves as a metacritique. *Supergirl*'s writers use the show's media outlets to directly engage with the audience and critics about the legacy of Supergirl past and the expectations of Supergirl present. Ultimately, just as Supergirl is "branded" by Cat Grant in the series, so too is Supergirl rebranded and reclaimed by the series writers as a complex pop-culture icon for the twenty-first century.

The "It" Girl: The CatCo Media Machine

In the series, the role of the media is defined by its relationship to Supergirl and vice versa. In parsing out the concept of media in the series, it would be impossible not to address the relationship between Cat Grant and Kara/Supergirl. For the purposes of this argument, I examine Cat's relationship with Supergirl through the lens of CatCo and the commodity-driven media market. We see this in the series when one character accurately summarized Cat's relationship with Supergirl as: "You've been a critic, you've been a cheerleader and some say that you are a friend."[4] As this description suggests, this relationship can be described best as dynamic, complex, and fluid.[5] Cat Grant the media mogul and Cat Grant the person are often difficult if not impossible to distinguish. This decision is obviously intentional not only by Cat Grant who brands CatCo with her name and in her image but also by the series' creators, writers, and directors who use her as a touchstone between Kara as a private person and Supergirl as a public persona.

The audience's first introduction to Supergirl is through the lens of CatCo Worldwide Media and Kara's position as the assistant to Cat. The first episode begins with Cat asking Kara to help her with the logistics of downsizing the *Tribune*. When Kara questions why the *Tribune* has to downsize but not their Metropolis-rival *The Daily Planet*, Cat reminds her of the realities of modern media: "Metropolis has a person who wears a cape and flies around performing heroic acts. *The Planet* puts this superlative man on the cover 54% of the time. You want to save the *Trib*? Go find me a hero, Kara."[6] In other words, modern media with its twenty-four hour news cycle is driven by interest stories, sound bites, and clickbait.[7] Superman fulfills all three of those needs, and thus, provides enough fodder for Metropolis to keep the talking heads safely employed. Cat's response positions her as a pragmatist when it comes to the industry. And while the audience will also come to see her in moments of optimism and perhaps even sentimentality, those moments are separated from corporate decision-making.[8] In this way, media is not an act of social justice or an attempt at conscious-building but a ratings-driven, financially-motivated industry where occasionally, important societal issues are viewed, analyzed, and discussed—so long as they turn a profit.[9] This is perhaps why we see Kara questioning her position at the company a few moments later: "I feel like I'm not living up to my potential. I went to work for Cat Grant because I thought working in a media company run by a powerful woman who actually shapes the way people think would be the way that I can make a difference."[10] Kara's idealistic outlook on the industry belies the fundamental truths about media that Cat expresses: media is a commodity, true, but it is also a consumer of culture with power to commodify things, ideas, and even people. Kara herself is a commodity in the media marketplace, whether that is as Cat's assistant or later as Supergirl.

For CatCo, the Supergirl brand is another product to be bought and sold. One example of Supergirl's commodification is when Cat berates Leslie Willis, "the shock jock National City loves to hate," for her demeaning commentary on Supergirl and its potential damage to the Supergirl brand: "But going after a young girl, insulting her body, how she dresses, her sexuality [...] I named her, Leslie. I am doing everything I can to cultivate a relationship between Supergirl and CatCo. If I could legally adopt her, I would."[11] While Cat's defense of Supergirl has the makings of altruism, it is wrapped into a conversation about branding and ownership for the good of company profits. After all, Cat is doing everything to cultivate a relationship between Supergirl and *CatCo*—not necessarily Cat Grant. Willis' attack on that relationship is really an attack on the CatCo brand and Cat's bottom line. Cat makes a similar remark about Supergirl-as-commodity later in the series when she reminds Supergirl: "I made you. And you are not going to let me down."[12] This exchange underlines the reality of the modern media machine where heroes are not born, they're made. Kara herself is uniquely aware of Supergirl's commodification when she tells James Olsen: "You know, I've seen so many pictures of myself recently, I'm kind of on a me overload. But this one feels different."[13] The "realness" of James' Supergirl is contrasted with the fakeness of Cat's Supergirl. One is a unique, candid work of art while the other is a saturating, mass-produced spectacle, respectively.

Later in the series, the audience sees the hero-as-commodity narrative come to fruition when Cat expresses doubts about the Supergirl brand. In the second episode, Supergirl accidentally breaks the bow of an oil tanker during an over-zealous rescue attempt, causing National City's bay to fill with oil. This incident makes for a politically awkward situation for Cat and CatCo who have created the Supergirl brand and subsequently tied their fortunes to her. Unsurprisingly, Cat's take on the scandal is one of financial interest coupled with worry about public perception of her reputation: "Now, when I branded her, there was implicit promise that she would be, at a minimum, above average. But in the past week, she has proved herself to be.... Oh, what is the opposite of super? #Terriblegirl?"[14] Cat's criticism here underscores Supergirl-as-media-brand and reinforces that the brand is the real commodity at stake, especially because it has slowly been synonymized with her own. Cat also alludes to the worldwide media outside of the series with the inclusion of the ubiquitous hashtag and the fickleness of public opinion in the age of viral posts, videos, and headlines. One day, Supergirl is a social media sensation; the next day, she is a hashtag campaign. While Cat's criticism is harsh, she does effectively make the point that with a mercurial media, branding is constant, fluid work.

To this end, the series consistently emphasizes the role of the media in shaping the narrative of public figures like Supergirl. Kara and Supergirl are constantly surrounded by versions of themselves in the news media, reinforcing the importance of the public's constant, watchful gaze. For instance, during the devastating earthquake, a distraught woman recalls to Kara, "I once saw a clip of Supergirl in the news. She flew someone over there to the hospital."[15] Kara, having lost her powers, is forced to see herself through the eyes of this woman whose father dies when Supergirl fails to show. The television coverage that once gave this woman and National City the solace of a superhero's seemingly omniscient presence is now a reminder of that superhero's absence. Like all acts of storytelling, the news coverage of Supergirl is made past as soon as it is present.[16]

Moreover, Kara often learns the difficulties of being a public figure and the impact the media can have on her relationship with the public. At the beginning of "Human for a Day," Supergirl has found herself battling a public-relations disaster following the accidental oil spill. Cat has decided to "take control of Supergirl's narrative. Save her from self-immolation, and scoop the *Planet*."[17] While Supergirl is the face of the brand, it is Cat's behind-the-scenes heroics that appear to save the day. All appears forgotten and forgiven by the end of the episode when a newscaster happily announces: "A dazzling display of heroics by the Girl of Steel now has a grateful National City asking, 'what oil spill?' Watch out, metropolis. Looks like we're about to give you a run for your superhero money!"[18] While there is some "television magic" happening here where problems can be resolved in an hour-or-less, it does serve as a reminder of how quickly a public figure can go from hero to villain and sometimes back again by understanding the media and working to control its narratives.

The audience sees a similar version of this media whiplash later in the first season when "Bizarro" Supergirl rampages the city. Again, Cat is forced to go back on defense: "All right people how are we going to frame this? Give me headlines that will grab eyeballs."[19] Reporters volley headlines like "Supergirl Gone Rogue" and "Supergirl? Super Menace?" at Cat who chides them for their lack of creativity.[20] It is not until Kara suggests, "Maybe it's not even Supergirl at all [...] Maybe it's an imposter? Pretending to be Supergirl? [...] I don't know, maybe it's someone trying to discredit her" that Cat decides to take a more positive approach: "I like that angle. It gives our girl the benefit of the doubt. It shows that we're choosing not to believe the worst in people. Yes, I can see the headline clearly now. The word Supergirl, with a question mark. As in, 'Supergirl?' That's good, that's good."[21] Again, while it may be tempting to read Cat's willingness to buy into Kara's more generous explanation as altruism, Cat is really defending the Super-"our"-girl brand.[22] Cat may want to believe the best in Supergirl, but the narrative Kara provides sounds at best far-fetched and a seasoned journalist like Cat should be loathed to pursue it, let alone it pursue it with such enthusiasm.[23] Unless, of course, like Cat, that seasoned journalist was working a brand narrative rather than an actual news story. Much like in previous episodes, Cat protects the Supergirl brand even when Supergirl seems like she's the one determined to destroy it. Cat's ability to "take control of Supergirl's narrative" throughout the series is a decided attempt to protect the commodity of Supergirl with the added benefit of protecting the super girl herself.

Other media outlets in the series are not always kind to their titular hero, and perhaps unlike Cat, hold her accountable to public opinion, helping to shape and reshape her as they do. Perhaps the best example of media as accountability monitor is the first season's most outspoken critic of Supergirl, Maxwell "Max" Lord. Kara describes Lord as "a showman who loves preening for the press" even while demonstrating a profound dislike for them.[24] He uses every opportunity to blast Supergirl in the media: "Forget about Supergirl's lack of experience, I'm talking about the trouble she'll bring to National City. Look at Metropolis. Since Superman's arrival, a veritable super bad guy war has been waged on that city. Their maintenance budgets have quadrupled. National City does not need Metropolis' problems."[25] His brand of fear-mongering is particularly suited for the twenty-four hour news cycle, which thrives on these kinds of sound-bites.[26] He uses an obvious analogy with Superman and Metropolis to draw attention away from the specifics of the situation—even while making sure to reference Supergirl's "lack of the experience"—to what he believes is the real issue of superheroes causing financial hardships in their cities and essentially inviting danger. He turns the very media that was used to acknowledge and celebrate Supergirl into a weapon against her.

Perhaps even more damaging to CatCo's narrative is Lord's uncanny ability to use media outlets as a platform for fear-mongering. He invokes such tactics later in the season after a devastating earthquake hits National City. Having depleted her powers in a previous fight, Supergirl is unable to heed the city's cry for help. Lord takes full advantage of the opportunity to criticize Supergirl's absence. Speaking to a news anchor, Lord tells viewers "this city's a powder keg" and "Just when the city needed her the most, she's nowhere to be found. The world's most unreliable superhero. Let this be a lesson to all of us. We need to rely on ourselves, not aliens in capes."[27] Lord's attacks on Supergirl damage the brand because they introduce paradoxes to the CatCo narrative: how can she be both savior and destroyer, citizen and alien, and hero and villain?[28] He does not need to prove any of these accusations because the accusations themselves are not the point. Rather, they plant questions, suspicions even, that will slowly erode the CatCo narrative. The damages he inflicts on the Supergirl brand is straight from the CatCo playbook, and he replaces National City's "unreliable" superhero with a much more consistent one: himself.

These moments also allow the series to engage in a metacritique of the way big personalities, like Lord, are given platforms to create fear and induce panic. He employs the rhetoric of fear that is a common formula within media circles: "Television news programs survive on scares. On local newscasts, where producers live by the dictum 'if it bleeds, it leads,' drug, crime, and disaster stories make up most of the news portion of the broadcasts."[29] Lord's "powder keg" rhetoric certainly applies this dictum while simultaneously weaponizing it against the "real" threat: Supergirl. He becomes the emblem of the fear-mongering media and exemplar of the damage it can do not only to the targets of its vitriol but also to the viewers of it.[30] Moreover, by giving Lord a platform from which to spout his negativity, the series criticizes a media who is too eager to promote the sensational over the substantial.[31] Lord, as both mouthpiece and symbol of the discourse of fear, acts as a reminder to the audience about the ways that media can be used by these larger-than-life personalities to shape, change, and propagandize for personal and financial gain. This certainly applies to celebrities like Supergirl whose public lives provide opportunities for such soap-boxing.

Unlike the real media, however, the show's media has a champion in Cat Grant who provides a counter-narrative to the toxicity of the Lord's rhetoric. Cat frames her entire counter-narrative as an alternative to Lord's discourse of fear: "There are real stories out there and they're not getting reported because Maxwell Lord is sucking up all the air with his negativity."[32] While Lord attempts to obfuscate his real motives, Cat sees the situation for what it is: "Look at Max. Using the earthquake as a branding opportunity. [...] well, I'm not going to let that bloviating narcissist knock my creation down just to build himself up. [...] we are going to counter Max's message about my girl."[33] Cat recognizes Lord's attempt to use the media to discredit the Supergirl brand in an effort to reinforce his own. Interestingly, her disgust towards Lord is not because he uses the media to achieve his own ends, but rather because he does so at the expense of Cat's own "creation." Like Lord, Cat sees the media as a personal marketing machine: she brands CatCo in her name, inextricably connects herself to the company, and seeks to reduplicate herself in her media protégés, including Kara, Leslie Willis, and later, Lucy Lane.[34] Her disgust for Max is that his branding is effective, potentially more effective than her own. To counter Lord's negativity and attempt to rebrand Supergirl, she employs the same spin, just in a more personally and professionally positive direction.

Cat's counter-narrative engages the viewing public by recycling Lord's "everyman" definition of heroism, but with some important differences. Instead of simply replacing Supergirl as the heroic figurehead for Lord, Cat appeals to the public to take on the mantle of hero: "We're all suffering through a major disaster. Now, you can react to this crisis by being petty and divisive or preying on other people's fears. And after all, it is human to be selfish. But isn't it also human to face our weaknesses and rise above them? Act like a superhero, even if you aren't one?"[35] Cat's layered rhetorical stance has a three-fold purpose. First, it undercuts Lord's attempt at branding, since he is the "petty and divisive" person "preying on other people's fears." Second, it positions Cat as the opposite of such persons since she is appealing to the audience's better natures to "rise above" human selfishness. Third, it reframes Lord's definition of superhero as something that anyone can achieve. Cat's retort to Lord's negativity also allows her defend "her creation" and deflect any damage to the brand that he attempts to inflict. She argues, "It's true. Supergirl has not been located yet. But her spirit stays with us, her insistence on seeing the best in people, a call for us to heed our better angels. Supergirl has faith in us. So let's have a little faith in her. Supergirl will return when we need her most."[36] Cat knows how fickle the viewing public can be and how easily they can turn on a once-beloved public figure, so she uses the media to rehabilitate Supergirl's brand. This move is an important one not just for Supergirl, of course, but also for Cat's company, which has come to rely on Supergirl brand to stay in business.

Cat's relationship with Supergirl mirrors the complex relationship between these characters and the Supergirl media narrative. It is no coincidence that Cat ends her response to Lord's "powder keg" speech with an appeal for positivity: "Call us, share your stories of heroism. Let's show the world what we're really made of. And, no, we can't do with Supergirl does, but we must choose to do what we can."[37] She knows the aphrodisiac of such feel-good stories, especially on a troubled viewing public.[38] Her motives are fairly obvious for media-watchers like Lord, who see the move as more about controlling the media and the messaging than a public service. When Kara tells him that she found his media blitz "a little surprising" and asks him if "people need a more positive message right now? Hope instead of fear?," he returns the question with "because Cat Grant says so? She might as well be Supergirl's PR flack, slapping that 'S' on everything just to make money."[39] Lord defends his stance as "realistic" rather than "cyclical," and while the audience might not wish to agree with Supergirl's nemesis, his point about Cat's drive to create and exploit the Supergirl brand is the very position Cat herself has articulated.[40] Cat is Supergirl's public relations manager in the first season. She even throws a release party for the magazine issue dedicated to Supergirl.[41] That is not to say that Cat does not care deeply for Kara or for

Supergirl, which she obviously does, but rather, these moments demonstrate Cat's savviness when it comes to using the media to encourage brand identity and loyalty.

The true test of CatCo's media narrative comes when Cat has to distance herself from Supergirl and allow her to finally take control over her own narrative. After being exposed to Red Kryptonite, Cat realizes that there is no positive spin to the Supergirl story and decides to "denounce her as a villain."[42] Kara, arguably Supergirl's other "PR flack," asks Cat to hold off her judgment, claiming that Supergirl will "be fine soon" and warning her that if she denounces her, "She'll have lost the city's trust."[43] In moment of humility, Cat speaks directly to the citizens of National City:

> As you all know, I have been Supergirl's most outspoken champion. So, you can imagine how difficult it is for me to tell you that I and CatCo can no longer stand behind Supergirl. I made you trust her. I gave you my word that she was safe, a friend. I was wrong. Supergirl has changed. She is unstable and extremely dangerous. [...] It's not easy being let down by our idols. Having someone who embodies our heroic ideals helps us believe that we can be heroes, too. Sometimes heroes fall. So, please, for your own safety, stay away from Supergirl.[44]

This public service announcement offers a hard lesson for CatCo and for Supergirl: media narratives are still accountable to the truth. No matter what spin CatCo puts on Supergirl, no matter how they "take control" of the narrative, there still has to be a plausible, identifiable truth to the story. As her "most outspoken champion," Cat takes responsible for her "creation" in a way that demonstrates true media accountability—not unlike what Lord advocated for.

Until this point, CatCo has been creating and controlling the Supergirl narrative. With this denunciation, Supergirl has to find a way to "win them back."[45] The only help she is going to get from Cat is this advice: "I said that it's not going to be easy. But I didn't say it would be impossible. Personally, I don't believe in failure. Not if you get back up and face the music. It takes time. But if anybody can win this city back.... It's you."[46] Supergirl does indeed have to work to regain the public's image and restore her sullied reputation. After the CatCo denunciation, a news anchor acts as the voice of National City citizens when saying,

> What was once a symbol of hope is now a symbol of fear [...] instead of the usual cheers, Supergirl's intervention was met with skepticism and fear. Some say Supergirl was under a mind-altering drug when she attacked the city. But she turned against our people once. The question on everyone's minds, what's to stop her from turning against us again?[47]

While this story does indeed provide Supergirl with the benefit of the doubt, it reinforces some of the same questions the audience heard from Lord.

For Supergirl, CatCo's denunciation becomes a defining moment not just for her public image, but also for ability to control her own story. Kara recounts her efforts as Supergirl to win back the city, including helping "a family assemble their IKEA table."[48] While earnest, these attempts do not sway public opinion enough to help recuperate her image. It is not until Supergirl risks her life to save the people of National City that she is able to finally turn the tide of public perception. Again, one of the National City reporters acts as the public's voice: "In one of the most remarkable displays of city unity I've ever seen, Supergirl's willingness to sacrifice her own life for the innocent has made her the hero of National City once again."[49] Supergirl has been able to change her legacy not by what she says, but by what she does. She does not have to rely on spin to help ingratiate herself with the people of National City and build her heroic persona, because she has (re)created her legacy based on her own work.

This moment also sets Supergirl up to use the media not only as a means of public relations but as an opportunity to further her legacy. At the end of the first season, the audience sees a much more media savvy Supergirl appear before them to warn them of an attack and to give them the "solace and consistency" that Cat tells her people they need from their heroes.[50] After Myriad takes over National City, Supergirl uses her new media prowess to alert the city: "People of National City. This is Supergirl and I hope you can hear me. We have been attacked. Mothers and fathers, friends and neighbors, children, everyone, suddenly stopped by a force of evil as great as this world has ever known."[51] In National City's darkest hour, Supergirl turns to the media as her greatest superpower. As television screens light up all over National City, the audience looks to Supergirl—literally to her face—to remember who they are. As her words fly through the airwaves, people turn away from Myriad and begin to reclaim themselves. With the Supergirl "S" appearing on monitors all over city, the brand and the icon literally save the day.

Throughout the first season, CatCo transforms Supergirl from "#Terriblegirl" into the "excellent" hero of National City. Supergirl becomes the hottest commodity in town because of Cat's efforts, and she is able to transcend her fifteen minutes of fame to become a household name. CatCo's "it" girl has withstood the proverbial slings and arrows of the media with no small help from the CatCo Worldwide Media machine. When the media machinery breaks down, Supergirl uses their formula to help spin and weave her own superhero story. Ultimately, like the series itself, Supergirl has to be the one to reclaim her own brand identity and transform it for the next generation.

The Icon: Reclaiming Supergirl's *Girl*

While Supergirl has Cat Grant and the CatCo Worldwide Media machine as "PR flack," the *Supergirl* series has no such champion in the real media to help it to reclaim, promote, and maintain the Supergirl brand. As we have seen, the media in the series functions as a space to unpack and repackage the Supergirl brand for the audience of National City. Of course, these are not the only audience members watching the narrative styling of CatCo. Series viewers also witness the way Supergirl and her brand emerge from relative obscurity to headline news. As such, the show's media spaces serve the dual function of creating and discussing the Supergirl brand and legacy for the audience, bringing viewers along on the same kind of narrative-building journey that happens at CatCo.

The series knowingly "brands" the Supergirl character by recontextualizing her for a twenty-first-century audience. Producer Greg Berlanti revealed the thinking behind the show's creation and its focus on Supergirl: "It should be strong and bold. That was our goal. One of the blessings of what we get to do is to introduce it to a new generation and that means changing key elements of the character and still keeping true to the core DNA of the character."[52] Part of confronting, and perhaps changing, the "core DNA of the character" is confronting that new generation's expectation of what makes a "good" superhero. One such expectation is to have a female superhero who can stand on her own and not be the "sidekick" to a stronger, more capable male counterpart. The series addresses these concerns in the scene showing Cat's and Kara's first tête-à-tête about Supergirl, a moment that producer Andrew Kreisberg, remembers as "We sort of wanted to have a conversation with our characters that we believed that the audience would be having, and that others might be having in terms of saying, 'Well, she's an adult woman—why isn't it called Superwoman?'"[53] Certainly, this moment stands out in the episode, leaving one critic to describe it as "stand[ing] out as a *bit* defensive" and that it, "seems to exist to preemptively stop real-life critics from bashing the 'girl' name, right?"[54] The moment is both preemptive and defensive, but it creates a confidence and determined line in the sand when it comes to the "new" Supergirl brand. The series producers were not so naïve to think that this argument would be enough to stop the critics entirely. After all, the series reprises the critique of the word "girl"—mimicking real-life critics—when Cat's mother, Katherine Grant, comes to visit: "Supergirl? Shouldn't she be called 'Superwoman'?"[55] Not only is this critique not new to the realities of the series, but it is also not new to Berlanti, who hears this line of criticism often: "We knew going in that Supergirl might imply a younger audience, but we felt we could take a powerful word back and participate in introducing that to a new generation and say that doesn't just mean young or inconsequential."⁵⁶ Moreover, as executive producer Ali Adler rightfully points out, Superwoman is also a different character in the DC Universe altogether.⁵⁷

Reclaiming Supergirl, however, is not as simple as reframing her for a new generation. Part of the rebranding efforts also had to account for expectations about a female superhero for a millennial generation. Again, Cat's mother provides a well-trod critique of the Supergirl brand: "So interesting, isn't it? A woman hero. I can't help but feel safer in Metropolis. Call me old-fashioned but I still prefer male doctors."⁵⁸ While her internalized female misogyny here is meant as an extreme, it does speak to criticisms of female superheroes and their strengths. Kreisberg provides a key insight into the decision-making process in creating a superhero who "isn't all-powerful" like the indomitable Superman: "There's a tendency with Superman to make him so powerful that there isn't really any danger. There are plenty of things besides Kryptonite that can take her down. It's not to diminish her, it's to make it feel like there's actual jeopardy to the show."⁵⁹ This explanation provides not only a logistical foundation to Supergirl's vulnerabilities, but also a cultural one: she's not a lesser-version of Superman, but rather, a more relatable one.⁶⁰

Moreover, the audience sees this reintroduction of Supergirl not only in Cat's defense of the word "girl," but also in the way the series uses media spaces writ large. In the first episode, a waitress watches a news report of Supergirl rescuing a doomed plane and tells Kara, "Can you believe it? A female hero. Nice for my daughter to have someone like that to look up to."⁶¹ The sentiment is aspirational, not only for the newly debuted superhero, but also for the series itself. Speaking past the Kara Danvers of the scene, the waitress addresses the hopes—and perhaps concerns—of its audience by addressing them directly. This "new" *Supergirl* understands the complex media nexus it is entering and the high-stakes for a character that is somehow both mainstream and marginal. The "Super" franchise is iconic in American popular culture, but the "girl" half has been an after-thought at best. Twenty-first-century audiences, spurred on by fourth-wave feminism, have demanded more diverse representations in a historically patriarchal superhero genre. Supergirl in the series and *Supergirl* in culture will be judged not only according to how they measure up to the history of superhero media, but also to these new standards of representation. This not-so-subtle moment does not just wink at this reality, but fully acknowledges the herculean task of rebranding the Supergirl legacy.

Supergirl herself wrestles not only with the Super*girl* narrative in the series, but with the concept of female heroes in the media in general. After being exposed to Red Kryptonite, Supergirl accuses Cat of pushing her into the same mold as other female superheroes: "You branded me in the media as a Girl Scout. 'Supergirl is brave, kind and strong.' Mmm-hmm? Isn't that kind of a stock characterization? Very two-dimensional. Everyone knows real people have a dark side."[62] Cat has indeed branded her in the media as the ultimate do-gooder and championed her as the exemplar of altruism, locking her into a narrative that makes her an "idea" rather than a person.[63] This moment also serves to deflect the criticism of audience and critics, who might wish to see Supergirl portrayed in a specific, singular way, rather than as a dynamic character. The accusation of turning Supergirl into a "very two-dimensional" character is a warning not only to Cat, but to the audience: this Supergirl is not going to fit nicely into any one narrative, so get used to it.

In addition to the Supergirl legacy, the series also confronts the gender roles, history, and impacts of its titular character. For instance, when Supergirl appears for an interview with Cat, Cat asks her a baiting question that is familiar to most women in the public eye: "Any of plans to start a family?"[64] Taking the bait, Supergirl responds that "Nobody ever asked my cousin these questions," which unwittingly provides Cat with the actual information she was digging for: the relationship between these two superhumans.[65] In this brief exchange, we see the Cat and Supergirl coopting some of the language and stances swirling in mainstream media about the sexist questions that female celebrities are asked during interviews, including questions about work-life balance and career versus family.[66] Viewers also see Cat intentionally invoking discussions of the media's gender bias and suspecting that as a millennial—especially the way that Cat defines them—Supergirl is likely to take the bait, which she does.

This exchange runs parallel to the next one between Cat and Kara, where questions about media portrayal of women and millennials again serve as metacommentary on the media within the series and mainstream media. In this scene, Cat has finished writing the article where the interview notes will appear and has given it to Kara for review—and praise. Kara's response, however, is far from adulatory, when she asks, "Isn't the tone kind of … a little nasty? Uh, I mean, the headline. Um, okay. 'Millennial Falcon. Every Generation Gets the Superhero it Deserves.' Supergirl didn't tell you how old she is. How do you know she's a millennial?"[67] As evidence, Kara reads the following excerpt: "'Supergirl embodies the worst traits of her generation. The earnestness without purpose, the unshakable belief that she has a right to be heard, even when she has nothing to say.'"[68] Kara accuses Cat of taking Supergirl "out of context" to which Cat defends her editorializing by saying, "I have given her context. I hate to break it to you, but the world is tough. What is she going to do when she has to face a real threat? Oh, I know, she'll call her cousin. Just like every other millennial who calls Mommy and Daddy the second things don't go their way."[69] In her retort, Cat draws on the narratives in the media that define millennials in a similar way: entitled, narcissistic, and self-important.[70]

Kara, however, provides a counter-narrative to Cat's and the media's spin on millennials, as well on Supergirl's place within these narratives. She claims that Supergirl "won't do that" in reference to Cat's accusation about millennials being codependent and weak, and in defense of herself and millennials, Kara argues, "I think maybe what she's trying to say is that when people are scared or hurt or in danger, they think of Superman. But that it's okay to think of her, too and not just as some consolation prize. She's every bit the hero he is. She just needs a chance to prove it."[71] First, Kara makes it a point to argue that Supergirl is not a "consolation prize" for National City, for Cat Grant, for critics, or for millennials. She's "every bit a hero" as those who have come before, and more importantly, she's a hero in her own way and on her own terms. If, according to Cat Grant's definition of millennials, that makes her the flag-bearer of her generation, then so be it. What Kara asks for, however, is a "chance to prove it." This volley is not only a defense against Cat's negative perceptions of Supergirl, but also against the media's dismissal of a still very young generation. Supergirl, like the millennial generation, has not really had her moment to "prove it" because people have not been willing to see her as a hero. When they are "scared or hurt or in danger," people have not yet given Supergirl a first or second thought, waiting instead for rescue to come in the form of Superman, an icon of a former generation. Kara asks simply for a fair consideration and not to be considered as a "consolation prize" in the eyes of the public.

In this way, her argument echoes some of the earliest writings about the millennial generation that positioned them as the "next great generation," celebrating them as civic-minded do-gooders who were going to change the face of American society.[72] Such arguments have given way to media accusations that millennials are responsible for "ruining" or "killing" the best parts of American society.[73] Kara's defense, however, seeks to reframe the media message, and turn Cat's headline, "Millennial Falcon. Every Generation Gets the Superhero it Deserves," from taunting allegation into truthful description: Supergirl *is* the hero that millennials deserve, and she is the hero that *Supergirl*'s audience deserves.

The relationship between Supergirl and media, whether inside or outside of the series, is fundamentally shaped and reconceptualized by the CatCo media machine. Within the confines of the series itself, the CatCo Worldwide Media machine churns out the brand identity for Supergirl. Cat Grant and her company create it, protect it, and advance it as a highly valuable commodity. Being the "it" girl, Supergirl must learn to navigate the media machine within the series in order to be taken seriously as a superhero and to create her reputation with the residents of National City. Beyond the walls of CatCo and the fourth wall of the series, CatCo does a similar service for the viewers of the series. Characters in the media space often speak beyond their immediate setting and directly to the show's audience and critics, and the series uses this space to address the hopes—and sometimes fears—of these viewers. Discussions about media and through media in the series help the show's creators and writers to address the Supergirl legacy past and present and allow them to draw very confident lines around their vision of Supergirl's future. CatCo's dual function for the fictional and real audience works to rebrand and reclaim Supergirl as a complex pop-culture icon for the twenty-first century.

Notes

1. *Supergirl*, "Pilot," season 1, episode 1, directed by Glen Winter, story by Greg Berlanti, Ali Adler, and Andrew Kreisberg, teleplay by Ali Adler, aired October 26, 2015, on CBS.
2. *Supergirl*, "Pilot," season 1, episode 1.
3. *Supergirl*, "Pilot," season 1, episode 1.
4. *Supergirl*, "Falling," season 1, episode 16, directed by Larry Teng, written by Robert Rovner and Jessica Queller, aired March 14, 2016, on CBS.
5. The audience also hears Supergirl's version of her complicated relationship with Cat during her Red-Kryptonite-fueled invective against her mentor: "You're the most arrogant, self-serving, mean-spirited person I know." While she is under the influence, the writers do not let her use that as an excuse, having Alex remind her that was some "truth" to what she said. *Supergirl*, "Falling," season 1, episode 16.
6. *Supergirl*, "Pilot," season 1, episode 1.
7. Cat understands the world of click-bait, as she says later in the series, "while bigots will always take the gold on the medal podium of my contempt, they make excellent click-bait." *Supergirl*, "Strange Visitor from Another Planet," season 1, episode 11, directed by Glen Winter, written by Michael Grassi and Caitlin Parrish, aired January 25, 2016, on CBS.
8. Using Cat's words, she reminds the audience, "You don't build a company like CatCo by being a wallflower not having an opinion and a strong point of view." *Supergirl*, "Hostile Takeover," season 1, episode 8, directed by Karen Gaviola, written by Roberto Aguirre-Sacasa and Caitlin Parrish, aired December 14, 2015, on CBS.
9. In speaking about the coverage of Senator Crane's much anticipated anti-alien rally, Grant demands that James Olsen "get us a quote that will offend virtually everyone." *Supergirl*, "Strange Visitor from Another Planet," season 1, episode 11.
10. *Supergirl*, "Fight or Flight," season 1, episode 3, directed by Dermott Downs, written by Michael Grassi and Rachel Shukert, aired November 9, 2015, on CBS.
11. *Supergirl*, "Livewire," season 1, episode 5, directed by Kevin Tancharoen, story by Roberto Aguirre-Sacasa and Caitlin Parrish, aired March 28, 2016, on CBS.
12. *Supergirl*, "Falling," season 1, episode 16.
13. *Supergirl*, "Human for a Day," season 1, episode 7, directed by Larry Teng, written by Yahlin Chang and Ted Sullivan, aired December 7, 2015, on CBS.
14. *Supergirl*, "Stronger Together," season 1, episode 2, directed by Glen Winter, story by Greg Berlanti and Andrew Kreisberg, teleplay by Andrew Kreisberg and Ali Adler, aired November 2, 2015, on CBS.
15. *Supergirl*, "Human for a Day," season 1, episode 7.
16. Later in the episode, Cat explains it this way to Supergirl: "You didn't scare me. But regular people, they're starting to depend on you. It's easy for them to feel abandoned. You have to understand most people out there spend most of their lives feeling isolated and alone. And when a tragedy strikes, they look to their heroes. Not only for rescue but for solace and consistency." *Supergirl*, "Human for a Day," season 1, episode 7.
17. *Supergirl*, "Human for a Day," season 1, episode 7.
18. *Supergirl*, "Human for a Day," season 1, episode 7.
19. *Supergirl*, "Bizarro," season 1, episode 12, directed by John Showalter, written by Roberto Aguirre-Sacasa and Rachel Shukert, aired February 1, 2016, on CBS.

20. *Supergirl*, "Bizarro," season 1, episode 12.
21. *Supergirl*, "Bizarro," season 1, episode 12.
22. The series also gives us other moments were Cat exploits her position and relationships to further CatCo. The audience sees this when Winn Schott is discovered as the Toyman's son, causing Cat to ask: "So, when can we set up the TV interview? He seems like a very sensitive boy. You think he can cry on cue?" *Supergirl*, "Childish Things," season 1, episode 10, directed by Jamie Babbit, written by Yahlin Chang, teleplay by Anna Musky-Goldwyn and James Dewille, aired January 18, 2016, on CBS. We also see this when she demands that Senator Crane be brought in for an interview after her change of heart about aliens even after calling her a bigot at the beginning of the episode. *Supergirl*, "Strange Visitor from Another Planet," season 1, episode 11.
23. The audience, of course, knows that Kara's narrative is correct, and that Cat's leap here will be proven to be not only risky but lucrative. It also paves the way for a later episode where Supergirl is exposed to Red Kryptonite and begins a rampage throughout the city, and Cat is able to brush it off as "Maybe it's another Bizarro." *Supergirl*, "Falling," season 1, episode 16.
24. *Supergirl*, "Human for a Day," season 1, episode 7.
25. *Supergirl*, "Stronger Together," season 1, episode 2.
26. We see some of the same tactics employed by Senator Crane during her rally speech: "Aliens. Extraterrestrials. Non-humans. Whether they're wearing a red cape or not, they are a threat to this country, our freedom, and our lives. Starting today, we need solutions. We need to know where they live, what they do and who they eat. Most importantly, we need to stop them from landing in our country. If it takes a dome, let's build a dome. It's time to stop talking and start acting. Monsters are coming for your families." *Supergirl*, "Strange Visitor from Another Planet," season 1, episode 11.
27. *Supergirl*, "Human for a Day," season 1, episode 7.
28. This question is never far away in the series, and the media is often used to give voice to such concerns. For instance, we hear the disembodied voice of an anchorman asking: "An unknown woman is hovering over CatCo Plaza with, it seems, the same powers of Supergirl. Does she mean us harm? Should we be concerned?" *Supergirl*, "Hostile Takeover."
29. Barry Glassner, *The Culture of Fear: Why Americans Are Afraid of the Wrong Things: Crime, Drugs, Minorities, Teen Moms, Killer Kids, Mutant Microbes, Plane Crashes, Road Rage & So Much More* (New York: Basic Books, 2010), xxix.
30. This line of argument is derived from media-effect theories in media studies, which is concisely explained by Dan Laughey: "'Effects' studies tend to have one of two main objectives. The first of these is a genuine social, moral and political objective to measure the power of media technologies to affect how individuals think, feel and act. The other objective—sometimes ulterior—is motivated by commercial interests and attempts to measure the effectiveness of media as vehicles for advertising and publicity campaigns. Media are often said to have effects but these can be benevolent as well as malign, depending on your point of view." Dan Laughey, *Key Themes in Media Theory* (New York: McGraw-Hill Education, 2007), 7.
31. Media critic David Altheide has argued, "Constructing the discourse of fear is a major accomplishment of the mass media and marks a significant change in the role of the mass media as a social institution. The mass media and popular culture to not merely report on events or issues. We do not merely obtain information from the mass media. Rather, a media logic and expansive communication formats have moved beyond the technology into the foundations of our daily lives. Virtually everyone is an audience member of some form of popular culture today." David Altheide, *Creating Fear: News and the Construction of Crisis* (New York: Aldine de Gruyter, 2002), 184.
32. *Supergirl*, "Human for a Day," season 1, episode 7.
33. *Supergirl*, "Human for a Day," season 1, episode 7.
34. As Cat's failed protégé, Willis provides an interesting contrast to Kara/Supergirl: "I should've pushed Leslie. Held her to a higher standard. The more awful she was, the more I rewarded her. Leslie turning into Livewire that started a long time ago. It's my fault. I turned her into a monster. I need to fix this. I need to talk to Supergirl." *Supergirl*, "How Does She

Do It?," season 1, episode 4, directed by Thor Freudenthal, written by Yahlin Chang and Ted Sullivan, aired November 23, 2015, on CBS.

35. *Supergirl*, "Human for a Day," season 1, episode 7.
36. *Supergirl*, "Human for a Day," season 1, episode 7.
37. *Supergirl*, "Human for a Day," season 1, episode 7.
38. This is not the first time Cat draws on the allure of feel-good stories. She turns to them in the previous episode after the debacle with Willis-Livewire: "About the paparazzi shots from over the weekend of the young stars and starlets, compromised in assorted humiliating ways. [...] The world is full of so much noise and snark, much of it we generate. Today, why don't we elevate the city's level of discourse instead with a photo essay of all the people who spent their holidays volunteering at soup kitchens and shelters. Let's not see if we can't bring some attention to those organizations." *Supergirl*, "Livewire," season 1, episode 5. She also says a version of this during an appearance on a local talk show: "Having a platform like mine is only worthwhile if I can use it to bring attention to the people who are really making a difference." *Supergirl*, "Falling," season 1, episode 16.
39. *Supergirl*, "Human for a Day," season 1, episode 7.
40. *Supergirl*, "Human for a Day," season 1, episode 7.
41. *Supergirl*, "Fight or Flight," season 1, episode 3.
42. *Supergirl*, "Falling," season 1, episode 16.
43. *Supergirl*, "Falling," season 1, episode 16.
44. *Supergirl*, "Falling," season 1, episode 16.
45. *Supergirl*, "Falling," season 1, episode 16.
46. *Supergirl*, "Falling," season 1, episode 16.
47. *Supergirl*, "Falling," season 1, episode 16.
48. *Supergirl*, "Human for a Day," season 1, episode 7.
49. *Supergirl*, "Human for a Day," season 1, episode 7.
50. *Supergirl*, "Human for a Day," season 1, episode 7.
51. *Supergirl*, "Better Angels," season 1, episode 20, directed by Larry Teng, written by Andrew Kreisberg and Ali Adler, teleplay by Robert Rovner and Jessica Queller, aired April 18, 2016, on CBS.
52. Natalie Abrams, "Supergirl vs Superwoman argument at CBS TCA," *Entertainment Weekly*, http://ew.com/article/2015/08/10/supergirl-superwoman-argument-cbs.
53. Emily Yahr, "Is the Term 'Supergirl' Offensive? The Story Behind That 'Girl vs. Woman' Speech in the Pilot," *The Washington Post*, www.washingtonpost.com/news/comic-riffs/wp/2015/10/27/is-the-term-supergirl-offensive-the-story-behind-that-girl-vs-woman-speech-in-the-pilot/?utm_term=.c3122c8dded7.
54. Yahr, "Is the Term 'Supergirl' Offensive?"
55. *Supergirl*, "Red Faced," season 1, episode 6, directed by Jesse Warn, written by Michael Grassi and Rachel Shukert, aired November 30, 2015, on CBS.
56. Abrams, "Supergirl vs Superwoman Argument at CBS TCA."
57. Abrams, "Supergirl vs Superwoman Argument at CBS TCA."
58. *Supergirl*, "Red Faced," season 1, episode 6.
59. Abrams, "Supergirl vs Superwoman Argument at CBS TCA."
60. In "Fight or Flight," Supergirl defeats Reactron, which is noted in the episode as something not even Superman was able to do. This moment identifies their abilities as comparable, but different.
61. *Supergirl*, "Pilot," season 1, episode 1.
62. *Supergirl*, "Falling," season 1, episode 16.
63. This moment references an earlier discussion Cat has on a local talk show where she describes Supergirl as, "everything you think she is. She's strong, she's brave. But the most remarkable thing about Supergirl is that she is the kindest person I have ever known. [...] She is an idea, she's inspiring us to be our best selves. Now, we can learn a lot from her. You can learn a lot from her. I have learned a lot from her. And I'm still learning." *Supergirl*, "Falling," season 1, episode 16.
64. *Supergirl*, "Fight or Flight," season 1, episode 3.
65. *Supergirl*, "Fight or Flight," season 1, episode 3.

66. There have been numerous social media campaigns, news articles, and opinion columns dedicated to the issue of the questions posed to female celebrities, including Alice Howarth, Claire Hodgson, and Charlotte Alter,.

67. *Supergirl*, "Fight or Flight," season 1, episode 3. We also see Cat having a discussion on millennials during a subsequent episode where she remarks on the historical realities of working women that millennial women seem to have just "discovered":

CAT GRANT: You have stumbled upon the most annoying question of the century, and you are so young that you do not even realize it. How do you juggle it all? You learn, that's how. You start with two balls before adding another. I figured out how to be brilliant in business and then I added being a brilliant mother. Far too many women burn out trying to do too much before they're ready.

KARA DANVERS: So you can have it all?

GRANT: Of course. Just not all at once, and not right away [*Supergirl*, "Crossfire," season 2, episode 5, directed by Glen Winter, written by Gabriel Llanas and Anna Musky-Goldwyn, aired November 7, 2016, on The CW].

68. *Supergirl*, "Fight or Flight," season 1, episode 3.
69. *Supergirl*, "Fight or Flight," season 1, episode 3.
70. Perhaps the most iconic example of this narrative is Joel Stein, "Millennials: The Me Me Me Generation." Other examples include Jean M. Twenge and W. Keith Campbell, *The Narcissism Epidemic: Living in the Age of Entitlement* (New York: Atria, 2009), and Christian Smith, *Lost in Transition: The Dark Side of Emerging Adulthood* (New York: Oxford University Press, 2011).
71. *Supergirl*, "Fight or Flight," season 1, episode 3.
72. The most influential writing on this topic was Neil Howe and William Strauss, *Millennials Rising: The Next Great Generation* (New York: Vintage, 2000). Other articles include Andrea Stone, "Civic Generation' Rolls Up Sleeves in Record Numbers," *USA Today*, https://usatoday30.usatoday.com/news/sharing/2009-04-13-millenial_N.htmeverything-a-millennials-confession/?utm_term=.9b5e5c622096 and Bob Herbert, "Here Come the Millennials," *New York Times*, http://www.nytimes.com/2008/05/13/opinion/13herbert.html?mcubz=0. These are emblematic of the positive, and perhaps, hopeful, perspective on millennials in the first years of the century.
73. These arguments have become so commonplace that it is now a point of humor, see Alendra Petri, "I Am Sorry for Killing Everything: A Millennial's Confession," *The Washington Post* (blog), https://www.washingtonpost.com/blogs/compost/wp/2017/08/10/i-am-sorry-for-killing-

SELECTED BIBLIOGRAPHY

Abrams, Natalie. "Supergirl Vs Superwoman Argument at CBS TCA." *Entertainment Weekly*. August 10, 2015, http://ew.com/article/2015/08/10/supergirl-superwoman-argument-cbs.

Alter, Charlotte. "Reese Witherspoon Slams Sexist Red Carpet Questions, Encourages Journalists to #AskHerMore." *Time Magazine*. February 22, 2015. http://time.com/3718008/oscars-2015-askhermore-reese-witherspoon.

Altheide, David. *Creating Fear: News and the Construction of Crisis*. New York: Aldine de Gruyter, 2002.

Glassner, Barry. *The Culture of Fear: Why Americans Are Afraid of the Wrong Things: Crime, Drugs, Minorities, Teen Moms, Killer Kids, Mutant Microbes, Plane Crashes, Road Rage & So Much More*. New York: Basic Books, 2010.

Herbert, Bob. "Here Come the Millennials." *New York Times*. May 13, 2008. http://www.nytimes.com/2008/05/13/opinion/13herbert.html?mcubz=0.

Hodgson, Claire. "The Avengers' Scarlett Johansson and Mark Ruffalo Answer Each-Others' Gender-Stereotypical Questions." *Cosmopolitan UK*. April 22, 2015, http://www.cosmopolitan.com/uk/entertainment/news/a35167/scarlett-johansson-mark-ruffalo-avengers-interview.

Howarth, Alice. "Ask Better Questions Calls Out Sexist Interviews." *Glamour Magazine UK*.

January 19, 2015. http://www.glamourmagazine.co.uk/article/askbetterquestions-sexism-in-film-movie-industry-woman.

Howe, Neil, and William Strauss. *Millennials Rising: The Next Great Generation*. New York: Vintage, 2000.

Laughey, Dan. *Key Themes in Media Theory*. New York: McGraw-Hill Education, 2007.

Petri, Alendra. "I Am Sorry for Killing Everything: A Millennial's Confession." *The Washington Post* (blog). August 10, 2017. https://www.washingtonpost.com/blogs/compost/wp/2017/08/10/i-am-sorry-for-killing-everything-a-millennials-confession/?utm_term=.02ff0129f4a7.

Smith, Christian. *Lost in Transition: The Dark Side of Emerging Adulthood*. New York: Oxford University Press, 2011.

Stein, Joel. "Millennials: The Me Me Me Generation." *Time Magazine*. May 20, 2013. http://time.com/247/millennials-the-me-me-me-generation.

Stone, Andrea. "'Civic Generation' Rolls Up Sleeves in Record Numbers." *USA Today*. April 13, 2009. https://usatoday30.usatoday.com/news/sharing/2009-04-13-millenial_N.htm everything-a-millennials-confession/?utm_term=.9b5e5c622096.

Tancharoen, Kevin, dir. *Supergirl*. Season 1, episode 5, "Livewire." Aired March 28, 2016, on CBS.

Twenge, Jean M., and W. Keith Campbell. *The Narcissism Epidemic: Living in the Age of Entitlement*. New York: Atria, 2009.

Warn, Jesse, dir. *Supergirl*. Season 1, episode 6, "Red Faced." Aired November 30, 2015, on CBS.

Yahr, Emily. "Is the Term 'Supergirl' Offensive? the Story Behind That 'Girl Vs. Woman' Speech in the Pilot." *The Washington Post*. October 27, 2015. https://www.washingtonpost.com/news/comic-riffs/wp/2015/10/27/is-the-term-supergirl-offensive-the-story-behind-that-girl-vs-woman-speech-in-the-pilot/?utm_term=.c3122c8dded7.

Lies, Damned Lies and Relationships

The Deceits and Secrets That Plague the Couples of Supergirl, Season 2

TIM RAYBORN

When *Supergirl* shifted networks at the end of its first season from CBS to The CW in 2016, a number of significant changes in content occurred that would see the show's sophomore season take on a different tone. In addition to a new filming location,[1] certain cast members departed and with them their characters—Cat Grant (except for the first two and final two episodes of the second season), Maxwell Lord, Lucy Lane, and others.[2] In response, new cast members were added, bringing several key supporting DC characters from the "Super" mythos into the story: most notably, Mon-El, Lena Luthor, Maggie Sawyer, Lillian Luthor, and M'gann M'orzz. Each of these new additions would have a significant impact on the show's main characters, whether as friends, lovers, or enemies, and sometimes a combination of all three. Attachments and enmity alike resulted in a large number of deceitful acts and outright lies between various characters, often with unfortunate and unhappy consequences. This essay will look at how those deceptions played out (particularly in romantic pairings), some of their causes, and their resolutions.

The Secrets at the Heart of the Series

One of the most significant changes in tone between the two seasons was a deeper focus on personal relationships, especially for the Danvers sisters, Kara and Alex. While Kara was given a "will they/won't they" plot with

James Olsen throughout the first season, this relationship was set aside at the beginning of the second season, with Kara expressing a desire to discover more about herself before embarking on a romance with anyone. In the first season, Alex, by contrast, was depicted as married to her work for the DEO and looking after Kara, with no time for a personal relationship or even a personal life of any note; much of her free time was spent at Kara's apartment.[3] Both women have their proverbial lives turned upside down by the entrance of new characters in the second season: Mon-El, a prince from the planet Daxam, and Maggie Sawyer, a police detective for National City's Science Division, respectively. Both of these characters have long and storied histories in DC Comics, and their introductions served to further expand the canon population in the multiverse of The CW's DC series.[4] Kara, after continually pushing away feelings for Mon-El, finally enters into a relationship with him during the second half of the season.[5] For Alex, meeting Maggie triggers long-suppressed feelings in her, and she begins the process of coming out as a lesbian, first to herself, and then to Kara and their mother Eliza, before also entering into a relationship with Maggie.[6] Thus, both sisters are given new social lives, independent of each other, a move that was applauded by some as a way for the characters to grow, and condemned by others as diminishing a crucial aspect of the series that had been carefully and extensively built up in the first season.

In addition to the two main characters gaining partners, two other first season regulars were also given relationships: Winn Schott and J'onn J'onzz. While Winn had secretly been in love with Kara as the first season opened, he eventually confessed his feelings to her, leading to a period of awkwardness between them before they were able to move forward as friends.[7] Subsequently, he entered into a relationship with a new and ambitious CatCo employee, Siobhan Smythe, who later became the supervillain, Banshee.[8] Winn's seeming bad luck with her foreshadows his further woes in the second season, when he is singled out for attention by an aggressive alien, Lyra Strayd, and enters into a whirlwind relationship, which proves problematic as the season progresses.[9] By contrast, J'onn, like Alex, was wedded to his work and even more so, his responsibilities as head of the DEO in the first season. Further, any "personal" role that he had was more akin to that of a surrogate father for Alex and Kara. In the second season, however, he meets M'gann M'orzz, another Martian.[10] J'onn presumed that he was the last of the Green Martians when they were massacred by a rival species, the White Martians. He survived, but his family did not, leaving him with tremendous grief and a feeling of unfillable emptiness. M'gann presents herself to him as a fellow Green Martian, but this later proves to be untrue.

Thus, Kara, Alex, J'onn, and Winn—four central characters on the series—find themselves navigating the difficulties of new relationships and the inevitable problems that arise in them. Of course, television loves nothing more than good melodrama, so the opportunity to inflict emotional angst and obstacles on each pairing was no doubt irresistible to the showrunners. The way that these four couples' hardships play out over the course of the second season is of particular interest, since many of them are linked by the common themes of lies, deceptions, and secrets.

Secrets and deception abound in the first season, and they carry on into new plots in the second season. First, there is the cat-and-mouse game between Lena and Lillian Luthor (wherein Lena pretends to support her mother's plans to murder National City's aliens, but thwarts them instead).[11] We also have President Marsdin's secret, hinted at early in the season,[12] before she is finally revealed to be an alien herself.[13] Next, Queen Rhea's schemes to bring back her son Mon-El (leading her to murder her husband, Lar Gand),[14] as well as her deceiving Lena in using Lena's technology to bring Daxamite ships to earth on a mission of conquest.[15] Thus, secrets and lies are clearly at the heart of the show's identity, so it is not surprising that they work their way into the personal relationships of the second season in various ways.

This essay will examine each relationship—Kara and Mon-El, Alex and Maggie, J'onn and M'gann, and Winn and Lyra—to see what specific acts of deception occur, note the reasons for them, and how such lies and secrets affect all four couples. It is worth noting that the deceptions are directed toward the main characters—Kara, Alex, J'onn, and Winn—by the new partners in their lives (and new to second season). While as we have seen, each of these established characters has engaged in spreading deceptions and keeping secrets of their own, in their romantic pairings, they are all victims. We will also look at some psychological theories of lying and philosophical approaches to untruths, and see how these apply to each of these new characters, all of whom have their own reasons for keeping their secrets and telling their lies; some of these are nobly intended, some less so.

Kara and Mon-El

A Kryptonian space pod similar to the ones that brought Kara and Clark to earth crash-lands in National City in the finale of the first season.[16] This event forms the cliff-hanger and is taken up again in the premier of the second season,[17] and the occupant is eventually revealed to be Mon-El,[18] a refugee from the planet Daxam that was also badly damaged when Krypton exploded. The Daxamites and the Kryptonians have a long history of antagonism, so Kara, while sympathetic to his plight, finds that she is unable to detach herself from her pre-existing prejudices about his people. She sees them as lazy, spoiled, and self-indulgent, if not outright evil, calling them "A race of bullies and hedonists, committed only to their own pleasure."[19] When she is reminded that Daxamites had slaves, Mon-El responds: "There were a lot of things there I didn't agree with."[20] This does not seem to impress her.

True to his supposed nature, Mon-El is initially care-free, careless, and obnoxious, being only interested in partying and having a good time.[21] Kara tries to convince him to use his yellow-sun induced powers for good like she does,[22] and at first, he has no interest at all, openly arguing with her about it.[23] Gradually, she brings him around to the idea of helping others and insists on training him after winning a bet with him that she could down the one alcoholic drink that would make her drunk in a single shot, a miscalculation that Alex finds highly amusing.[24] Mon-El agrees, and slowly begins to trust Kara, but he has a dark secret he is loath to tell her: he is not just any Daxamite, he is the prince, the son of King Lar Gand and Queen Rhea, who was hastily ushered into a Kryptonian escape pod (meant for Krypton's ambassador) and launched from the planet just as the shards of Krypton begin to reign down on Daxam.[25] Knowing that Kara could never accept him if she knew the truth, he keeps this secret, though he almost confesses when they are both prisoners of the organization Cadmus, and he fears they will not escape alive.[26] Shortly after this affair, he realizes that he is developing romantic feelings for Kara,[27] which makes his situation even more untenable and unbearable. He and Kara share a kiss, but he later lies to her and tells her that he does not remember anything. She reinforces that lie and assures him that nothing happened, even though both of them know that this is not true. They maintain the fiction of having no interest in each other for several more episodes.

Mon-El continues to conceal his background from Kara, even after they enter into a romantic relationship with each other. However, Mon-El's parents, Lar Gand and Rhea, arrive to bring him back to Daxam that has become habitable again, and when Kara agrees to accompany Mon-El to their ship, she learns that he is actually their son.[28] Naturally, Kara is devastated and Mon-El explains is that she never would have accepted him if she had known the truth. He also argues she would not have been able to believe that he could change into a better person, given her prejudice against Daxamites. This break-up proves to be short-lived, however, being resolved on the next episode of *The Flash* where she forgives Mon-El for his deception when she nearly dies, and he helps save her.[29]

Alex and Maggie

Of all of the pairings in second season, that of Alex and Maggie met with perhaps the widest acclaim and enthusiasm. From her introduction in the third episode, police detective Maggie Sawyer seemed a natural fit for the series, especially in her interactions with Alex.[30] In their first contentious encounter at an airport, following a presumed alien attack on the life of the president, Alex must maintain the deception about her identity. The scene shows her ID badge (held behind her back) digitally change to instead identify her as part of the president's secret service, and it is this fake ID that she shows to Maggie. Later in the episode, Maggie reveals that she has already deduced that Alex works for the DEO, telling her, "I'm a detective Agent Danvers; I detect."

Despite the friction of their first encounter,[31] Maggie trusts Alex enough to take her to an alien speakeasy dive bar (complete with a password for entry), where she shows Alex a hidden setting in which "offworlders" can relax and just be themselves without fear of persecution. She refers to them as "hardworking immigrants" who just want a home and to make a life for themselves. She also reveals that she is a lesbian, and that growing up in conservative Nebraska, she "may as well have been from Mars."[32] She can feel as alien as any of those around her. Alex later returns this trust by taking Maggie to the DEO for medical treatment after she is injured during a battle with the villain, Scorcher.[33] Thus, both women reveal secrets to each other in their first interactions, a sign of their growing trust in one another. They engage in breezy banter again before Maggie departs, with Maggie telling Alex that she has a "hot date" and that she does not "want to leave the lady waiting."[34] Alex's lingering glance at her new friend as she leaves telegraphs what is on the horizon for both of them.

The first true test of their eventual romantic relationship comes several episodes later, when Kara mysteriously vanishes, and all of Alex's teenage fears and anxieties about her adoptive sister come rushing back.[35] In a hasty decision, she breaks up with Maggie so that she can focus on the mission of finding Kara, scolding herself for even thinking that she could ever be happy. At this point, they have been together for only a little more than a month. After the episode's resolution and Kara's return, Alex rethinks her mistake and nervously invites Maggie over to her apartment; Maggie reluctantly agrees to see her, but clearly is in no mood to be there. Sitting in a supplicating position (she is normally taller than Maggie), Alex explains her foolish and hurtful behavior, born out of an almost overwhelming sense of duty and a need to put herself second all the time. Maggie flat-out tells her that this is because her sister is Supergirl, which shocks Alex. Once again, Maggie has "detected," and the implication is that she knows Alex has been keeping this secret from her for some time. Maggie explains that Kara is the only person Alex gets that upset over, and "plus, the glasses don't help,"[36] an amusing nod to the often-ridiculed idea that simply wearing a pair of glasses could conceal Supergirl's or Superman's identity. Alex agrees that it is ridiculous, and after they share a laugh, she tells Maggie that she is glad Maggie knows, "because I don't want there to be any secrets."[37] Maggie's response is curious and telling; instead of agreeing, she looks down, almost guilty, and then quickly changes the subject back to Alex's rash decision to break-up. For the viewer, this is a clear indication that she is hiding something, and indeed, we find out more later in the season.

Having patched up their relationship, they encounter their next obstacle four episodes later: Valentine's Day.[38] Alex is looking forward to spending the day with her new girlfriend and doing "all the cheesy things that couples do" after having been single for so many years (and unaware of her repressed sexual orientation). Unfortunately, Maggie wants nothing to do with the day, calling it "manufactured" and declaring that she hates the whole concept. Alex is disappointed, but after some nudging from Kara, she tries to entice Maggie into celebrating it anyway with an offering of gifts of some of her favorite things (scotch, tiramisu, and a bonsai tree) as well as herself in lingerie. Unfortunately, Maggie is immediately hostile. She threatens to leave and only stays because Alex asserts herself, insisting they talk through it. Here, Maggie reveals one of the secrets she has kept from Alex. She had initially encouraged Alex to come out to her family, telling her that she came out to her own father and mother and they were "pretty good" with it. Maggie now confesses that this was a lie. She angrily and tearfully tells Alex that when she was outed against her will on Valentine's Day at the age of fourteen, her father kicked her out of the house and she had to go and live with a (presumably) more sympathetic aunt until she was an adult.[39] When Alex apologizes and asks why Maggie lied to her, Maggie replies that she did not want to scare Alex: "I wanted it to be better for you."[40] She wanted Alex to have a positive experience, so she was willing to lie about her own coming-out to make it better for her girlfriend.

This selfless lie is supplanted by a more selfish secret based on fear later in the season. While walking from a yoga class, Maggie and Alex have a chance encounter with Emily, an ex-girlfriend of Maggie's, and Alex pressures Maggie into agreeing to meet up with her for dinner, proudly stating, "see how cool I'm being about this?"[41] Emily stands them up, and Alex angrily confronts Emily, only to be told that Maggie cheated on her while they were together—which is why they broke up—and she just wants to put it all behind her. When Alex brings up the subject with Maggie, Maggie becomes defensive again, but Alex is not looking for a fight. Rather, she explains that she believes this secrecy to be part of a pattern, one that comes from Maggie's inability to trust others after the betrayal by her parents. Maggie agrees with this assessment and is comforted that Alex does not think of her as "a horrible person," and Alex is relieved that Maggie is not perfect.

Maggie's secrets do not have the high stakes that Alex's do, but they are important enough to her that she is prepared to keep them from the person she arguably loves the most. Despite using her deductive skills to tease out some of Alex's most closely-guarded secrets, she is remarkably reluctant to reveal her own and it is only through a realization that she can be loved regardless of her flaws that she is able to let go of them. It may or may not be significant that they do not say "I love you" to one another until after Alex nearly drowns.[42] The realization that they nearly lost each other finally breaks down that emotional barrier.

J'onn and M'gann

J'onn is often portrayed as the main father figure of the series, a mentor to both Kara and Alex. He is also portrayed as a tragic figure having fled Mars following the extermination of his people, the Green Martians, by a larger and more hostile people, the White Martians. Alone, J'onn has lived on earth as a refugee for centuries. Being both psychic and having the ability to shape-shift, he has kept himself alive by assuming human forms, most recently that of Hank Henshaw, the director of the DEO. It comes as a great surprise to him, then, when he meets M'gann M'orzz working at the alien bar, who reveals herself to be Martian, as well.[43] M'gann explains that she escaped the genocide with the assistance of a White Martian who helped smuggle her off Mars. This is a lie; she was, in fact, the White Martian who tried to help the Greens. Not knowing this, J'onn offers to establish a psychic link with her, but she shrugs him off.[44] She hastily withdraws, obviously not wanting him to learn the truth about her. Initially annoyed, J'onn is soon forced to fight M'gann in an underground alien fight club, but they refuse to kill each other, and instead unite to help Kara, Alex, and Maggie bring the club down. Later, he visits her at her home, telling her he accepts that she does not want to share the bond with him, but still offers his friendship, if she wants it.[45] J'onn is soon injured and needs a blood transfusion. M'gann is the only one who can give it to him, but she is obviously terrified of doing so, since an infusion of her blood will transform J'onn into a White Martian. She tells Alex, "If J'onn knew, he would not want this,"[46] but Alex insists, saying that there are no other options as she also does not know M'gann's true identity.

After his recovery, J'onn begins to hallucinate and realizes that something is wrong. He deduces the truth and confronts M'gann. When she finally confesses to being a White Martian, J'onn is furious, not only because she has lied to him, but also because he now carries her "tainted" blood. He threatens to kill her, saying, "I want to look my enemy in the eye as I avenge the deaths of my wife and daughters."[47] She tells him that she could not stomach what her people were doing, that she was the White Martian who helped the Green Martians escape, but obviously, this makes little difference to J'onn. She also reveals there are other White Martians who agree with her and want to change things for the better. J'onn spares her life but locks her up at the DEO "to rot in this cell for all eternity."[48] He is eventually cured of his infection and remains a Green Martian.[49]

Later, when M'gann is psychically attacked, J'onn agrees to bond with her, where they share a moving experience together: a flashback to the horrific events on Mars. J'onn is able to let go of his hate and offer her his forgiveness.[50] Unfortunately for J'onn, M'gann feels a duty to return to Mars and try to persuade other White Martians to change, to abandon hatred.[51] J'onn reluctantly lets her go and they share a romantic bonding moment before parting.[52] At this point, their story ends, but M'gann returns in the second season finale with a host of other good White Martians to help repel to Daxamite invasion. In the final moments of the episode as the two reflect on things at the DEO, she tells him that she wants to stay, the implication being that she wants to explore a romance with him, and they exit with arms around each other.[53] Unlike the other couples in the second season, these two only enter into a relationship with each other after the deception has been exposed and after taking a much longer time to reflect on the pros and cons of such a pairing. This cautious approach stands in stark contrast to the mess in which Winn Schott finds himself.

Winn and Lyra

The whirlwind relationship between Winn and Lyra came as a surprise not only to Winn himself, but also to many of the show's fans. Worked into the Valentine's Day episode, Winn finds himself the subject of sudden attention by an intriguing alien, Lyra Strayd, recently arrived from a planet called Starhaven.[54] Lyra aggressively pursues Winn after saving him in a fight at the alien bar (the speakeasy that became a mainstay set of the series after Maggie introduced it to Alex). Their interactions are passionate, hot, heavy, and in the moment, but it all seems a bit too good to be true, and given Winn's history, this is soon proven to be the case. A few weeks into the relationship, Winn receives a phone call from Maggie, asking him to come down to the police station.[55] There she shows him security camera footage proving that Winn was at an art museum the same night that a valuable Van Gogh painting was stolen. Winn admits to being there and having snuck in with Lyra after hours, but he denies having anything to do with the theft, and is surprised that Lyra isn't in the footage—it turns out that her species does not show up on film. Maggie, once again "detecting," surmises that Lyra has framed Winn, stealing the painting while invisible to the camera, and letting Winn take the fall for it. Winn reluctantly agrees with this theory and despairs over falling for a female villain a second time.

Given the chance to correct things and clear his name, Winn angrily confronts Lyra with James/Guardian and Alex as his backup. She readily admits to engaging him in a long con, though says it was not personal. Winn does not believe her at first, saying, "if you can tell me that you didn't care for me, that I'm just some mark, then I will walk away right now." She replies, "You were a mark."[56] She later reveals that she was pressured into the theft (and into duping Winn) in order to save her brother from the machinations of an alien art smuggler who will kill her brother unless she delivers the painting to him. She also says that they are refugees from Starhaven—the planet whose air once smelled like cinnamon, but also was badly damaged by the fallout from Krypton's destruction.

Lyra's deception is one of criminal intent—the long con—even though she is compelled to undertake it out of concern for her brother's life. She and Winn reconcile, and she reveals that she does have feelings for him after all. Lyra's temper and aggressive nature still come to the fore afterward, however, showing that these were not just a part of the role she assumed to deceive him. In a later episode, she becomes angry with both James and Winn while out on patrol with them, defying James' wish not to rough up a robbery suspect and later threatening Winn and yelling at him when he suggests that she and James/Guardian are probably not a good crime-fighting match.[57] This hostile and even abusive nature is troubling and hints at further secrets and problems.

Theories and Motivations for Lying

These four couples thus face numerous challenges and stresses as the season unfolds. A large amount of this angst is due to one simply being untrue to the other; in this case, as we have seen, each of the new characters deceives or lies to an established character. Such deceit is a common problem in most relationships of all kinds, and it is worth discussing some of the motivations for such actions. Why do people, who in theory love each other and strive to be honest and open, so often resort to keeping secrets, if not straight-out lying? There are many different philosophical and scientific approaches to lying, why we do it, the ethics involved, and other related topics. Deception seems to be coded into our genes over millions of years and humans are far from the only animals who engage in it. In the larger animal world, such trickery is essential for survival, as is the ability to recognize it. Travis Riddle notes:

A frog which successfully fakes its croak to make itself seem bigger will be more likely to succeed in life than a similarly sized one which unsuccessfully fakes its croak. However, the ability to detect deception is just as important as the ability to deceive. A female frog with a talent for detecting deception will be more likely to mate with the actual biggest frog in the pond, rather than the one which only sounds the biggest, ensuring a greater likelihood of success for her genes.[58]

Deception goes beyond just the need to reproduce, however. The *New York Times* reported more than thirty years ago: "Jane Goodall, working in Tanzania in the 70s, first reported chimpanzee guile in the wild when she described how one male led others away from a pile of bananas, then sneaked back alone to eat."[59] Anthropologist Frans de Waal further noted, "Deception seems to permeate all aspects of chimpanzee social life, and chimpanzee skills in deceit are a match for human lie-detection abilities."[60] If our closest cousins engage in such behaviors, what hope do we have in avoiding them? Very little, it seems. Studies suggest that children may begin deceiving as early as six months of age—before they can even talk—in order to gain what they want and need.[61] This suggests that deception has evolutionary advantages and is likely hardwired into us.

As long ago as 1977, Jerald M. Jellison of USC posited that the average person is lied to up to 200 times a day,[62] an astonishing number that has been borne out in subsequent studies, one of which suggests that 60 percent of American adults cannot hold a conversation for ten minutes without lying at least once.[63] Many in the study were completely unaware that they lied until it was pointed out to them afterward. It seems that lying is so much a part of our nature that we can engage in it on "auto pilot." Given this remarkable evolutionary predilection to indulge in falsehoods, it is only natural that personal relationships would suffer from them, as well. White lies, lies to spare their partner's feelings, lies about their true thoughts on a contentious issue ... all of these are common in relationships, but the act of mating itself is some ways a grand lie. From birds ruffling up their feathers to twenty-somethings choosing just the right outfit for a Friday night, the act of attracting partners and mates comes with a hefty dose of misrepresentation, in the hopes of standing out from the competition. Trickery and deceit often seem necessary to win the initial attention of a desired mate; we frequently view these actions as benign and sometimes even humorous. Many a funny story and situation comedy has been based around just this predicament.

As such, there is no reason to believe that a couple, once together, would discontinue the practices that have been drummed into them by culture and evolution. Sometimes these falsehoods are innocuous; sometimes they have very bad consequences. Much of how and why lies and deceit occur in a given relationship derives from the intent of the person in question, as we will see. Humanity has long recognized and thought about its tendency to lie. Philosophers have tackled the problem of lying for as long as there has been philosophical inquiry. Though a full discussion of the philosophy of lying in the Western tradition is obviously (and absurdly!) out of the realm of possibility here, it is worth briefly mentioning a few of the more famous schools of thought. While earlier thinkers such as Plato, Aristotle, Augustine, and Thomas Aquinas approached the problem of lying and deception in various ways, Immanuel Kant is perhaps the best known of the more recent philosophers to delve into the topic in depth.[64] Kant's view is generally that lying is unacceptable, even in extreme circumstances, such as to protect someone's life. This harsh, unyielding rigidity has often been criticized, but it oversimplifies other statements that he made across various writings.[65] He noted, for example, "if we were to be at all times punctiliously truthful we might often become victims of the wickedness of others who were ready to abuse our truthfulness."[66] He is here differentiating between a "lie" and an "untruth." An untruth can be told ethically when there is no expectation from the listener that the teller is actually telling the truth, for example.[67] If we sign a letter with "best wishes," we may not be sending the recipient our actual best wishes, but they do not care, and neither do we. This is a harmless untruth masquerading as a social convention.

Nevertheless, Kant is still adhered to strict beliefs that lying is in most cases, wrong. His views (and Augustine's before him) belong to a school of ethics known as Deontology, which advocates for universal laws which govern right and wrong (though Kant was not interested in a religious foundation for these, unlike his medieval predecessors), but of course, the crucial question is: who gets to determine just what these laws are, and can they always apply in every situation? Clearly not. Other important schools of thought include Utilitarianism and Virtue Ethics. The Utilitarian view looks at the consequences of each act; if a lie results in a good outcome, it is not necessarily bad. The problem with this approach is that there is no way to predict all possible outcomes. A lie told with the intent of helping a person or situation could easily backfire and make things worse. Virtue Ethics focuses on character development and making a person the best they can be.[68] Lying is therefore discouraged for its lack of virtue, but the problem arises that it might sometimes be necessary for someone to lie to achieve a more desirable outcome (saving a life, or even simply sparing one's feelings). Is this form of lie "virtuous" or not?[69] The debate continues.

In considering a more practical question, is there a difference between a "deception" and a "lie"? In some cases, lying is more active and deception is potentially more passive, though deception can also include lying and might be better thought of as an umbrella term that contains the act of lying. Neglecting to reveal something, or keeping information secret does not always require the same effort as an outright lie, but the intent is much the same in many cases.⁷⁰ A standard definition of a lie is: "a statement made by one who does not believe it with the intention that someone else shall be led to believe it"⁷¹ Further, there are four conditions to a given lie:

> First, lying requires that a person make a statement (statement condition). Second, lying requires that the person believe the statement to be false; that is, lying requires that the statement be untruthful (untruthfulness condition). Third, lying requires that the untruthful statement be made to another person (addressee condition). Fourth, lying requires that the person intend that that other person believe the untruthful statement to be true (intention to deceive the addressee condition).⁷²>

By contrast, a deception can be defined as: "to intentionally cause to have a false belief that is known or believed to be false."⁷³ A deception is further characterized by a very important feature: its success. It can only be considered to be an "actual" deception if the intended recipients are, in fact, deceived. A lie can be disbelieved and still be a lie, a deception cannot; if it is not believed, then no one was deceived. Deceptions can be committed without words: dressing up and impersonating as a medical doctor or police officer when one is not, for example. Paradoxically, deception can also be achieved by telling the truth: using selective facts to put a particular spin on a news story, for example.⁷⁴

However, deception does not always have a malevolent intent. A stage magician practices deception, for example, by misdirecting an audience's attention; this deception causes viewers to believe that they have seen something they have not, that they have witnessed "magic." The intent is for the audience to marvel and have fun by suspending their disbelief; they are willingly deceived and left to wonder how the magic trick was accomplished.

As noted, deception can be passive. If someone were to withhold the information that they had spent time in prison, for example, this is different than actively insisting that the incarceration had never taken place—which would be a lie—but the intent is essentially the same: to misdirect and deceive someone else (or a group) into believing something other than the truth. We do not normally assume that everyone we meet has spent time behind bars, so it is easier for someone to keep such a fact secret, at least for a while, but eventually, as in an active lie, the risk increases that the truth will be found out. Ultimately, the intention of the individual who lies or deceives can be the same.

What are those intentions? What makes people commonly want to lie or deceive? In their study, "Motivation and Consequences of Lying. A Qualitative Analysis of Everyday Lying,"⁷⁵ Arcimowicz, Cantarero, and Soroko identify broad categories of lying that are very useful for general classification and can be applied to the story lines discussed in this essay. This study denote lies as being primarily beneficial or protective: "A beneficial lie is associated with the objective or benefit the liar wants to achieve.... Protective motivation is rather about guarding the liar from the unpleasant effects of revealing the truth."[76]

Beneficial and protective motivations can both be divided into two additional categories: self-oriented and other-oriented. Beneficial self-oriented lies are about personal gain, whether material (a job, money, and so on) or psychological (praise, prestige, social standing, acquiring romantic or sexual partners, and so on). The person in question lies or deceives to gain something for him or herself. Beneficial other-oriented lies are created to please others, such as those that one cares about: complimenting someone when they don't deserve it, lying about how good someone looks in a certain set of clothes; this is particularly true when such lies are told to avoid conflict, or to help remove distress and worry, rather than being merely insincere compliments (these latter kinds of encouraging lies are told to children all the time to enforce self-esteem and motivate them, for example; there is generally no ill intent). Protective self-oriented lies are, as the name implies, intended to protect oneself. These can include lies to avoid some consequence or punishment (denying committing a crime when one is accused, for example, even if one is guilty), to hide one's own perceived faults, to keep secrets about events in one's past that one is ashamed of, to avoid taking responsibility, and so on. Protective other-oriented lies are told to shelter others, to spare their feelings, to save them from worry, or even to protect them from harm (the hiding of slaves in the Underground Railroad, for example, or hiding those fleeing Nazi persecution).[77] Most lies fall into one of these categories and sometimes, they overlap, which is certainly true of the examples on *Supergirl*, as we will see below.

Types of Lying on *Supergirl*

Having looked at various types of lies and the motivations for engaging in them, as well as certain philosophies about them, we can see how these categorizations work well in classifying the various deceptions at work on the series, especially those between the romantic couples. Mon-El's withholding of his true history from Kara is a protective self-oriented deception; he fears her reaction if she were to learn the truth and he is ashamed of his past. The longer he waits to tell her, of course, the worse the situation becomes and the more likely she will reject him, which is just what she does when the truth comes out against his will. He makes the consequence he fears (and that caused him to withhold information about himself to begin with) eventually come true by his actions. His deception is authentic, because Kara believes him to be a palace bodyguard, rather than the Prince of Daxam. The schools of thought we have examined would view this deception and the lies spun out of it as wrong on all counts.

Maggie's lie to Alex, that her coming-out was easy and her parents accepted her, is one of protective other-oriented motivation; she wants to protect Alex and create a safe space for her while she is going through her own unique situation. Maggie fears that if Alex knew the truth, it might scare her away from telling her family that she is gay, or instill anxiety about the coming-out process in general. Thus, it is a lie born out of care and compassion. From the point of view of Virtue Ethics and Utilitarian belief, this might be seen as an acceptable action to take, even though it is still untrue and undermines trust. On the other hand, Maggie's secret, hiding that she had cheated on a former girlfriend, comes from protective self-oriented motivation; she fears that if the truth is revealed, Alex will no longer love her and accept her. Maggie's traumatic experience as a teenager causes her to push away those she is closest to (presumably why she cheated on her former girlfriend), and Alex has to reassure her that (unlike the situation with Kara and Mon-El) her fear will not be realized this time. It is a successful deception, but one which probably would have been discovered eventually and which would not be held to be virtuous or ultimately useful.

Lyra's long con of Winn is interesting, in that it reveals overlapping categorizations. Her deceit has the elements of beneficial self-orientation; she misrepresents herself to Winn in order to gain something (a valuable painting) while framing him for stealing it. This seems to be a purely selfish motivation from a dishonest art thief who spotted an easy mark and took advantage of him, pretending to be attracted to him. Underneath, however, is another layer, that of protective other-orientation, as she is trying to prevent her brother from being murdered by Mandrax, and her motivation is revealed to be that the entire long con was set up to save his life. Winn is an unfortunate casualty of this situation, but one that Lyra seemingly regrets; she did not plan on developing feelings for him and regrets involving him. From the point of view of Virtue Ethics, her regret over her actions might be a sign that she is striving to become a better person.

M'gann's deception likewise has more than one component. The main reason to hide who she is from J'onn obviously comes from protective self-orientation. Her true identity as a White Martian would certainly doom any friendship that she might develop with J'onn, to say nothing of anything more romantic. Further, given his hatred of her species, he would most likely try to kill her, so her need for self-preservation occurs on at least two levels, emotional and physical. However, as we learn more about her, we can also see that this secret is kept in part to help spare J'onn any further pain. The very existence of a White Martian on earth and in his presence would be enough to cause him terrible anguish and she clearly wants to keep from doing this, especially as she is wracked by guilt over what her people have done.[78] Again, Virtue Ethics might see this guilt as a sign that she is trying to become a better individual, after rejecting a horrific past.

The application of these designations works with the other lies and deceptions on the series, most importantly, with those surrounding Kara. She protects her secret identity (arguably one of the main themes of the entire series) for two reasons: first, there is protective self-orientation. Her need to keep the Supergirl part of her life a secret exists to protect her. A public identity would simply put a target on her back for any would-be villain that wanted to take up the challenge. Her life could become a living hell of constantly fending off challenges as Kara Danvers.

Second, there is also a strong element of protective other-orientation in maintaining the fiction that Kara and Supergirl are two different individuals. This fiction protects those close to her, many of whom (Alex, Winn, and James) are "only" human and would be vulnerable to attack, kidnapping, and other forms of harm from any adversary who sought to hurt Kara at a deeper level. The kidnapping of Alex by Rick Malverne, a former high school classmate who learned Kara's secret identity, is a prime example of that danger. It ultimately necessitated that J'onn psychically wipe Rick's memory of all of the events of the kidnapping and his discoveries in order to protect Kara's identity and the existence of the DEO.[79]

Thus, the Deontological model of lying as always being wrong cannot possibly apply here, as the consequences of Kara's telling the truth about her identity would put many innocents in danger. The lie she maintains is far more ethical than the possible outcomes of revealing the truth, which could leave many injured or dead. Virtue Ethicists would probably see that Kara is striving for betterment not only for herself, but also for everyone. Utilitarians would agree that the consequences of this grand deception are far more beneficial than not.

Deception and lies are at the core of many of the storylines of *Supergirl*'s first two seasons. Some are designed to protect individuals or whole groups of people while others are merely self-interested indulgences. Most result in unpredictable outcomes and cause considerable stress to those who perpetuate them; even the most nobly-intended lie (such as Kara's secret identity) can be a source of considerable pain and hardship in maintaining it. Each of the four relationships explored in the second season is affected by one or more acts of deception: misrepresentation, secrets, and outright lies threaten the survival of each relationship. However, it is significant that each couple survives these trials and in theory, grows stronger; forgiveness is also at the heart of the series. Perhaps because we all know on some level that we each have the tendency to lie—even frequently—there is a part of us more willing to forgive such behavior in others. This is may the case with these romantic pairings, as each wronged individual (Kara, Alex, J'onn, and Winn) has their own reasons for offering that forgiveness and understanding, however differently they may arrive at it. Learning to live in a world of secrets with vast implications is the price that each heroic character on *Supergirl* must pay to serve a greater good. Understanding that other kinds of deceptions often spill over into their personal lives as a result of the world that they live in is a difficult challenge that each faces in unique ways.

Notes

1. Vancouver, as opposed to the Los Angeles sets of season 1, which allowed the show to integrate more easily with the CW's other DC shows.

2. The difficulties for some cast members who resided in Los Angeles but would have had to commute on a regular basis to Vancouver were certainly among the main reasons that several of them departed after the first season.

3. Alex's own apartment was never shown in season 1; it was a specially built set for season 2 and became a major setting for her interactions with Maggie Sawyer. As one queer internet user joked: "She was given an apartment for gay reasons."

4. An early version of Mon-El first appeared in *Superboy* # #89 (June 1961), though his role would change in the 1980s and '90s, after the *Crisis on Infinite Earths* mini-series (1985–86). Maggie first appeared in John Byrne's revamp of *Superman*, in issue #4 (1987), but did not come out as a lesbian until issue #15 (1988). She was later romantically involved with Kate Kane (Batwoman) in the *New 52* run of *Batwoman* (2010–15); the two were engaged to be married, but DC's chiefs decided to cancel all plans for any of their heroes (homosexual or heterosexual) to have a proverbial happy ending. Story-wise, the two broke up, and Maggie left Gotham and moved back to Metropolis. There was a strong fan and even creator backlash against this company-wide decision.

5. *Supergirl*, "Mr. & Mrs. Mxyzptlk," season 2, episode 13, directed by Stefan Pleszczynski, written by Jessica Queller and Sterling Gates, aired February 20, 2017, on The CW.

6. This highly praised story arc ran from episodes 4 to 8 of season 2, and earned the show widespread praise, including a GLAAD nomination. See http://tvline.com/2017/01/31/glaad-media-awards-nominations-supergirl-shadowhunters-black-mirror/ and https://www.glaad.org/mediaawards/nominees.

7. *Supergirl*, "Childish Things," season 1, episode 10, directed by Jamie Babbit, written by Yahlin Chang, teleplay by Anna Musky-Goldwyn and James Dewille, aired January 18, 2016, on CBS.

8. Played by Italia Ricci; this season 1 story arc ran from episodes 14 to 18.

9. Lyra first appears in season 2, episode 13, "Mr. & Mrs. Mxyzptlk," a Valentine's Day–themed episode that focused on the main character's relationships.

10. M'gann, also known as "Miss Martian," is a relative newcomer to the DC Universe, having been introduced in *Teen Titans* #37 in 2006.

11. *Supergirl*, "Crossfire," season 2, episode 5, directed by Glen Winter, written by Gabriel Llanas and Anna Musky-Goldwyn, aired November 7, 2016, on The CW.

12. *Supergirl*, "Welcome to Earth," season 2, episode 3, directed by Rachel Talalay, written by Jessica Queller and Derek Simon, aired October 24, 2016, on The CW.

13. *Supergirl*, "Exodus," season 2, episode 15, directed by Michael Allowitz, written by Paula Yoo and Eric Carrasco, aired March 6, 2017, on The CW.

14. *Supergirl*, "Distant Sun," season 2, episode 17, directed by Kevin Smith, written by Gabriel Llanas and Anna Musky-Goldwyn, aired March 27, 2017, on The CW.

15. *Supergirl*, "Alex," season 2, episode 19, directed by Rob Greenlea, written by Eric Carrasco and Greg Baldwin, aired May 1, 2017, on The CW.

16. *Supergirl*, "Better Angels," season 1, episode 20, directed by Larry Teng, written by Andrew Kreisberg and Ali Adler, teleplay by Robert Rovner and Jessica Queller, aired April 18, 2016, on CBS.

17. *Supergirl*, "The Adventures of Supergirl," season 2, episode 1, directed by Glen Winter, story by Greg Berlanti and Andrew Kreisberg, teleplay by Andrew Kreisberg and Jessica Queller, aired October 10, 2016, on The CW.
18. Mon-El's actual name in the comics is Lar Gand, but this name is instead given to his father (played by Kevin Sorbo) in the television series. The fact that "El" is a Kryptonian name, the name of the family from which both Clark and Kara come raises the question as to why Mon-El, born and raised on another planet, would be named as such, but this not addressed in the second season.
19. *Supergirl*, "Survivors," season 2, episode 4, directed by James Marshall and James Bamford, written by Paula Yoo and Eric Carrasco, aired October 31, 2016, on The CW.
20. *Supergirl*, "Supergirl Lives," season 2, episode 9, directed by Kevin Smith, story by Andrew Kreisberg, teleplay by Eric Carrasco and Jess Kardos, aired January 23, 2017, on The CW. In episode 16, "Star Crossed," directed by John Medlen, written by Katie Rose Rogers and Jess Kardos (aired March 20, 2017), Rhea justifies slavery by telling Kara that they were loved and had been lifted up out of a life of misery for something much better. Again, she is not impressed.
21. See, for example, "Survivors," season 2, episode 4, where Mon-El convinces Winn to come out with him to the alien bar. See also, "Crossfire," season 2, episode 5, where Mon-El's attempts to work at CatCo go badly wrong.
22. Like Kara, Mon-El gains enhanced abilities from Earth's yellow sun, though because he is from a different species, they are not as pronounced. He has extra strength, for example, but cannot fly and doesn't have Kara's heat vision.
23. *Supergirl*, "Changing," season 2, episode 6, directed by Larry Teng, story by Greg Berlanti, teleplay by Andrew Kreisberg and Caitlin Parrish, aired November 14, 2016, The CW.
24. *Supergirl*, "Changing," season 2, episode 6.
25. This is later revealed in full in "Star-Crossed," season 2, episode 16.
26. *Supergirl*, "The Darkest Place," season 2, episode 7, directed by Glen Winter, written by Robert Rovner and Paula Yoo, aired November 21, 2016, on The CW.
27. *Supergirl*, "Medusa," season 2, episode 8, directed by Stefan Pleszczynnski, written by Jessica Queller and Derek Simon, aired November 28, 2016, on The CW.
28. *Supergirl*, "Star-Crossed," season 2, episode 16, directed by John Medlen, written by Katie Rose Rogers and Jess Kardos, aired March 20, 2017, on The CW.
29. *The Flash*, "Duet," season 3, episode 17, written by Dermott Daniel Downs, written by Greg Berlanti, Andrew Kreisberg, Aaron Helbing, Todd Helbing, aired March 21, 2017, on The CW. Many fans and critics were unhappy with this story, because it involved the resolution of a major plot line on another show; not everyone watches all of the DC shows on the CW. Further, many felt that such quick forgiveness for a very large deception was unrealistic and did not reflect what someone would "really" do.
30. *Supergirl*, "Welcome to Earth," season 2, episode 3, directed by Rachel Talalay, written by Jessica Queller and Derek Simon, aired October 24, 2016, on The CW. The two actresses, Chyler Leigh and Floriana Lima, immediately received considerable praise for their chemistry. Executive producer Andrew Kreisberg was quoted as saying that if "you could bottle and sell" said chemistry, "you could rule the world." See Natalie Abrams, "Supergirl Winter Finale: What's Next?" *Entertainment Weekly* (online), November 28, 2016: http://ew.com/article/2016/11/28/supergirl-kara-mon-el-kiss-alex-maggie-spoilers. Leigh has recounted how Lima was chosen for the role, based off of how well they got on when they first met for a reading. See Natalie Abrams, "'Supergirl' star Chyler Leigh opens up about Alex's coming-out story," February 27, 2017: https://www.yahoo.com/entertainment/supergirl-star-chyler-leigh-opens-140057629.html.
31. Despite their confrontation, Maggie is noticeably flirtatious with Alex, telegraphing their later relationship.
32. Perhaps significantly, this episode is also where M'gann reveals her origin to J'onn as being from Mars, but not telling him the whole truth.
33. *Supergirl*, "Welcome to Earth," season 2, episode 3.
34. *Supergirl*, "Welcome to Earth," season 2, episode 3.

35. *Supergirl,* "Supergirl Lives," season 2, episode 9.
36. *Supergirl,* "Supergirl Lives," season 2, episode 9.
37. *Supergirl,* "Supergirl Lives," season 2, episode 9.
38. *Supergirl,* "Mr. & Mrs. Mxyzptlk," season 2, episode 13.
39. Lima's acting in this scene was highly praised for its realness and for the important message that it conveyed about the plight of LGBT teenagers facing similar circumstances, though others criticized the show for not giving this issue better closure, either by the episode's end or later in the season.
40. *Supergirl,* "Mr. & Mrs. Mxyzptlk," season 2, episode 13.
41. *Supergirl,* "Distant Sun," season 2, episode 17.
42. *Supergirl,* "Alex," season 2, episode 19.
43. *Supergirl,* "Welcome to Earth," season 2, episode 3. M'gann is often referred to as "Miss Martian" in the comics, and does not have a romantic connection to J'onn.
44. *Supergirl,* "Survivors," season 2, episode 4.
45. *Supergirl,* "Survivors," season 2, episode 4.
46. *Supergirl,* "Changing," season 2, episode 6.
47. *Supergirl,* "The Darkest Place," season 2, episode 7.
48. *Supergirl,* "The Darkest Place," season 2, episode 7.
49. *Supergirl,* "Medusa," season 2, episode 8, a cure that some fans felt was achieved a bit too easily and missed the potential for some additional drama in subsequent episodes.
50. *Supergirl,* "We Can Be Heroes," season 2, episode 10, directed by Rebecca Johnson, written by Caitlin Parrish and Katie Rose Rogers, aired January 30, 2017, on The CW.
51. *Supergirl,* "The Martian Chronicles," season 2, episode 11, directed by David McWhirter, written by Gabriel Llanas and Anna Musky-Goldwyn, aired February 6, 2017, on The CW.
52. Some have likened it to a form of Martian sex.
53. *Supergirl,* "Nevertheless, She Persisted," season 2, episode 22, directed by Glen Winter, story by Andrew Kreisberg and Jessica Queller, teleplay by Robert Rovner and Caitlin Parrish, aired May 22, 2017, on The CW.
54. *Supergirl,* "Mr. & Mrs. Mxyzptlk," season 2, episode 13.
55. *Supergirl,* "Star-Crossed," season 2, episode 16.
56. *Supergirl,* "Star-Crossed," season 2, episode 16.
57. *Supergirl,* "Ace Reporter," season 2, episode 18, directed by Armen V. Kevorkian, written by Paula Yoo and Caitlin Parrish, aired April 24, 2017, on The CW.
58. Travis Riddle, "Liars: It Takes One to Know One," *Scientific American* (online), July 24, 2012: https://www.scientificamerican.com/article/liars-it-takes-one-to-know-one/.
59. Erick Eckholm, "Deceit Found Pervasive in the Natural World," *New York Times,* January 14, 1986: http://www.nytimes.com/1986/01/14/science/deceit-found-pervasive-in-the-natural-world.html?pagewanted=all. For deceptive behavior in dogs, see Brian Owens, "Dogs Use Deception to Get What They Want from Humans (a Sausage)," *New Scientist* (March 2017): https://www.newscientist.com/article/2124087-dogs-use-deception-to-get-what-they-want-from-humans-a-sausage.
60. Eckholm, "Deceit." For further study, see Frans de Waal, "Intentional Deception in Primates," *Evolutionary Anthropology: Issues, News, and Reviews,* 1 no. 3 (June 2005): 86–92, and William A. Searcy and, Stephen Nowicki, *The Evolution of Animal Communication Reliability and Deception in Signaling Systems* (Princeton: Princeton University Press, 2005).
61. See Vasudevi Reddy, *How Infants Know Minds* (Cambridge, MA: Harvard University Press, 2008), for further information.
62. Jerald M. Jellison, *I'm Sorry, I Didn't Mean To, and Other Lies We Love to Tell* (New York: Chatham Square Press, 1977).
63. See, for example, Robert Feldman's study in the prevalence of lying, summarized in "UMass Amherst Researcher Finds Most People Lie in Everyday Conversation," *UMass Amherst,* June 10, 2002: https://www.umass.edu/newsoffice/article/umass-amherst-researcher-finds-most-people-lie-everyday-conversation. See also Robert Feldman, *The Liar in Your Life: The Way to Truthful Relationships* (New York: Twelve, 2009).
64. See Kant, *Lectures on Ethics,* trans. Louis Infield. (Indianapolis: Hackett, 1963).

65. For a thorough discussion of this topic, see Randolph Wheeler, "Kant on Untruths and Lying: The *Falsiloquium* and the *Mendacium*," *Ethics Journal* 8 no.1 (2007): 51–65: https://www.uvu.edu/ethics/seac/Wheeler-KantonUntruthsandLying.pdf.
66. Kant, *Lectures on Ethics*, 228, quoted by Wheeler, "Kant on Untruths," 52.
67. For detailed examples of such a scenario, see Wheeler, "Kant on Untruths," 52 and 54.
68. Aristotle was an early proponent of this thought. See his *Nicomachean Ethics*: http://classics.mit.edu/Aristotle/nicomachaen.html.
69. For further discussion of these schools of thought, see Tim C. Mazur, "Lying," *Issues in Ethics* 6 no. 1 (1993): https://www.scu.edu/ethics/ethics-resources/ethical-decision-making/lying/. See also the BBC's "Ethics Guide": http://www.bbc.co.uk/ethics/lying/lying_1.shtml.
70. For an exhaustive discussion, see "The Definition of Lying and Deception," *Stanford Encyclopedia of Philosophy*: https://plato.stanford.edu/entries/lying-definition/#DecVsNonDecAboLyi.
71. Arnold Isenberg, "Deontology and the Ethics of Lying," *Aesthetics and Theory of Criticism: Selected Essays of Arnold Isenberg* (Chicago: University of Chicago Press, 1973), 248.
72. "The Definition of Lying and Deception," section 1, *Stanford Encyclopedia of Philosophy*: https://plato.stanford.edu/entries/lying-definition/#DecVsNonDecAboLyi.
73. "The Definition of Lying," section 3.
74. An all-too-common phenomenon these days in the U.S. media.
75. From the website for *Forum: Qualitative Social Research*: "This project was financed by the Polish Ministry of Science and Higher Education under the National Program for the Development of Humanities, No. 21H11 0002 80, 'Anthropology of Lying in Everyday Life.'" *Forum: Qualitative Social Research*, 16 no. 3 art. 31, September 2015: http://www.qualitative-research.net/index.php/fqs/article/view/2311/3892.
76. Beata Arcimowicz, Katarzyna Cantarero, and Emilia Soroko, "Motivation and Consequences of Lying: A Qualitative Analysis of Everyday Lying," and *Forum: Qualitative Social Research*.
77. A graph and further discussion of these categories can be found at *Forum: Qualitative Social Research*.
78. *Supergirl*, "We Can Be Heroes," season 2, episode 10.
79. *Supergirl*, "Alex," season 2, episode 19.

Selected Bibliography

Abrams, Natalie. "'Supergirl' Star Chyler Leigh Opens Up About Alex's Coming-Out Story," February 27, 2017: https://www.yahoo.com/entertainment/supergirl-star-chyler-leigh-opens-140057629.html Arcimowicz, Beata, Katarzyna Cantarero, and Emilia Soroko, "Motivation and Consequences of Lying. a Qualitative Analysis of Everyday Lying," *Forum: Qualitative Social Research*. 16 no. 3. art. 31. September 2015: http://www.qualitativeresearch.net/index.php/fqs/article/view/2311/3892.
_____. "Supergirl Winter Finale: What's Next?" *Entertainment Weekly*. (online) November 28, 2016: http://ew.com/article/2016/11/28/supergirl-kara-mon-el-kiss-alex-maggie-spoilers.
Aristotle, *Nicomachean Ethics*: http://classics.mit.edu/Aristotle/nicomachaen.html.
BBC, "Ethics Guide": http://www.bbc.co.uk/ethics/lying/lying_1.shtml.
Carson, Thomas L. *Lying and Deception: Theory and Practice*. Oxford: Oxford University Press, 2010.
"The Definition of Lying and Deception." *Stanford Encyclopedia of Philosophy*: https://plato.stanford.edu/entries/lying-definition/#DecVsNonDecAboLyi.
de Waal, Frans. "Intentional Deception in Primates." *Evolutionary Anthropology: Issues, News, and Review*. 1 no. 3. June 2005: 86–92.
Eckholm, Erick. "Deceit Found Pervasive in the Natural World." *New York Times*. January 14, 1986: http://www.nytimes.com/1986/01/14/science/deceit-found-pervasive-in-the-natural-world.html?pagewanted=all.
Feldman, Robert. *The Liar in Your Life: The Way to Truthful Relationship*. New York: Twelve, 2009./ Isenberg, Arnold. "Deontology and the Ethics of Lying." In *Aesthetics and Theory*

of Criticism: Selected Essays of Arnold Isenberg. Chicago: University of Chicago Press, 1973. pgs. 245–64.

———. "UMass Amherst Researcher Finds Most People Lie in Everyday Conversation," *UMass Amherst*. June 10, 2002: https://www.umass.edu/newsoffice/article/umass-amherst-researcher-finds-most-people-lie-everyday-conversation.

Jellison, Jerald M. *I'm Sorry, I Didn't Mean To, and Other Lies We Love to Tell*. New York: Chatham Square Press, 1977.

Kant, Immanuel. *Lectures on Ethics*. trans. Louis Infield. Indianapolis: Hackett, 1963.

Mazur, Tim C. "Lying." *Issues in Ethics*. 6 no. 1. 1993: https://www.scu.edu/ethics/ethics-resources/ethical-decision-making/lying.

Reddy, Vasudevi. *How Infants Know Minds*. Cambridge, MA: Harvard University Press, 2008.

Riddle, Travis. "Liars: It Takes One to Know One." *Scientific American*. (online) July 24, 2012: https://www.scientificamerican.com/article/liars-it-takes-one-to-know-one.

Searcy, William A., and Stephen Nowicki. *The Evolution of Animal Communication Reliability and Deception in Signaling Systems*. Princeton: Princeton University Press, 2005.

Wheeler, Randolph. "Kant on Untruths and Lying: The Falsiloquium and the Mendacium." *Ethics Journal*. 8 no. 1. 2007: 51–65.

Supergirl and Lena Luthor
Constructing Public and Private Personas
Johanna Church

"[H]ow one identifies *and* how one *is identified by others* has a mutual impact on the range of identities from which one chooses a position ... names and labels have associations, and in employing them we confer or withdraw their legitimacy [emphasis added]."[1]

Supergirl, cousin of Superman, is living in the shadow of the most physically powerful man on the planet, and she is eager to prove that she is just as capable as her superhero cousin. Lena Luthor, the CEO of L-Corp (formally Luthor Corp), finds herself living in the shadow of her famously evil brother, Lex Luthor. She tries to prove that she is not like him and that L-Corp has changed its ways. Both women are struggling to carve out careers and identities in the world outside of their associations with the men in their lives. To do so, both women use the same strategy: they project different and distinct personas that they use to navigate the difficult societal and personal expectations of their public identities. This is a common situation for public women as Tessa Pfafman notes, "expectations that professional women be both assertive and polite constitute a paradox, as the act of performing assertiveness undermines the success of polite communication."[2] Lena and Kara, as L-Corp's CEO and Supergirl respectively, live this paradox, and their persona-creation is necessary to ward off attacks from a male-dominated society that wants to destroy them, their reputations, and sometimes their very bodies.

Yet privately, while in each other's company, both are able to take off these masks to show their true selves, complete with emotions and weaknesses they cannot show the world. Supergirl assumes the persona of Kara Danvers, a mild-mannered reporter for CoCat Worldwide Media. Wearing this mask, Supergirl (now Kara) is able to get close to Lena. Her unthreatening nature allows Lena to let her guard down, take off her own public persona, and admit her struggles. What the world may view as weakness, Lena can be herself with Kara behind the closed doors of her office and away from the prying eyes of society. Supergirl, wearing the mask of Kara Danvers, can express her insecurities to Lena without judgement.[3] Applying the true self/false self theory, Lena and Kara demonstrate the ways women are forced to wear masks as part of the public roles they play. As Robert Park notes, "It is probably no mere historical accident that the word person, in its meaning, is a mask. It is rather a recognition of the fact that everyone is always and everywhere, more or less consciously, playing a role ... it is in these roles that we know each other, it is in these roles that we know ourselves."[4] This essay analyzes Kara Danvers/Supergirl/Kara Zor-El's and Lena Luthor's personas as case studies through the lens of psychoanalysis and argues that these personas are representative of a necessary coping mechanism related to women's roles in society.

Lena, Kara and True Self/False Self Theory

The true self/false self theory is a psychoanalytic theory proposed by D.W. Winnicott around 1960 with Carl Rogers and Wendy Doniger later expanding on his research.[5] Winnicott theorizes that people create a false self to navigate everyday existence as a means of compliance.[6] Both "selves" must work more diligently to return to the "true self" while also reconstructing, internally and externally, a culture within which the individuals can flourish. Once an individual is able to maintain a homeostasis or internal stability of his/her "true self," then the person is able to utilize his/her culture or experience, thus reinforcing the "true self."

Individuals desire to distinguish between themselves and others. For example, Winnicott theorizes that infants born into trauma were not given the opportunity to identify and establish a "true self," and with a limited true self, there is an inability to develop meaningful intimate relationships. Thus, intrapersonal limitations lead to interpersonal instability. Psychoanalyst Alfred Adler's identity formation theory adheres to the idea that "once the beliefs and goals that mediate behavior are identified, it is possible to predict behavior in a given social setting."[7] An individual searches for a group or place that he/she can predict interactions, thus reducing stress. This helps create positive social interactions, nurturing feelings of belonging. Adler's theory also posits that people uncover a truth about themselves through a series of transformations and masquerade. Doniger expands on this concept, arguing, "each of us is already a lot of people [...] and, so, when failing to be the other person we hoped to change into, we return to our default position, we find a different form of ourself [...] when we put on a mask we have a choice of 1000 faces, and in a very real sense they are our own."[8] This phenomenon occurs in the series when Kara Zor-El—"the original" Kara—crafts her default position as the awkward, shy, dorky Kara Danvers as well as when Lena Luthor creates her own default position as the tough, unemotional CEO of L-Corp.

Kara and Lena are important case studies for the true self/false theory because in addition to personal traumas, they have also been affected by their experiences in larger social settings, and they have used these experiences to maneuver in these contexts: "each of us behaves in accordance with our subjective awareness of ourselves and of the world around us [...] at the same time the individual chooses; his or her behavior is being determined by all the relevant conditions that exist."[9] For example, Kara Zor-El has observed modern, American attitudes regarding women's roles in society so that her persona (Kara Danvers) is easily assimilated into it. Using her observation of these norms, she assumes the persona of a klutzy, female, millennial assistant to Cat Grant. Lena, conversely, constructs her "normal" public persona as a stereotypical CEO based on her own experiences: she is guarded with those around her and apprehensive towards trusting them. Both are responding to societal assumptions of how females and millennials would behave in contemporary society, and use these assumptions to create a false self for the public that are interpretations necessary for assimilation.

These characters are also important case studies for this theory because they ask the audience to investigate whether the characters are active or passive within these roles. B.F. Skinner's observations on man and society may help explain their psychological formation:

> Even when "self-determination" appears to be at work, the real control still resides in environmental conditions and in the past and present experiences of the person; even when the individual's behaviors alter the environment, the environment still influences the person's behaviors. We may escape or avoid aversive conditions by behaving in various ways (thereby "exerting self-control"), but the new conditions produced by these behaviors will affect our subsequent actions.... When we choose or decide, we are simply behaving—and that behavior is influenced by the situations, behaviors, and behavioral consequences of the past and present.[10]

When applied to the characters, we see distinct differences in the ways different environments impacted their behaviors. For example, Lena's adoptive environment is toxic; she has to choose between following in her family's infamous footsteps or becoming her own person. Lena mimicked the behaviors and attitudes of her mother and Lex until they both turned evil, leaving her friends at school as the major influencers of her formative years. Lena mentions having gone to boarding school with the villain Roulette, but did not interact with her because of her distaste for Roulette's alien fight club.[11] Conversely, Kara's adoptive environment is largely positive; she is placed with the Danvers family who love and support her. She has an older adoptive sister, Alex, who helps her understand societal norms and is charged with protecting her. In these characters, we see the ways that characters react differently to external stimuli; their false selves being crafted to not contain a "truth" regarding their true selves. Moreover, we also Skinner's observations manifesting in the backstories of these main protagonists. In the series, Lena constantly worries that her Luthor-upbringing has made too lasting an impression on her and that her Luthor-ness is her "true" self. She admits she fears that it will emerge eventually. However, by interacting with Kara, she is able to do what is right and reject her mother's suspect values (at least as far as we know). Thus, when applying Skinner's theory, we see that these private interactions between Kara and Lena are in many ways "true."

As case studies, these characters also demonstrate the role of repression in persona creation. For instance, Kara Zor-El's true self is difficult to analyze because she wears three masks—Kara Zor-El, Kara Danvers, and Supergirl—that force her to constantly be repressing parts of her true self. The earth's yellow sun transforms Kara Zor-El from a typical Kryptonian into a superpowerful alien. At the same time, she must hide this power if she is to protect her friends, her privacy, even her life. For Kara Zor-El, it appears that "If the normal face is already a mask [which it is for viewers watching the TV show] then the mask may free the true self, lure it out of its repression, and create a safe-house for it to live."[12] So, her "normal" face—Kara Danvers—is a mask, but so too is Supergirl. Kara Zor-El—a blend of both Kara Danvers and Supergirl—is closest to her true self but is really only known (and really only can be known) to a handful of characters on the show, making this persona also the most repressed part of the self.

We also see these characters repressing different aspects of their true selves as well as the consequences for repressing their identities. For instance, the unconscious seepage between Kara/Kara Zor-El/Supergirl identities comes to fruition in the first season when Kara comes under the influence of Red Kryptonite.[13] This substance makes Supergirl behave aggressively without the normal restraints of her socialization. It takes her deepest, darkest thoughts and allows her to act on them, and as a result, the city is soon afraid of her and quickly turn against her:

> The particularly hidden or repressed or subversive parts of the self may emerge most easily in a masquerade, which makes accessible parts of the experience that are not always available. Then to take off the mask might be to get further from the truth not nearer. Sometimes the mask is more of the truth than the truth because it covers up the conscious lie and reveals the unconscious lie.[14]

In this episode, Kara Danvers yells at boss and mentor, Cat Grant, who recites that women are not allowed to get angry, so they must express it in different ways.[15] Taking this advice, she decides to express her anger by punching cars, demonstrating a seepage between personas. Moreover, the feelings that she suppresses everyday are ultimately exposed, and she has to face the negative consequences for allowing her persona to slip. For Lena, her public/private masks work much differently. Rather than suppress her power draw from anger, Lena has to constantly suppress her vulnerability and insecurities from the public. As a CEO of a billion-dollar company, she cannot afford to be seen as weak or emotional. She also cannot express anger because National City's citizens are wary of her family's psychotic history. On an individual level, the series suggests that like these characters, we all have parts of ourselves that we repress to either protect others or ourselves. On a more symbolic level, it also highlights society's fear of strong, powerful women as demonstrated by National City's reaction to these characters as well as the characters' need to repress their true selves.

Supergirl: A Masked Hero

Supergirl's comic history is packed with instances of her masking her hero persona and abilities from the world. The Supergirl character in the original DC Comics is often seen as simply a female Superman. In Alex Link's article, "The Secret of Supergirl's Success," he observes:

> [Supergirl's] unique success is attributable in part to the way in which she presents a rich and subtle critique of mid-twentieth century American idealizations of femininity. Close attention to her early adventures [in comics] reveals ways in which readers are more specifically invited to emulate her efforts to secure limited freedom while under the watchful gaze of patriarchy.[16]

When Supergirl was introduced in *Action Comics* #252 in 1959, the career roles of women consisted mostly of nurse, schoolteacher, and secretary; a life outside the home was limited. For female readers, Link argues, "Supergirl's shared secret with readers is not the specific identity of her mundane alter ego—as with readers who know Superman's secret identity—but that any mundane girl might be more powerful than she seems."[17] Thus, readers are complicit in the understanding that women are strong and powerful, but they must hide it from others, as it is socially unacceptable for women to be powerful. He continues, "Much of Supergirl's early career concerns the management of performances in general, while she tries to keep a low profile living as Linda Lee at the Midvale Orphanage."[18] In the comics, her true self is constantly being repressed by family and workplace obligations: "By trying to live within Superman's restrictions, Supergirl literalizes Friedan's sense that American women are forbidden 'to use [their] own abilities in the world,' and forbidden to 'accept or gratify their basic need to grow and fulfill their potentialities as human beings.'"[19] Patriarchal society constantly keeps women from fulfilling their potential, and in the series, we see this in Kara's struggle to differentiate herself from her famous cousin.

From the first episode, however, the series highlights Kara's desire to distance herself from Superman and succeed on her own terms. Kara's adoptive family encourages her to keep her powers hidden and not use them, especially in public. They believe that if she hides them, she will be safer, and so she is initially only able to present part of her true self to the world. It is not until Alex's plane is about to crash that Kara unleashes her full powers in order to save her sister. Alex's response is to be angry with her for "outing" herself to the world. In the pilot episode, she says, "You exposed yourself to the world. You're out there now and you can't take that back.... What if people figure out who you are ... what you are? It's not safe for you to do anything like that."[20] The message is here that society is afraid of strong women. Conversely, Clark (Superman) is encouraged to save people, while Kara (Supergirl) is not only discouraged from using her powers, she is told to repress them at all costs. Yet, the audience learns that Kara does not want to repress her powers; she wants to finally embrace who she in the same ways as her cousin.

However, Kara's experience of releasing her true self into the world is fraught with consequences. In the second episode, she accidentally outs herself as Superman's cousin adding unwanted attention to her life as Supergirl. Alex is not happy about her public exposure, as it may put Kara's secret identity in danger. Yet, Kara still decides to embrace this side of herself and share it with her friend Winn. When she is subdued and brought to the Department of Extranormal Operations (DEO), Kara responds to learning about the DEO and Alex's involvement, saying, "You told me every single day not to be who I really am."[21] She is obviously furious by Alex's own use of the true/false self-paradigm and uses that experience to commit to continuing her own true self (Supergirl)/false self (Kara Danvers) existence.

Moreover, in order for Kara Zor-El to successfully navigate the world first as Kara Danvers and later as Supergirl, she often mimics society's views of Superman and female millennials, respectively. Famously, Jacques Lacan defined mimicry as a revelation: "Mimicry reveals something in so far as it is distinct from what might be called an itself that is behind. The effect of mimicry is camouflage ... it is not a question of harmonizing with the background, but against a mottled background, of becoming mottled—exactly like the technique of camouflage practiced by human warfare."[22] Kara Danvers is a societal construct. As an alien, Kara Zor-El literally creates a human mask named Kara Danvers. She mimics the other children in Midvale and humans from television and pop culture in order to blend in with the other children. Later, she mimics American society's idea of how a twenty-five-year-old female millennial would behave and possibly dress (though her attire is mocked by Cat Grant frequently as being too boring and conservative). Kara works hard to be hardly noticed, knowing that if she were discovered, she would be in danger. While this danger could be viewed as an abstract threat, the reality of it becomes clear when, years later, she reveals her Supergirl persona. This has severe implications on Alex and her work at the DEO, and Kara Zor-El learns that coming out as Supergirl does not just affect her life, but also the lives of those around her.

Maintaining a true self and a false self is exhausting. Link observes, "Supergirl shows readers the super-effort required to maintain a posture of inferiority."[23] Kara must constantly keep her powers hidden while inhabiting her Kara Danvers persona. Her senses as Supergirl are heightened and her abilities are exceptional, but as Kara Danvers, she is a klutz, insecure, quiet, and submissive. Also, as we have seen, anger has dire consequences for her. Anger for women in a male-dominated society is frowned upon, and for powerful women, it is even less acceptable. Kara has superpowers, so if she gets mad or loses control, people could die. She has moments when she wants to assert herself but knows she risks exposure.

Once Supergirl decides to join the DEO, she is subjected to numerous tests to prove her worth.[24] But when word of Supergirl's existence is mentioned, most people are excited about the idea of a superpowered being in National City.[25] In the pilot episode, James Olsen says, "If she's anything like him (Superman), she's a hero."[26] Her comparison to Superman begins, and she must focus on proving she is her own entity and does not want to exist in his shadow. She must prove her worth as a woman living in a man's shadow. Regarding Supergirl's comic book narrative, Link says, "While Supergirl is committed to following a gender script in her stories, she still, with many a knowing wink, lays bare for a reader of them, making the reader's conventional privileged knowledge of the superhero's double-identity into a window on the everyday workings of gender and power."[27] Multiple discussions between Kara and Cat Grant focus on these very issues. In the episode "Red-Faced," Kara gets angry with Cat Grant and asks her, "Why are you so mean?"[28] She apologizes for being angry, but Cat tells her:

> Here's the thing, Kara: Everybody gets angry. Everybody. And there's no pill that will eradicate this particular emotion. I know this, because if there were such a pill, I would be popping those babies like Pez.... This is about work, and anger. Whatever you do, you cannot get angry at work. Especially when you're a girl.[29]

At CatCo, Kara Zor-El works diligently to return to her false self while also reconstructing, internally and externally, a culture within which the personalities can flourish. For Kara Danvers, it appears that "If the normal face is already a mask [which it is for viewers] then the mask may free the true self, lure it out of its repression, and create a safe-house for it to live."[30] The "selves" portrayed allow Kara to release parts of her true self. Once an individual is able to maintain a homeostasis of his/her true self, then the person is able to utilize his/her societal norms thus reinforcing the true self. Individuals need to distinguish between themselves and others, which is why some of Kara Zor-El's attributes help Kara Danvers distinguish herself from others in the workplace.

As stated previously, maintaining deception is exhausting and inevitable seepage will occur. Philosopher Friedrich Nietzsche said that "deception, far from distorting the truth, operates a double negation by ... concealing the secret that there is no secret ... sometimes the mask turns out to have been the same face all along."[31]

As the series progresses, the Kara Danvers mask becomes more similar (if not the same as) Kara Zor-El. Kara's interactions with Lena Luthor give us the most insight into this true self/false self dichotomy. As the friendship becomes deeper, Kara feels more comfortable interacting with Lena. Parts of Kara Zor-El are present underneath all the masks, a composite of her various personas: sister, alien, reporter, friend, and the like. Parts of her various personas theoretically make up the true Kara Zor-El. But the series asks another important question: which persona of Kara's does society value more? Many would say Supergirl, and this is best represented by Kara's interactions with Cat Grant. As Cat begins to figure out that Kara is Supergirl and threatens to fire her if she does not reveal her identity:

> CAT: Every minute that you waste playing assistant in here is a minute that someone out there is not getting saved.
> KARA: Ms. Grant, what are you saying?
> CAT: I'm saying that I will not partake in this ruse any longer. So you either prove to me that you are not Supergirl, or you can clean out your desk tomorrow.[32]

Cat assumes Kara Danvers is not important—or at least not as important—as her Supergirl persona, and that Supergirl is the only component of Kara Zor-El that is of value to the world. But both personas provide her with the strength to survive and navigate her new planet and having to choose one over the other is appalling to her. She needs Kara Danvers as much as she needs Supergirl because they both serve different needs.[33] In the finale for the second season, Superman says that Supergirl is physically and mentally stronger than he is, and the viewer recognizes that she has surpassed the very man whose shadow she was under. In this moment, the series demonstrates that Supergirl will now focusing on creating a new superhero narrative, one distinctly feminine.

"You are not your family": Lena Luthor's Masks

Lena Luthor must similarly work to create her own narrative, free from comparisons to her brother Lex. Lex is, of course, Superman's nemesis, so by extension one would assume Lena is or will become Supergirl's nemesis. Instead of a nemesis, Kara Danvers discovers a friend. The two characters do not seem to have much in common at first, but both women are trying to differentiate themselves from their male relatives, which is why Kara reminds Lena: "You are not your family." In the comics, Lena Luthor was introduced in *Superman's Girlfriend Lois Lane* Volume #23 in February 1961:

> She was a toddler when her brother became a notorious criminal mastermind in his teenage years. Lex and Lena's parents were so ashamed of their son's crimes and reputation that they moved away from their home in Smallville with Lena and changed their surname to "Thorul"—"Luthor" inverted. Lena grew up with no knowledge of the fact that she had a brother or that he had become the arch-nemesis of Superman.[34]

In contrast, on the *Supergirl* television show, Lex is not disowned by his parents; in fact, his mother embraces him. However, Lena is essentially disowned because she wants nothing to do with Lex's or her mother's plans.[35] Moreover, in their characterization of him, *Supergirl* draws on the Lex from *Crisis on Infinite Earths*.[36] Lex does not make an appearance in the first or second season, but his character was referenced repeatedly—as shadow looming over Lena and show. However, *Supergirl* does use the idea that Lena was young when Lex went insane and that she at least has disavowed her brother's actions. When she is introduced on the show, Lena is twenty-four years old and the new CEO of L-Corp. The television show does not follow Lena's *Justice League* narrative arc, but instead, more closely follows *Superman Family* and *Superman's Girlfriend Lois Lane*.[37]

In the series, Lena was born in 1993 in Metropolis. Her mother is unknown but her father is Lionel Luthor. This knowledge is kept from her until the middle of season two when Lillian needs Luthor DNA.[38] Lena is adopted by the Luthors when she is four years old after he mother dies. While Lex welcomes her with open arms, Lillian (her stepmother) does not, and as a result, Lena is never considered a "real" Luthor. She went to MIT and was still close with Lex until he started becoming obsessed with Superman. She tried to help him, but he ended up in jail, serving thirty-seven life terms. Lena takes over LuthorCorp and moves to National City. In the television show: "Despite being raised by Lillian; following Lionel's death, Lena is a stark contrast to what the public perceives to be a Luthor. Whereas they are delusional, egotistical, amoral, and murderous, Lena is kind, caring, dutiful, selfless, moral and honorable."[39] She is also an engineer, computer programmer, and genius who is also skilled with firearms.

On *Supergirl*, viewers are introduced to Lena when Clark and Kara go to interview her for a newspaper article in the first episode of the second season. When we meet Lena, she is trying to prove that she is not like Lex, and she is determined to use her company for good rather than evil. Viewers also see her walking the fine line between her private insecurities and vulnerabilities and her public life as a strong CEO. In third episode of the season, Kara meets Lena because she was asked to interview: "The sister of the most notorious alien hater."[40] Lena's identity is once again overshadowed by her brother's legacy. Later, when it is revealed that Lena has developed an alien detection device, Kara worries that it—and Lena—will be used for evil. Lena defends herself, saying that there are bad aliens out there, and that she is not doing it to be malicious. Lena is fully aware of the public's perception of her and how L-Corp is negatively linked to Lex, and she is tirelessly working to change it. Clark assumes that Lena is just like her brother, but Lena responds to the acquisition by saying, "You wouldn't be asking me if my last name was Smith" to which Clark replies, "But it's not, it's Luthor."[41] Lena continues by explaining that she was adopted; therefore, the public perception of her as a Luthor is unwarranted because she is not a Luthor by birth. She renames Luthor Corp as "L-Corp" to further distance herself from the family's negative history and Lex's notoriety because, as she says, "I'm just a person trying to make a name herself outside her family. Can you understand that?"[42] Here Lena's false self has been assigned to her. Society has decided that she is evil and untrustworthy. Her true self, however, is the opposite. Even though Kara constantly defends Lena, her friends are suspicious. Winn says, "The Luthors are pretty good actors. Or, well, sociopaths. Either way they know how to fool people."[43] Kara is infuriated because she has seen the "real" Lena and does not believe she is evil at all.

The television show also explores Lena's motives.[44] For instance, Kara writes an article about women of power and the mothers who molded them. She is fishing for information regarding Lena's involvement with her mother's evil plans. Kara believes Lena is innocent, but her friends are not so sure. Lena is hurt that Kara would even suspect her. When Supergirl arrives to save Lena from her mother she says, "Kara Danvers believes in you," which is interesting. Why did she not say, "I believe in you?"[45] This is an interesting maintenance of the two selves. Kara is keeping her Supergirl persona separate from Lena and focusing on her friendship with Lena as Kara Danvers. Lena Luthor is trying to expand her outside friendships, and Kara is a friend and she wants to maintain her human friendship. When Lena asks Supergirl for help and Supergirl questions her motives, Lena asks, "Are you one of those people that believes there is no such thing as a good Luthor?" Lena later says, "Who would've believed it, a Luthor and a Super working together."[46] Lena says this with a glowing smile on her face. She truly relishes working with the Super and it provides her with hope for a positive future away from the negativity her family name arouses. Supergirl responds by saying, "I'm someone who believes in judging someone on their own merits."[47] Lena does not have the luxury of showing her vulnerable side at work. Nor does she have anyone to share her vulnerabilities with until Kara comes along.

But she can only share so much, as she must deny involvement in her mother's schemes, and she cannot discuss her mother with Kara. Lena and her mother have an interesting dynamic. At times, Lena is openly disdainful of her mother and the Luthor's obsession with aliens. Lena wears a mask when interacting with her mother because she does not agree with Lillian's views of aliens. She must pretend to be helping her mother release a toxic virus into the atmosphere to kill all the aliens. She must also pretend to Kara that she is working with her mother. This is the mask the world has given her: "anti-alien, psychotic Luthor." However, she assumes this persona with her mother in order to ultimately ruin her plans.[48] Supergirl says, "You are not like your mother."[49] Now Lena must separate herself from comparisons between her mother, Lex, and herself. Lillian, Lena's mother, believes that Lena is smarter than Lex and says that she "backed the wrong Luthor."[50] Now, Lillian sees her as separate from Lex and not just a poor substitute.

Of course, this reveal is tainted by her motives. Lillian is clearly psychotic and blinded by her hatred for aliens. She does not believe that Lena will stay away from Lex's values and the Luthor family's anti-alien rhetoric. But Lena is confident in her abilities when she says to Beth Breen:

> BETH: You know it's true what they say, behind every great man is a strong woman.
> LENA: Wouldn't know, I've never stood behind a man.[51]

She is overshadowed by him in the press, but never personally. Here, she implies that Lex is not a great man; if he were, she would not have responded this way. It is because she is in Lex's shadow that Lena is regularly exposed to anti–Luthor sentiment due to her brother's past behavior. Her phrasing provides some insight into her self-perception. She considers herself separate from the Luthor business. Amy Ratcliffe observes that after Lena has to kill her ex-boyfriend in order to save Supergirl:

> Lena is poised to fall over the side. She's experienced a significant amount of loss and hardship ... so it's not a surprise for her to feel like she can't catch a break. I hardly expect her to face the world with bright eyes and an overly optimistic attitude after what she's gone through, but she's swinging to the opposite end of the spectrum. She believes she'll go to a bad place because of her last name. The path for other Luthors has ended in criminal action, and she doesn't think she can go another direction. Because Lena expects a negative outcome, it's more likely to happen. Her focus will determine her reality.[52]

The question for her future is whether or not Lena embraces or turns to the "dark" side. Lena has overcome other hardships in the past and seems determined to fight against her mother's anti-alien organization, Cadmus. But at what point does someone simply embrace the expectations of others because it is an easier route to pursue? Lena's determination has been evident all season, but can she sustain it?

The Masks of Kara and Lena

Both Kara and Lena have experienced significant loss: they have both lost a family, a home, and a sense of self. Both have suffered through traumas and have crafted new personas as a result of those experiences. Lena worries that the latest trauma of her boyfriend Jack's death will change her psychically: "Lena told Kara loss does strange things to her family, and she's afraid of whom she'd be. She's letting herself be pushed by fate and the past rather than taking control. Lena's too grounded and strong for that sort of behavior, but she thinks she can't overcome her past."[53] Likewise, Kara has also suffered the loss of her boyfriend, Mon-El. Their ability to survive through trauma has allowed them to succeed together, but with these new traumas, what made them similar may eventually make them grow apart.

An individual's personality may change over time. Various social interactions may cause an individual to adjust their personas to suit various audiences. Symbolically, personalities are in flux. Goffman observes, "The self, then, as a performance character, is not an organic thing that has a specific location, whose fundamental fate is to be born, to mature, and to die; it is a dramatic effect arising diffusely from a scene that is presented, and the characteristic issue, the crucial concern, is whether it is credited or discredited."[54] Personalities change from interaction to interaction. People have "work selves," "private selves," and other "selves" for different situations. Both Lena and Kara do not just change from scenario to scenario but with each person they interact with. This is no doubt a source of stress for both women. Kara frequently catches herself mixing personas. For example, she tells Lena that she "flew here ... on a bus."[55] After such slips, she must backtrack and clarify her meanings; she can rarely relax. Likewise, Lena always has her guard up and does not trust anyone.

Both Kara and Lena experience guilt at times while wearing their false selves. Kara had a good relationship with her mother before she left Krypton, but has since learned more about her, which has made her become disillusioned. Lena feels guilty that she is not the perfect daughter or does not have the societally defined "mother/daughter" relationship. She is appalled by her mother's behaviors as the head of the anti-alien terrorist group Cadmus. Lena and Kara feel guilty because generally a daughter may feel that she should worship or fully support her mother. Beth Livingston theorizes, "Thus, individuals who adhere to traditionally accepted norms of gender are more likely to feel guilty when their family responsibilities interfere with their work responsibilities but are less likely to feel guilty when their responsibilities interfere with their family responsibilities."[56] However, Kara is not completely honest with Lena because she is still hiding her Supergirl persona from one of her best friends. Actor Katie McGrath explained the dynamic between Kara and Lena in a phone interview:

> Lillian seems pretty sure that Lena will figure out that Supergirl and Kara are one in the same, and that it will upset her to know that that was kept from her. How do you think she'll react, and what would it take for her to be okay with that lie?
> McGrath: [...] The thing that I like about the relationship is that neither of them has to be the other person when they're together. Supergirl is only Kara when she's around Lena, and Lena is only Lena. It's based on them being real human beings, flawed and wonderful, but not the head of a company and not a superhero.
> I think if Lena ever finds out, it will be hard for her not to feel betrayed that her best friend didn't tell her that. But then, she's also a very smart woman and she has to understand that it is very difficult for a superhero to be that open and honest about that secret with a Luthor.... Ultimately, I'm hopeful that she will feel betrayed and hurt, but accepting of her best friend.[57]

The friendship between Lena and Kara is an integral part of their identities because they get to be their true selves. They share their vulnerabilities and insecurities. They support each other professionally and personally. Kara writes articles about L-Corp and how Lena tries to make the company a force for good. She defends Lena's actions to her sister and friends. Lena gives Kara first dibs on stories and supports her journalistic career, but Kara is not all she appears to be to Lena. Kara, of course, is also Supergirl. Lena has been completely honest with Kara, but Lena's mother and Rhea (Mon-El's mother) have both deceived her in the second season, possibly making it difficult for Lena to forgive Kara.

So, who are the real Kara and Lena? Viewers may never truly know because the characters themselves do not truly know. They, like others, have personalities that are always in flux: "The self, then, as a performance character, is not an organic thing that has a specific location, whose fundamental fate is to be born, to mature, and to die; it is a dramatic effect arising diffusely from a scene that is presented, and the characteristic issue, the crucial concern, is whether it is credited or discredited."[58] Lena, for example, must draw on her negative, manipulative childhood lessons in order to trick her mother. She can assume that persona at will because it is a part of her, however, she chooses to suppress it overall.[59] *Supergirl* is a series comprised of women stuck in the bind the true self/false self dichotomy. Kara Danvers/Supergirl/

78 Why Not Superwoman? Constructing the Feminism of *Supergirl*

Kara Zor-El, Alex Danvers/Sister/Scientist/DEO Agent, Lena Luthor/CEO, and Cat Grant/CatCo/CEO are all women are all trying to balance society's perceptions and expectations of women in public and private spaces. After her ex-boyfriend dies, Lena says, "I think when I feel things again, I'm going to be very, very afraid ... about the person I might be."[60] It is prescient because Kara feels the same loss of her boyfriend in the second season finale and the third season trailer says that she will be dropping her Kara Danvers persona as a result. Perhaps it is a sign of both characters' transformations and the shedding of false selves.

Notes

1. Katya Gibel Azoulay, "Outside Our Parents' House: Race, Culture, and Identity," *Research in African American Literatures* 27, no. 1 (1996): 129–142.
2. Tessa M. Pfafman and Bree McEwan, "Polite Women at Work: Negotiating Professional Identity Through Strategic Assertiveness," *Women's Studies in Communication*, 37 no. 2 (2014): 202.
3. *Supergirl*, "Ace Reporter," season 2, episode 18, directed by Armen V. Kevorkian, written by Paula Yoo and Caitlin Parrish, aired April 24, 2017, on The CW.
4. Erving Goffman, *The Presentation of Self in Everyday Life* (New York: Anchor Books, 1956), 19.
5. Winnicott's research focuses on an individual's development when faced with opposition or traumatic events, and he states that early trauma leads to feelings of anxiety and anxious individuals have lessened or reduced perceptions of both themselves and society. This lessens an individual's overall ability to "reality test," meaning that an individual is unable to see what is *really* happening with respect to being accepted by societal norms. Thus, an individual interprets something that is unacceptable by the larger society to be acceptable. According to this theory, an individual consists of a "true self" and a "false self."
6. It is created in order to assimilate more effectively into society or groups. The false self is the one that society projects onto the individual and after decades of being portrayed and treated negatively by the dominant power, the individual loses more of the "true self" needed to cope with the surroundings.
7. Hildegard Adler, "Recall and Repetition of a Severe Childhood Trauma," *The International Journal of Psychoanalysis*, 76 (1995): 931.
8. Wendy Doniger, "Self-Impersonation in World Literature," *The Kenyon Review*, 26 no. 2 (2004): 115.
9. Robert Nye, *Three Psychologies: Perspectives from Freud, Skinner, and Rogers*, 6th ed. (Belmont, CA: Cengage Learning, 1999), 101, 103.
10. Robert Nye, *Three Psychologies*, 78, 81.
11. *Supergirl*, "Survivors," season 2, episode 4, directed by James Marshall and James Bamford, written by Paula Yoo and Eric Carrasco, aired October 31, 2016, on The CW.
12. Doniger, "Self-Impersonation," 117.
13. *Supergirl*, "Red Faced," season 1, episode 6, directed by Jesse Warn, written by Michael Grassi and Rachel Shukert, aired November 30, 2015, on CBS.
14. Doniger, "Self-Impersonation," 117.
15. *Supergirl*, "Falling," season 1, episode 16, directed by Larry Teng, written by Robert Rovner and Jessica Queller, aired March 14, 2016, on CBS.
16. Link, "The Secret of Supergirl's Success," *The Journal of Popular Culture*, 46, no. 6 (2013): 1177.
17. Link, "The Secret of Supergirl's Success," 1178.
18. Link, "The Secret of Supergirl's Success," 1179.
19. Link, "The Secret of Supergirl's Success," 1179.

20. *Supergirl*, "Pilot," season 1, episode 1, directed by Glen Winter, story by Greg Berlanti, Ali Adler, and Andrew Kreisberg, teleplay by Ali Adler, aired October 26, 2015, on CBS.
21. *Supergirl*, "Pilot," Season 1, episode 1.
22. Xu Ping, "Irigaray's Mimicry and the Problem of Essentialism," *Hypatia*, 10 no. 4 (1995): 76–89. https://www.jstor.org/stable/3810206.
23. Link, "The Secret of Supergirl's Success," 1179.
24. The DEO makes her perform flying speed tests as well as learn proper fighting techniques to make sure she is not a liability to the organization.
25. Cat Grant is extremely excited about having a superhero and so she crafts a marketing campaign and names Kara, Supergirl. Season 1, episode 2 "Stronger Together," directed by Glen Winter, written by Greg Berlanti and Andrew Kreisberg, Andrew Kreisberg, and Ali Adler. CBS, November 2, 2015. Cat Grant is extremely excited about having a superhero and so she crafts a marketing campaign and names Kara, Supergirl.
26. *Supergirl*, "Pilot," season 1, episode 1.
27. Link, "The Secret of Supergirl's Success," 1179.
28. *Supergirl*, "Red Faced," season 1, episode 6.
29. *Supergirl*, "Red Faced," season 1, episode 6.
30. Doniger, "Self-Impersonation," 117.
31. Friedrich Wilhelm Nietzsche and Helen Zimmern, *Beyond Good and Evil: Prelude to a Philosophy of the Future* (London: Global Classics, 2008), 113.
32. *Supergirl*, "Blood Bonds," season 1, episode 9, directed by Steve Shill, written by Ted Sullivan and Derek Simon, aired January 4, 2016, on CBS.
33. In the comics, Supergirl's identity undergoes an intense pressure typical of American women living under the burden of feminine mystique. The pressures of living in such a maze of contradictions, of public limited power and private infinite power; of shoring up the performance of masculine power that at the same time actualizes it as effective power; of spending so much of one's energies on maintaining the invisibility of those very energies; of living a double life of power and ability without opportunity or recognition; and of exercising power covertly, without hope of direct and unmitigated agency except, ultimately, by the good graces of an authority that might one day choose to share itself, takes a toll … as a double life has its price. Link, "The Secret of Supergirl's Success," 1186.
34. Jamie Hari, "Lena Luthor Prime Earth," *DC* (wiki), July, 15, 2017: http://dc.wikia.com/wiki/Lena_Luthor (Prime_Earth).
35. According to S. Atkinson, "In the newer comics, Lena and Linda Lee [Supergirl's alias in the Silver and Bronze Age of comics] become friends in a high school science club, where a scientist is testing for ESP, and, when Lee sees Luthor get every question right, she's intrigued. When Lena falls in with a criminal set, Supergirl is concerned she's responding to her rejection by the FBI (due to her relation to Lex) by becoming just like her brother, but Supergirl shouldn't have worried; Lena Luthor was just going undercover to bring the criminals to justice. Like Supergirl, we shouldn't assume that simply because Lena's related to supervillain Lex Luthor that they'll be on the same side. In fact, in Justice League #41, which dropped last year [2015], Lena puts a couple of bullets in her brother." S. Atkinson, "Who is Lena Luthor?" *Bustle*, June 8, /2017: https://www.bustle.com/articles/165710-who-is-lena-luthor-supergirl-season-2-adds-an-interesting-comic-book-character.
36. The DC Wiki mentions, "Following the 1985 limited series Crisis on Infinite Earth, the character was re-imagined as a Machiavellian industrialist and white-collar criminal, even briefly serving as President of the United States. In recent years, various writers have revived Luthor's mad scientist persona from the 1940s." Anonymous, "Lex Luthor," *DC Villains* (wiki), July 10, 2017: http://dcvillains.wikia.com/wiki/Lex_Luthor. Moreover, Lex Luthor is often described as "Driven by jealousy masked with hate over what he perceives to be his stolen place as humanity's true savior, Luthor constantly attempts to destroy and humiliate Superman at every possible opportunity. He's willing to lie, cheat, steal, manipulate and go to any extreme necessary to accomplish his goals, not caring one bit about who he hurts. He is a man who not only wants to be seen as a god, but who has convinced himself he's the only one this world needs." Anonymous, "Lex Luthor," *DC* (wiki), July 20, 2017: http://dccomics.com.

37. Jamie Hari, "Superman Family Vol. 1 #214," *DC* (wiki), July 15, 2017: http://dc.wikia.com/wiki/Superman_Family_Vol_1_214.
38. *Supergirl*, "Luthors," season 2, episode 12, directed by Tawnia McKiernan, written by Robert Rovner and Cindy Lichtman, aired February 13, 2017, on The CW.
39. "Lena Luthor (Earth Fifty)," *Memorydelta* (wiki), http://memorydelta.wikia.com/wiki/Lena_Luthor_(Earth_Fifty).
40. *Supergirl*, "Welcome to Earth," season 2, episode 3, directed by Rachel Talalay, written by Jessica Queller and Derek Simon, aired October 24, 2016, on The CW.
41. *Supergirl*, "Welcome to Earth," season 2, episode 3.
42. *Supergirl*, "The Adventures of Supergirl," season 2, episode 1, directed by Glen Winter, story by Greg Berlanti and Andrew Kreisberg, teleplay by Andrew Kreisberg and Jessica Queller, aired October 10, 2016, on The CW.
43. *Supergirl*, "Medusa," season 2, episode 8, directed by Stefan Pleszczynnski, written by Jessica Queller and Derek Simon, aired November 28, 2016, on The CW.
44. *Supergirl*, "Medusa," season 2, episode 8.
45. *Supergirl*, "Luthors," season 2, episode 12.
46. *Supergirl*, "Crossfire," season 2, episode 5, directed by Glen Winter, written by Gabriel Llanas and Anna Musky-Goldwyn, aired November 7, 2016, on The CW.
47. *Supergirl*, "Crossfire," season 2, episode 5.
48. *Supergirl*, "Medusa," season 2, episode 8.
49. *Supergirl*, "Medusa," season 2, episode 8.
50. *Supergirl*, "Nevertheless, She Persisted," season 2, episode 22, directed by Glen Winter, story by Andrew Kreisberg and Jessica Queller, teleplay by Robert Rovner and Caitlin Parrish, aired May 22, 2017, on The CW.
51. *Supergirl*, "Ace Reporter," season 2, episode 18.
52. Amy Ratcliffe, "Looking Out for Lena Luthor," *DC Comics* (blog), April 24, 2017: http://www.dccomics.com/blog/2017/04/24/supergirl-looking-out-for-lena-luthor.
53. Amy Ratcliffe, "Looking Out for Lena Luthor."
54. Goffman, *The Presentation of Self*, 252–53.
55. *Supergirl*, "Welcome to Earth," season 2, episode 3, directed by Rachel Talalay, written by Jessica Queller and Derek Simon, aired October 24, 2016, on The CW.
56. Beth A. Livingston and Timothy A. Judge, Livingston, "Emotional Responses to Work-Family Conflict: An Examination of Gender Role Orientation Among Working Men and Women," *Journal of Applied Psychology* 1, no. 93 (2008): 207–16.
57. Katie McGrath, "'Supergirl': Katie McGrath on Season 2 and Lena Luthor's Future," interview by Christina Radish, *Collider*, May 22, 2017, http://collider.com/supergirl-season-2-katie-mcgrath-interview/#images.
58. Goffman, *The Presentation of Self*, 252–53.
59. In Hélène Cixous's argument, "woman must counteract her unhistory and speak always in the present and to the present: 'At risk of losing oneself the risk is necessary.'" Adams, Tessa and Andrea Duncan, eds., *The Feminine Case: Jung, Aesthetics and Creative Process* (London: Routledge, 2003).
60. *Supergirl*, season 2, episode 18, "Ace Reporter."

Selected Bibliography

Adams, Tessa, and Andrea Duncan, eds. *The Feminine Case: Jung, Aesthetics and Creative Process*. London: Routledge, 2003.
Adler, Hildegard. "Recall and Repetition of a Severe Childhood Trauma." *The International Journal of Psychoanalysis* 76 (1995): 927–42.
Atkinson, S. "Who Is Lena Luthor? 'Supergirl' Season 2 Adds an Interesting Comic Book Character." Bustle.com, June 8, 2016, https://www.bustle.com/articles/165710-who-is-lena-luthor-supergirl-season-2-adds-an-interesting-comic-book-character.
Azoulay, Katya Gibel. "Outside Our Parents' House: Race, Culture, and Identity." *Research in African American Literatures* 27, no. 1 (1996): 129–142.
Dinkmeyer, Don, and Don Dinkmeyer, Jr. "Adlerian Psychotherapy and Counseling." In *Con-

temporary Models and Methods, ed. Steven Jay Lynn and John P. Garske, 117–54. New York: A. Bell and Howell Co., 1985.
Dinkmeyer, Don, and Len Sperry. *Adlerian Counseling and Psychotherapy*. 2nd ed. Columbus, Ohio: Merrill Publishing Company, 1987.
Doniger, Wendy. "Self-Impersonation in World Literature." *The Kenyon Review*, New, 26, no. 2 (2004): 101–25.
Goffman, Erving. *The Presentation of Self in Everyday Life*. New York: Random House, 1956.
Hari, Jamie. "Lena Luthor Prime Earth." *DC* (wiki). July 15, 2017, http://dc.wikia.com/wiki/Lena_Luthor (Prime_Earth).
_____. "Superman Family Vol. 1 #214." *DC* (wiki). July 15, 2017, http://dc.wikia.com/wiki/Superman_Family_Vol_1_214.
"Lena Luthor (Earth Fifty)." *Memorydelta* (wiki). http://memorydelta.wikia.com/wiki/Lena_Luthor_(Earth_Fifty).
"Lex Luthor." *DC Villains* (wiki). http://dcvillains.wikia.com/wiki/Lex_Luthor.
Link, Alex. "The Secret of Supergirl's Success." *The Journal of Popular Culture*. 46, no. 6 (2013): 1177–1198.
Livingston, Beth, and Timothy Judge. "Emotional Responses to Work-Family Conflict: An Examination of Gender Role Orientation Among Working Men and Women." *Journal of Applied Psychology* 1, no. 93 (2008): 207–16.
McGrath, Katie. "'Supergirl': Katie McGrath on Season 2 and Lena Luthor's Future." Interview by Christina Radish. *Collider*, May 22, 2017. http://collider.com/supergirl-season-2-katie-mcgrath-interview/#images.
Nietzsche, Friedrich Wilhelm, and Helen Zimmern. *Beyond Good and Evil: Prelude to a Philosophy of the Future*. London: Global Classics, 2008.
Nye, Robert. *Three Psychologies: Perspectives from Freud, Skinner, and Rogers*. 6th ed. Belmont, CA: Cengage Learning, 1999.
Pfafman, Tessa M., and Bree McEwan. "Polite Women at Work: Negotiating Professional Identity Through Strategic Assertiveness." *Women's Studies in Communication*. 37 no. 2 (2014): 202–219. https://doi-org.jwupvdz.idm.oclc.org/10.1080/07491409.2014.911231
Ping, Xu. "Irigaray's Mimicry and the Problem of Essentialism." *Hypatia*. 10 no. 4 (1995): 76–89. https://www.jstor.org/stable/3810206
Pollock, Donald. "Masks and the Semiotics of Identity." *Journal of the Royal Anthropological Institute*. 1, no. 3 (1995).
Ratcliffe, Amy. "Looking Out for Lena Luthor." *DC Comics* (blog). April 24, 2017, http://www.dccomics.com/blog/2017/04/24/supergirl-looking-out-for-lena-luthor.

Female Otherness and Intersectionality in *Supergirl*

"Pull up your big-girl pants, and own your power"

Feminist Anger and the Working Woman in The CW's Supergirl

Justin Wigard

One of the most striking characteristics about *Supergirl* is the prominence of the workplace to Kara's/Supergirl's life. She works at CatCo Worldwide Media as a personal assistant to CEO Cat Grant, as well as at the Department of Extranormal Operations (DEO) assisting Director Hank Henshaw (also known as the Martian J'onn J'onzz).[1] While at the DEO, Kara dons the mantle of Supergirl, essentially working through the DEO to stop crimes and protect people in a governmentally-sanctioned role. Because of her position as a superhero, Kara extends her workplace beyond the offices of both CatCo and the DEO to wherever she operates as a superhero out in the field. Despite the show's relative success and popularity, CBS opted not to renew *Supergirl*, and instead, the show landed with The CW, which CBS co-owns with Warner Bros. Entertainment. Kara's employment fluctuates in season two of *Supergirl* as Cat Grant steps down, offering an opportunity for Kara to choose a new profession within the company as a result. Each episode's overarching plot generally involves Kara saving National City from an extraterrestrial threat or natural disaster, yet many episodes also feature storylines about workplace conflict and drama, whether in the form of difficult assignments at CatCo or strife in the DEO. Within these episodes, there are notable instances in which Kara expresses anger; not stress, nor frustration, but outright anger, an emotion not traditionally associated with traditional superhero norms and an emotion with a politically-fraught history with respect to women in the workplace.

This essay explores issues of anger as they manifest within *Supergirl* through a critical feminist lens, looking to anger as an emotion of political and social change for working women in The CW television show. Here, I am particularly concerned with the mode in which feminist anger is depicted from season to season (and network to network) as the different workspaces go through drastic changes, including new coworkers and a shift from a female CEO to a male one at CatCo Worldwide Media. Drawing upon feminist literature, emotion criticism, and social surveys of workplace dynamics, I look to pivotal examples of Supergirl expressing anger and whether this emotion is represented constructively or detrimentally in terms of feminist politics. I focus first on unsuccessful expressions before moving onto Supergirl's productive uses of anger. Ultimately, Supergirl's position as an avatar of women in the workplace, particularly as it relates to her experiences expressing feminist anger (positive and negative, successful and unsuccessful) offers critical insight into issues of the modern working woman through her cross-season superhero narrative.

Feminist Anger

Any discussion of feminist anger would be remiss without acknowledging, and working from the considerable foundation built by Audre Lorde in her 1981 keynote address, "The Uses of Anger: Women Responding to Racism." Speaking on the explicit and veiled racism that Black women face, Lorde spoke on the practical purpose of anger, explaining that "every woman has a well-stocked arsenal of anger" through which to effect change.[2] What Lorde advocates for is not a simple release of pressures built up from a strenuous day of work, but for women to focus and channel anger designed to radically alter a specific aspect of life. Since her keynote, Lorde's concept of anger has been expanded to understanding how oppressed peoples can come to terms with their own productive power. Anger is that emotion bridling up when confronted with oppression, individual or institutional; by tapping into such a powerful emotion tied to an external threat or system of oppression, women can become empowered if their anger is channeled effectively to enact change. Therefore, when women express anger, it becomes imperative to look at what aspects of their lives are radically altered (signifying productive anger) or not (signifying unproductive anger).

Sylvia Burrow expands on Lorde's foundation of anger as a "politically and epistemologically subversive response to oppressive practices" by investigating the abusive practice of emotionally dismissing anger.[3] In viewing anger as a mode of communication, particularly as a communicative expression, Burrow points to instances of denying anger as another party interpreting an individual's emotions, judging that emotion as negative or otherwise beneath acknowledgment, and thus worthy of being dismissed. Viewed this way, the denial of anger is an oppressive, almost abusive, action. Elizabeth Spelman further notes that dominant groups are typically not the ones being suppressed; instead, oppressed groups (minorities and women) are having their anger denied.[4] When denials of anger occur, these interactions can be read in terms of a representative of a dominant group interpreting the emotions of a member of an oppressed group, rather than understanding the emotion as intended. The danger here isn't simply that anger is being denied, but that an emotion charged with potential for political action and change is silenced.

This is often seen when men, as representatives of patriarchal power within the workplace, listen to women's expression of anger, then deny that anger through dismissal or outright shaming.[5] Commonly known as gaslighting, the insidious act occurs when men dismiss women's expressions as irrational to such a degree that the women experience a disorienting state of self-doubt and helplessness. The purposeful misinterpretation of female expressions and their subsequent dismissal acts as a mode of oppression; within the workplace, these suppressive acts are often covert in their execution, necessitating closer examinations of workplace relations within *Supergirl*.

An important distinction must be made at this time between *rage* and *anger*, particularly as it relates to feminist politics. In recent years, the phrase "feminist rage" has been appropriated by proponents of toxic masculinity as an attempt to undermine the foundations of feminism. More than simple gaslighting, "feminist rage" is applied in a derogatory manner to instances of feminists speaking out against the norm, quelling their voices, and dismissing their emotions.[6] While more research is needed detailing the insidious nature of toxic masculinity, Kimberly Flemke and Katherine R. Allen provide a much-needed and succinct distinction between the two terms: "Rage is described as an overwhelming experience with particular physiological and cognitive changes that takes control of a woman's emotions and actions. In contrast, anger is described as a controllable emotion with a specific termination point."[7] Thus, what many might perceive to be rage is, in actuality, anger. The key delineation between these two emotions revolves around the presence of control (or lack thereof): when control is present, one is tapping into anger while remaining logical or rational; when control is overwhelmed, or absent, one is tapping into rage while logic and reason are ignored. Making a similar distinction between "hatred" and anger, Lorde notes that hatred is driven by anger at oppressors with the intent of "destruction," whereas anger is motivated by a desire for change.[8] Thus, the instances of *Supergirl* in which anger is channeled (not hatred or rage) for a productive purpose or to a productive end are the primary consideration of this investigation, with a secondary focus on examples featuring rage as distinguished from anger.

Feminist anger has been explored in many different societal contexts, but of particular attention is that which bears heavily on *Supergirl*: the workplace. Theresa A. Domagalski and Lisa A. Steelman find that within the workplace, women are socially "labeled the more emotional sex" while facing societal pressure to suppress emotions indirectly, particularly when it comes to anger.[9] The same cannot be said for men, who "are permitted, and perhaps expected, to display their anger directly, if not aggressively" at work.[10] What this signals is a serious discrepancy between how gender affects the expression of anger, particularly as it relates to the conditioning of employees in the workplace.

Domagalski and Steelman further note that anger in the workplace can have both short-term and long-term consequences on both individual and organizational levels, particularly when the anger goes unresolved. Unresolved anger correlates to a deterioration of personal relationships as well as degenerative personal health in the form of heart problems or poor sleep patterns, issues which can affect the individual's personal work-life. Past the immediate individual concerns, that unresolved anger can lead to counterproductive work behavior and poor work ethics on up to employment dismissal, or even violence in the workplace. As a result, the appearance of these effects within *Supergirl* merits close analysis in order to determine whether these effects are specifically related to anger within the show's fictionalized workplaces.[11]

Superheroes have often been analyzed regarding their positions within the workplace, particularly female superheroes during the 1960s and 1970s. According to Laura Mattoon D'Amore, these earlier superheroines not only acted as representations of cultural empowerment, but "acted out a burgeoning feminist fantasy in their roles as women working in a man's world."[12] These superheroines working among men operate as idealized representations of feminism, championing equality for women through their working narratives. Characters such as the Invisible Woman, Wonder Woman, and on occasion, Storm, are shown alongside men, both within typical workplace environments (offices, for example) and atypical or superheroic environments (cosmic worlds and alternate planes of existence), while Brett White notes that, in her first solo series in 1977, Ms. Marvel was "unapologetically feminist," becoming "a force to be reckoned with, as she fought battles in Boston, outer space, and everywhere in between."[13] Though these representations are often problematic in other ways, D'Amore's insight highlights the key roles that the working woman played in early superhero narratives. For example, the Invisible Woman has a long history of representing and embodying conflicting traits of feminine weakness and strength, as her power allows her to become invisible as well as project impenetrable force fields. While D'Amore focuses more on the competing roles that both maternity and employment play in superheroine narratives between 1963 and 1980, her work serves as a critical connector between the realm of feminist anger and superhero narratives. D'Amore notes that "superheroines were a critical component of superhero comics during the 1960s and 1970s, and they acted out a burgeoning feminist future in their roles as women working in a men's world."[14] Given the current zeitgeist of superhero film and television properties and franchises of the late 2000s/early 2010s, it becomes critical to investigate what these popular avatars of the human condition signify in popular culture, particularly with *Supergirl*, an incredibly popular female-led superhero television show.[15]

The DEO and Unproductive Anger

When adopting the mantle of mild-mannered "Kerah"[16] at CatCo, Kara suppresses her powers, adopting the mantle instead of her alter-ego. She works primarily in an office setting, with many of her workplace narratives revolving around interpersonal relationships with Ms. Grant or with her other coworkers, James Olsen and Winn Schott. While in the labyrinthine and expansive hub of the DEO, Kara operates as a fully-fledged superhero alongside J'onn and others, learning from their tactical expertise and offering Kryptonian insight. Out in the field, or more specifically, whenever Kara dons the mantle of Supergirl, her superpowers allow her to operate outside of any existing workplace constraints. Interesting similarities occur when the two jobs are compared, particularly as each of Kara's chosen jobs involves assisting others on a daily basis. The work environment of CatCo embodies that of a fast-paced office in the media/journalism sector where she meets with coworkers in supply closets or attends meetings in Grant's office, yet Kara's time in the DEO reflects a higher-stakes governmental setting. Perhaps the most notable structure of this space is the circular command console, featuring prominently in many episodes. J'onn frequently calls meetings to order around this console, inviting Supergirl, Winn, Alex, and other high-ranking members of the DEO to gather around, shown through a floating and rotating camera perspective. The meetings at the console reflect a kind of board meeting, with many different participants all operating on more or less an even keel with respect to responsibilities within the DEO, though still reporting to J'onn. Grant calls similar meetings in her office, but during these meetings, Kara must simply act as an assistant, one who does not hold the same weight as most of her colleagues. Further, Grant addresses her employees, including Kara, as subordinates from her position of power at her desk, as opposed to the more equal round-table setting of the DEO. Distinguishing between these workspaces helps clarify Kara's role in them, whether as subordinate assistant or authoritative superhero, in turn bringing into focus how Kara's anger is received by those around her, an aspect that becomes much more apparent through close examination of two key episodes in *Supergirl's* first season.

Unlike most episodes of *Supergirl*, anger is at the center of episode "Red-Faced," which opens with Supergirl using excessive force to stop an escalating instance of road rage between two men. After Supergirl stops two cars driving dangerously on a highway, one of the drivers angrily yells at Supergirl for damaging his car and swings a fist at Supergirl, which prompts Supergirl to grab the driver's fist mid-swing, hurting his fist in the process. Upon returning to the DEO headquarters, she is soundly lectured by Hank/J'onn:

> SUPERGIRL: It's always men who go crazy behind the wheel.
> J'ONN: You cannot lose control like that!
> SUPERGIRL: Those two idiots nearly killed people, and you're getting mad at me?
> J'ONN: That's the thing Miss Danvers, I am not mad.... I am controlling my anger. I suggest you get into the habit. You know, I once told you, there are people out there who fear your cousin ... because of what he might do them if he lost his temper.[17]

Kara begins this conversation by bringing up gendered anger in the workplace which prompts J'onn to respond angrily. Three points stand out from this short and heated dialogue: first, Supergirl expresses anger in the workplace; second, her male supervisor chides her over this outburst; third, J'onn attempts to rationalize his emotional suppression through a cautionary tale. Supergirl's anger, a source of feminist power according to Lorde, effectively becomes nullified here.[18] This is further supported by Burrow, who notes, "The control of another's expression of emotion undermines that person's confidence and may reduce or remove the possibility for engaging in actions significant to her life," meaning that J'onn's suppression acts as a means of control over the superpowered feminist.[19] In this capacity, J'onn intends to uphold Supergirl's public image as a perfect avatar of hope, strength, and safety without allowing Kara the agency to express her own anger, gaslighting her intentionally or unintentionally in the process. Kara's initial outburst of anger about gendered stereotypes proves unproductive and unsuccessful, in large part due to J'onn's emotional suppression.

Kara is made to feel inferior through this interaction, questioning her own judgment of whether the emotional expression was socially acceptable or not. At the same time, J'onn's successful expression of anger is rationalized by Domagalski and Steelman's findings that women are conditioned to repress their emotions, particularly anger, in the workplace while men are able to express these emotions without fear of repercussion.[20] Since J'onn is a male director of a large government-sponsored military organization, he is therefore able to express anger without fear of short-term or long-term effects. He scolds Supergirl in anger, then hypocritically tells her not to get angry. According to Lorde, this unsuccessful expression of anger stems from a lack of productive goal.[21] As it stands, Supergirl's expression of anger is ultimately unsuccessful in this instance, suggesting that powerful women should not express anger ... at all.

In this first case, Kara is expressing anger towards a male supervisor while being scolded for said expression: Kara is told expressly how to avoid acting by way of a cautionary tale about her male cousin and fellow superhero, Superman. Because superheroes act as cultural signifiers, J'onn's warning to Supergirl to control her anger signals male suppression of feminist anger. The message is clear for Kara: express anger in public and risk public condemnation, or stifle anger and follow directions, specifically those given by J'onn. By controlling Kara's emotions, J'onn can exert a control over Supergirl. This interaction signals that even though Supergirl contains a great inner strength as an avatar of the working woman in the twenty-first-century, she is conditioned to keep her feminist anger to herself. From this position of signification, *Supergirl* seems to convey, through Supergirl's interactions with Director J'onn, that anger from women is not acceptable in the workplace, no matter the productive nature.

CatCo and Productive Anger

This same episode displays not just feminist anger towards/in dialogue with men, but between women in the workplace. While at CatCo, Kara is angrily scolded at length by Cat Grant for being late, during which Grant talks down to Kara, ending with a barrage of negative descriptors like "pointless, sad, pathetic, little." At this point, Kara cuts Grant off, and rebuffs her negative criticism in her own outburst of anger: "Don't talk to me like that! Please! I work so hard for you. I don't ask questions, I don't complain, and all you do is yell at me and tell me I'm not good enough. And it's mean! Why are you so mean?"[22] As Grant's assistant, Kara is subjected to Grant's verbal tirades daily, rarely earning a compliment amidst Grant's constant criticisms (though, in this case, Kara was indeed, late). Mary Holmes states that anger is not emancipatory in its own right, but ambivalent: one must be angry with an eye towards progress, lest the emotion inhibit, rather than assist.[23] Grant uses anger as a tool of belittlement, rather than creating change. Grant's anger is inhibiting and unproductive, rather than productive, berating Kara with no eye towards change as she does not offer suggestions to improve workplace behavior and instead channels anger wantonly.

Kara's statement, however, emulates Lorde's notion of productive anger aimed at ending this sisterly oppression: "If I participate, knowingly or otherwise, in my sister's oppression and she calls me on it, to answer her anger with my own only blankets the substance of our exchange with reaction."[24] Contrary to J'onn's reaction towards Supergirl's anger, which is to say, suppression through overt rationalization, Grant does not escalate the conflict or suppress Kara's anger; instead, she takes Kara out for a drink. Here, Grant offers seasoned advice to Kara: "Everybody gets angry. Everybody. But this is about work. And anger. Whatever you do, you cannot get angry at work. Especially when you're a girl. It is professional and cultural suicide."[25] Grant elaborates with an anecdote about a male coworker who got angry and tossed a chair through a window during a meeting, noting that the coworker was not reprimanded or punished; Grant surmises that had she committed the same act of anger, she may have been fired based on her gender. *Supergirl* seems to indicate that Grant's situation acts as an example of what many women in the workplace face, as "the consequences for females who express their anger directly are far more damaging than they are for males."[26] Kara called out Grant's unjust treatment within the workplace in an effort to earn better treatment, and as a result, Grant moves forward positively by viewing the conflict as an opportunity for mutual growth within the workplace. Rather than berating her, Cat defends Kara later in the episode, extolling her work ethic, skillset, and dedication to CatCo. Even though Kara brought about meaningful change in the workplace by using her feminist anger to demand better treatment by her boss, Kara's anger is still socially and professionally cautioned against by her employers.

At two different points in this episode, Kara's supervisors warn her against expressing her anger in the workplace, pushing the issue to the point of offering cautionary tales to prove their point. In the first case, Kara is warned not to express anger in case other people become afraid of her. In the second case, Kara expressing feminist anger at her female supervisor plays out differently when Kara's anger is acknowledged by Grant, though this scene also ends with a cautionary tale. Both people who caution her to control her anger use men as examples—she is forced to measure her own anger and behavior against men. The repetition of these examples within this episode suggest that men are the barometer for appropriate behavior within the workplace, potentially leaving women with the distinct impression that the only emotions acceptable at work are those sanctioned by their employers.

Yet, Kara's actions offer a much more significant point concerning the show's agenda. Given Kara's success within the episode through expressing anger and achieving positive change, it becomes apparent that anger, when expressed with productive purpose, effects change in the workplace. This point of productive purpose, hearkening back to Lorde, is hammered home later in season one, suggesting that anger without purpose, that is, rage, is what proves ultimately damaging.

Red Kryptonite and Rage

While the previous episode, "Red Faced," engages with both productive and unproductive anger within the workplace, a later episode in the first season of *Supergirl* titled "Falling" deals with the social and political ramifications of tapping into rage, not anger, at work.[27] The episode finds Kara encountering Red Kryptonite, which does not weaken her physically but weakens her inhibitions to the point of nonexistence. Flemke and Allen find that rage has three precursors, in no particular order: (1) feeling threatened or feeling fear; (2) overwhelming emotions linked with the appearance of tears; (3) a lack of control.[28] Only the last precursor, "lack of control," is present throughout the bulk of the episode, originating with the Red Kryptonite and manifesting in her actions. Prior to encountering the foreign substance (and throughout the series), Kara is quite in control of her emotions. Immediately after encountering the red crystal, visual and narrative cues signal a shift in Kara's demeanor. Rather than calmly turning off her alarm in the morning, she unleashes super strength, smashing the clock to pieces.

Kara's exposure to Red Kryptonite begins eroding her inhibitions as she leaves behind her typical demure work attire for a tight-fitting and fashion-forward dress as she enters CatCo. When a superhero changes their costume (or their alter ego's day-to-day clothes), correlative changes are occurring on an emotional or mental level. Kara's workplace outfits, both before and during this episode, correspond to personality traits. Pre–Red Kryptonite, Kara dresses conservatively and acts the part in CatCo, primarily submitting willingly to Grant's domineering model of employment. Under the effects of the same substance, Kara dresses assertively on entering CatCo, visually signaling that she will be taking charge of her workplace life. This has positive short-term effects, as she is rewarded with exclusive dance club tickets from Grant. The issue, however, is that Kara seems to be emphasizing control over some aspects of her work life while losing control over her emotions.

Over the course of the episode, Kara's status worsens the longer that the Red Kryptonite, and by proxy the rage, stays in her system. She uses excessive force to stop villains attacking National City, yet lets one of these supervillains go free on purpose. One CatCo coworker, Siobhan, typically does not get along well with Kara, often bullying Kara while working together. When Kara finds out that Siobhan captures footage of Supergirl letting the supervillain free with the intention of sending it to a rival newspaper syndicate, Kara vindictively gets the coworker fired by showing the damning "scoop" evidence to Grant. When Kara does this, there is an element of spitefulness behind her actions, as she could have resorted to any number of approaches to ensure the video evidence did not reach its intended audience without getting Siobhan fired in the process. The action here stems from a lack of control over interpersonal communication, resulting in rage-based woman-on-woman workplace aggression. This shows a damaging visual example of anger in the workplace, in which women are not only working against each other in an office setting, but trying to get each other fired for personal reasons.

Later, Kara calls out J'onn for scolding her at the DEO: "We're in a good place when I do what I'm told. When I don't, you come down on me, and I'm tired of it!" On her way out, Kara slams her fist into the wall, seemingly unaware that she has expressed her emotions so viscerally as to physically create a fist-sized crater in concrete. Conversing with J'onn in this manner has the trademarks of her previous conversations in "Red-Faced," where she expresses anger, but certain fundamental aspects of Lorde's foundation remain absent, most notably Lorde's emphasis on purposefully using anger for progress. She calls out Director J'onn's pointed control, yet storms out without pursuing the matter further. Later in the episode, Kara (as Supergirl) unloads more emotions on Grant, complaining about enabling the citizens of National City to routinely act as victims as a consequence of saving them over and over. Cat suggests therapy to help Supergirl control her emotions; in response, Supergirl becomes enraged, and in order to prove who holds more power between them, throws Cat off of a skyscraper, catching her at the last minute. This conversation between Cat and Kara is an inversion of the one from "Red-Faced," in that Cat began by offering aid to Kara only for Kara to respond in anger.

Another symbolic act of Kara's rage-filled personality involves donning a new costume and simultaneously burning away her old workplace attire. When her sister Alex visits to check in on her, Kara appears wearing a tight-fitting black leather jumpsuit instead of her Supergirl costume or her workplace clothes, complete with a small red "S" symbol over one breast. Kara blames Alex for "pushing those dowdy sweaters" on her, before burning them all with her heat vision. Barbara Brownie and Danny Gordon assert that superhero costumes are emblematic of a superhero's identity. Accordingly, the bright, primary colors of red, blue, and yellow can be seen as "signifying the same openness and honesty of [her] exposed face," in that "both the bright colors and the lack of mask invite close engagement, challenging onlookers to scrutinize [her] actions."[29] Because of this, switching from bright colors to the dark bodysuit reflects two noteworthy changes: first, Kara is leaving behind her old personalities, both the submissive assistant role and the altruistic superhero role; second, Kara has embraced a dark power within her, manifesting in a visually dark superheroic costume. There is no mask to hide her identity while the classic "S" symbol (representing the Kryptonian house of El) stays on the bodysuit, thus making the change transparent for both the public and the people who know Kara: Supergirl embodies rage, instead of hope.

The citizens of National City and Kara's coworkers see these changes within her, and interpret her actions as evil, instead of stemming from a well of rage. She tries several times in the episode to elicit productive change, but her lack of control continually results in short-term and long-term consequences. At CatCo, Kara suffers the short-term consequences of weakened workplace friendships, as well as short-term guilt over getting Siobhan fired (in subsequent episodes). She manages to hurt her friendship with her love interest at the time, James Olsen, though the two repair their relationship before the end of the season. Her actions while as Supergirl, however, have far more damaging short-term and long-term consequences. Grant publicly denounces Supergirl while explaining the incident, warning the public that Supergirl is not so much a savior as she is dangerous to those around her. This essentially fulfills Director J'onn's cautionary tale from "Red-Faced": Supergirl abused her power from a position of rage, and the public came to fear her just as J'onn warned might happen.

The show is explicit in its critique of rage, showing that the emotion is not only unproductive, but ultimately damaging. In order to stop Kara's rampage through the streets of National City, J'onn publicly transforms into his Martian persona of the Martian Manhunter, outing himself to the citizens of National City as well as to other members of the DEO. As a result, J'onn is taken into custody just after subduing Supergirl. Kara wakes up in the aftermath of her rage episode, asking questions about what she did ("Did I kill anyone?") and expressing sorrow over hurting those around her, crying that "It was so horrible, Alex. It was so bad. It was so horrible. Every bad thought I've ever had, it just came to the surface. I couldn't stop it."[30] Kara apologizes profusely to Alex, who intimates that while Kara hurt her physically and emotionally during her episode of rage, "there was some truth" to what Kara said. Alex is the only one to forgive Kara in the episode, as James Olsen and Cat Grant avoid absolving Kara of guilt for her rage-filled actions. The episode ends without a happy ending, and without Kara effecting positive change in the office environment or her larger workspace of National City as Supergirl, moralistically showing that rage is largely ineffective no matter the conditions.

Snapper Carr and Misplaced Anger

Upon arriving to The CW Network, *Supergirl* undergoes some significant changes beginning with a decrease in screen time of CatCo, often featuring the DEO base more heavily than the office environment of CatCo. This may not come as a surprise given the prominence of the superhero stronghold to other CW superheroes shows, including *Arrow* (Oliver Queen's base), *The Flash* (S.T.A.R. Labs in Central City), and *Legends of Tomorrow* (The Waverider spaceship), but the change is notable nonetheless as it means that the few times when CatCo does get featured are rendered more significant. After the move to The CW from CBS, *Supergirl*'s second season sees the departure of Cat Grant as CEO and subsequent promotion of James Olsen to CEO in her stead. Before she leaves, Grant offers Kara any job within CatCo in recognition of her outstanding work as an assistant. Kara undergoes a career shift, transferring from her old position as Grant's assistant to one that may not surprise longtime comic book fans of Supergirl: journalism. Kara signs on with the journalism staff at CatCo, beginning work as a fledgling reporter under her editor, Snapper Carr.

In "The Last Children of Krypton," Carr exhibits similar traits of workplace anger as Cat Grant, lashing out at employees for late writing and yelling for coffee at whoever is nearby. Initially, when Kara reports for duty, Carr pointedly tells her that she has no job with him, going so far as to threaten her by saying "Now get your entitled ass out of my office before I channel my last divorce and break you emotionally." Kara sputters and stammers in visible frustration, "You.... You...," gives a frustrated sigh, and storms off.[31] This moment is a far cry from the articulate and politically charged instance of anger in "Red-Faced" that Kara expresses toward J'onn, not to mention the focused outburst she directs towards Cat later in that same episode. Instead, this aligns with Lorde's warning of expressing anger without an eye for change or progress. Kara has no aim in her expression, and therefore, finds her anger not only unproductive but ultimately denied by Carr as he says, "Thanks for killing the lingering notion that you might speak or write well" on her way out of the room.

Carr's dismissal and diversion of Kara's anger is more sinister than a simple rejection of employment might suggest, given this discussion of the politics of anger within superhero narratives. The final sentiment from Carr regarding Kara's anger equates her outward expression of anger with the inability to communicate properly, signaling that her feminist anger essentially renders her inadequate at her profession. Burrow looks to this mode of shutting down feminist anger as a form of emotional abuse, stating that the "implication is that the person raising the issue is herself inadequate to express that concern or she is to blame for how she raised the issue."[32] Rather than reporting to a tough but firm female CEO who acts as a mentor, Kara instead finds herself subject to an emotionally abusive male editor who rejects her claim for employment and silences her in the process.

Just after this, Kara appeals to Cat, venting her frustrations out loud and asking for help when the following exchange ensues:

CAT: You want me to instruct your new boss to be nice to you because you don't know how to stand up for yourself?
KARA: Um ... yes.
CAT: Um ... no. No, no, and no. I will not go talk to your boss. I will not fix things for you, Kara. You are a grown woman. You are smart and talented and astonishing. How many times am I going to have to tell you this for you to accept who you are? I just need you to pull up your big-girl pants, Kara, and own your power ... now. I want you to go in there, and show that son of a bitch Snapper what you are made of.[33]

In an inversion of their earlier exchange in season one's "Red-Faced," Cat is the one expressing anger at Kara in order to enact change. Reversing her original opinion of how and when to express anger in the workplace (which is to say, "never"), Cat urges Kara to own her power, tap into her arsenal of feminist anger, and challenge the institutional oppression she is currently struggling with. By the end of the episode, Kara angrily delivers a short, succinct, and well-written article to Carr, securing her position as a member of the journalism staff. This showcases a triumphant exercise in productive anger, channeling her emotion through the proper protocol in order to enact change.

Kara struggles with Carr continue throughout the season, coming to a head in season two's "Exodus" as the two battle over the ethics of journalistic publishing.[34] Kara is determined to publish an article exposing the organization Cadmus as an evil terrorist organization, though her only source is her own firsthand experiences fighting the organization as Supergirl. She fears that unless the public knows the truth about Cadmus, people all over the world will continue to suffer at the hands of this organization. Carr challenges her to build the article up through additional sources, noting that a single unnamed source, even if that source may be Supergirl, does not count as a journalistic smoking gun. She refuses to listen, instead publishing her article through her own website. Mary Holmes notes that the manner in which anger is "taken up," or manifests, is crucial to the success of the expression, stating that anger is typically more successful when based on inequalities and "a sense of process, rather than of past grievances versus future utopia."[35] Here, Kara is frustrated with the journalistic process, particularly with the conundrum of working two jobs (at CatCo and as Supergirl), one of which must be kept secret. This act is grounded in past grievances with her male superior: rather than addressing the errors found in her work or confronting Carr over her feelings of unequal treatment (as she did with Cat Grant), Kara's unresolved anger emerges in the form of publishing her article through her own outlet, instead of following Carr's journalistic protocol, resulting in her termination from CatCo. Whereas Kara's actions in "Red-Faced" showed that misplaced rage can have long-lasting consequences on personal and professional relationships in the workplace, her interactions with Carr and CatCo reveal that misplaced anger is often unproductive, leading to costly personal and professional repercussions. Kara eventually returns to work at CatCo under Snapper Carr, but not before learning to follow the organizational protocols in place for journalistic pursuit, eventually writing a piece that stands up to Carr's expectations of properly cited references.

Conclusion

These findings suggest that *Supergirl* offers nuanced insights into feminist anger, using Kara's narrative as a metatextual cautionary tale for women in the workplace. Though Kara's supervisors warn her against getting angry in season one, she recognizes that anger is not only an appropriate vehicle for change, but the only one in some instances. Her marked progress indicates that anger, when productive, is socially acceptable. However, the show's representation of rage further cautions audiences about the professional and personal risks of relying too much on anger or losing control of that particular emotive tool. Using Kara as a litmus test, the show explores the varied ramifications of rage within the workplace, offering her narrative as a cautionary tale evocative of the same cautionary tales that Kara is given early in season one. Upon moving from CBS to The CW, Kara's anger has been neutered in the workplace: there are much fewer instances of Kara expressing anger while at CatCo, and virtually no significant, positive examples on the same level as those in "Red-Faced" or "Falling." Kara expresses anger at Snapper Carr successfully through writing, then manages to reverse that success by independently publishing an inadequate journalistic piece in a fit of rage.

While the third season of *Supergirl* is unfolding at the time of writing, two moments stand out from the season three premiere, "Girl of Steel": Kara leaves CatCo, only to join Lena Luthor's company.[36] During the premiere, the audience sees Kara fully embracing her superhero side at the expense of her traditional job as a journalist for CatCo. This comes to a head when James confronts Kara after she misses a deadline, and in fiery response, Kara quits. When Alex critiques Kara for quitting her job at CatCo, Kara angrily asks "Cat moved on, why can't I?" Kara's question resonates particularly strongly given her feminist anger: why work for a patriarchal organization, when she doesn't have to work as a subordinate as Supergirl? She continues channeling her anger into productive uses, saving National City from villain-of-the-week Bloodsport, eventually deciding to work with (not for) Lena Luthor, who has become the new CEO of CatCo. The juxtaposition is clear: Kara's anger throughout season two was directed towards challenging men in positions of power at CatCo, whereas she feels comfortable working at CatCo under the direction of her friend, Luthor. It remains to be seen how present (or absent) feminist anger will be in season three of *Supergirl*, but with the first two seasons of *Supergirl* as evidence, the implication is that feminist anger can be incredibly powerful for the working woman ... when channeled productively.

NOTES

1. Though the character is initially introduced as "Hank Henshaw," it is revealed some episodes later that he is, in fact, J'onn J'onzz, and is most often referred to as J'onn by other characters throughout the rest of the series.
2. Audre Lorde, "The Uses of Anger: Women Responding to Racism," National Women's Studies Association Conference, Storrs, CT, June 1981.
3. Sylvia Burrow, "The Political Structure of Emotion: From Dismissal to Dialogue," *Hypatia* 20, no. 4 (2005): 27.
4. Elizabeth V. Spelman, "Anger and Insubordination," in *Women, Knowledge and Reality: Explorations in Feminist Philosophy*, Ann Garry and Marilyn Pearsall, eds. (London: Unwin Hyman, 1989), 270.
5. Paul Benson, "Free Agency and Self-Worth," *The Journal of Philosophy* 91, no. 12 (1994): 657–658.
6. In the wake of events such as "Gamergate" and the uploading of 'Feminist Rage' YouTube compilation videos, the term has been co-opted by anonymous internet trolls to gaslight feminists on the internet. This can be seen in YouTube videos in which men's rights advocates engage with feminists in public places, gaslighting them while filming their reactions. See for example, BOTI, "Ultimate Feminist Rage Compilation 2016 || Best of Feminist Rages," Film 2016, YouTube video, 10:24, Posted Dec.6, 2016, https://www.YouTube.com/watch?v=OlvjycG_wdU (accessed October 15, 2017.)
7. Kimberly Flemke and Katherine R. Allen, "Women's Experience of Rage: A Critical Feminist Analysis," *Journal of Marital and Family Therapy* 34, no. 1 (2008): 58.
8. Lorde, "The Uses of Anger."
9. Theresa A. Domagalski and Lisa A. Steelman, "The Impact of Gender and Organizational Status on Workplace Anger Expression," *Management Communication Quarterly* 20, no. 3 (2007): 309.
10. Domagalski and Steelman, "The Impact of Gender," 311.
11. Domagalski and Steelman, "The Impact of Gender," 299, 311.
12. Laura Mattoon D'amore, "The Accidental Supermom: Superheroines and Maternal Performativity, 1963–1980," *The Journal of Popular Culture* 45, no. 6 (2012): 1227.
13. Brett White, "Marvel Women of the 70's: Ms. Marvel," Marvel, Jul. 9, 2014: https://news.marvel.com/comics/22834/marvel_women_of_the_70s_ms_marvel/ (accessed October 15, 2017.)
14. Laura Mattoon D'amore, "The Accidental Supermom," 1227.
15. During its first season on CBS, Supergirl was ranked 39th out of 150 television shows with an average of 9.81 million viewers, which dropped to a rank of 115th out of 150 shows with an average of 3.12 million viewers during its first season on The CW, debuting ahead of popular CW shows like *Arrow*, *Legends of Tomorrow*, and *Supernatural*. Lisa de Moraes, "Final 2016–17 TV Rankings: 'Sunday Night Football' Winning Streak Continues," *Deadline*, May 30, 2017: deadline.com/2017/05/2016-2017-tv-season-ratings-series-rankings-list-1202102340 and Lisa de Moraes, "Full 2015–16 TV Season Series Rankings: 'Blindspot,' 'Life in Pieces' & 'Quantico' Lead Newcomers," Deadline, May 26, 2016: deadline.com/2016/05/tv-season-2015-2016-series-rankings-shows-full-list-1201763189.
16. In the "Pilot" episode, it is revealed that "Kerah" is Cat Grant's name for Kara Danvers, simultaneously characterizing Grant's lack of caring for her employee's full names as well as Kara's meekness through her unwillingness to correct Grant. *Supergirl*, "Pilot," season 1, episode 1, directed by Glen Winter, story by Greg Berlanti, Ali Adler, and Andrew Kreisberg, teleplay by Ali Adler, aired October 26, 2015, on CBS.

17. *Supergirl*, "Red Faced," season 1, episode 6, directed by Jesse Warn, written by Michael Grassi and Rachel Shukert, aired November 30, 2015, on CBS.
18. Lorde, "The Uses of Anger."
19. Burrow, "The Political Structure of Emotion," 28.
20. Domagalski and Steelman, "The Impact of Gender," 304.
21. Lorde, "The Uses of Anger."
22. *Supergirl*, "Red Faced," season 1, episode 6.
23. Mary Holmes, "Feeling Beyond Rules: Politicizing the Sociology of Emotion and Anger in Feminist Politics," *European Journal of Social Theory* 7, no. 2 (2004): 223.
24. Lorde, "The Uses of Anger."
25. *Supergirl*, "Red Faced," season 1, episode 6.
26. Domagalski and Steelman, "The Impact of Gender," 311.
27. *Supergirl*, "Falling," season 1, episode 16, directed by Larry Teng, written by Robert Rovner and Jessica Queller, aired March 14, 2016, on CBS.
28. Flemke and Allen, "Women's Experience of Rage," 69.
29. Barbara Brownie and Danny Graydon, *The Superhero Costume: Identity and Disguise in Fact and Fiction (Dress, Body, Culture)* (Bloomsbury Academic, 2015) Kindle: loc. 544.
30. *Supergirl*, "Falling," season 1, episode 16.
31. *Supergirl*, "The Last Children of Krypton," season 2, episode 2, directed by Glen Winter, written by Robert Rovner and Caitlin Parrish, aired October 17, 2016, on The CW.
32. Sylvia Burrow, "The Political Structure of Emotion," 31.
33. *Supergirl*, "The Last Children of Krypton," season 2, episode 2.
34. *Supergirl*, "Exodus," season 2, episode 15, directed by Michael Allowitz, written by Paula Yoo and Eric Carrasco, aired March 6, 2017, on The CW.
35. Mary Holmes, "Feeling Beyond Rules," 224.
36. *Supergirl*, "Girl of Steel," season 3, episode 1, directed by Jesse Warn, story by Andrew Kreisberg, teleplay by Robert Rovner and Caitlin Parrish, aired October 9, 2017, on The CW.

Selected Bibliography

Acu, Adrian. "Time to Work for a Living: The Marvel Cinematic Universe and the Organized Superhero." *Journal of Popular Film and Television* 44, no. 4 (2016): 195–205.
Benson, Paul. "Free Agency and Self-Worth." *The Journal of Philosophy* 91, no. 12 (1994): 650–668.
BOTI. "Ultimate Feminist Rage Compilation 2016 || Best of Feminist Rages." Filmed 2016, YouTube video, 10:24. Posted Dec.6, 2016: https://www.YouTube.com/watch?v=OlvjycG_wdU.
Brownie, Barbara, and Danny Graydon. *The Superhero Costume: Identity and Disguise in Fact and Fiction (Dress, Body, Culture)*. Bloomsbury Academic, 2015. Kindle.
Burrow, Sylvia. "The Political Structure of Emotion: From Dismissal to Dialogue." *Hypatia* 20, no. 4 (2005): 27–43.
D'Amore, Laura Mattoon. "The Accidental Supermom: Superheroines and Maternal Performativity, 1963–1980." *The Journal of Popular Culture* 45, no. 6 (2012): 1226–1248.
_____. Invisible Girl's Quest for Visibility: Early Second-Wave Feminism and the Comic Book Superheroine." *The Journal of American Popular Culture, 1900–Present* 7, no. 2 (2008): n.p.
Domagalski, Theresa, and Lisa Steelman. "The Impact of Gender and Organizational Status on Workplace Anger Expression." *Management Communication Quarterly* 20, no. 3 (2017): 297–315.
Flemke, Kimberly, and Katherine R. Allen. "Women's Experience of Rage: A Critical Feminist Analysis." *Journal of Marital and Family Therapy* 34, no.1 (2008): 58–74.
Fischer, Ann R., and Glenn E. Good. "Women's Feminist Consciousness, Anger, and Psychological Distress." *Journal of Counseling Psychology* 51, no. 4 (2004): 437–446.
Holmes, Mary. "Feeling Beyond Rules: Politicizing the Sociology of Emotion and Anger in Feminist Politics." *European Journal of Social Theory* 7, no. 2 (2004): 209–227.

Link, Alex. "The Secret of Supergirl's Success." *The Journal of Popular Culture* 46, no. 6 (2013): 1177–1197.

Lorde, Audre. "The Uses of Anger: Women Responding to Racism." National Women's Studies Association Conference, Storrs, CT, June 1981.

Moraes, Lisa de. "Final 2016–17 TV Rankings: 'Sunday Night Football' Winning Streak Continues." *Deadline*, 30 May 2017. deadline.com/2017/05/2016-2017-tv-season-ratings-series-rankings-list-1202102340.

———. "Full 2015–16 TV Season Series Rankings: 'Blindspot,' 'Life in Pieces' & 'Quantico' Lead Newcomers." *Deadline*, 26 May 2016. deadline.com/2016/05/tv-season-2015-2016-series-rankings-shows-full-list-1201763189.

Spelman, Elizabeth V. "Anger and Insubordination." In *Women, Knowledge and Reality: Explorations in Feminist Philosophy*, ed. Ann Garry and Marilyn Pearsall, 263–273. London: Unwin Hyman, 1989.

Taylor, Tiffany, and Barbara J. Risman. "Doing Deference or Speaking Up: Deconstructing the Experience and Expression of Anger." *Race, Gender & Class* 13, no. 3 (2006): 60–80.

White, Brett. "Marvel Women of the 70's: Ms. Marvel." *Marvel*, Jul. 9, 2014: https://news.marvel.com/comics/22834/marvel_women_of_the_70s_ms_marvel.

Krypton's Rage

Contrasting the Emotions and Powers of Supergirl in Television and the New 52

Nicholas William Moll

When the first season of *Supergirl* premiered in 2016, audiences were introduced to an upbeat Kara Danvers finding her first feet as a superhero. For consumers of the concurrently published comic book series of the same title, this Supergirl differed drastically from the super-charged and destructive Kara Zor-El introduced in 2011 under DC's *New 52* banner. The distinction between the two differing characterizations of Supergirl was highlighted in a contrasting use of the Superman narrative. Similar to Clark Kent, Kara Danvers arrives on Earth as a child and is raised by a human family. Within a domestic, Anglo-American family unit, Kara learns to control her powers and become a functioning member of human society. Distinctly, Kara Zor-El of the *New 52* lands as an adult, having circled the sun with the effect of supercharging her powers. Emerging, Kara Zor-El's powers are initially uncontrollable. Due to the difficulty in controlling her abilities and the trauma of Krypton's loss, Kara struggles to integrate with human society. With her powers and emotions unable to attain the ease learnt by Kara Danvers of the television series, Kara Zor-El seems violent and dangerous. Yet, while the characterization of Supergirl is contrastingly distinct between media, expressions of rage, pain and anger are not alien to television's Kara. Rather, they are used to punctuate moments of stress and tension and are accompanied by the use of superpowers.

The linkage of emotion to powers is furthermore unique to Kara as a female superhero when contrasted with Superman or Martian Manhunter as experienced male figures who maintain a distinction of their emotions and powers. This essay argues that the connection of superpowers and emotion is presented consistently as central to Supergirl's characterization in both television and comic books. In doing so, it frames this portrayal as alternating between a strength and flaw for Kara in both productions. This essay draws on media and franchise theories to explore the use of characters from the expanded DC Universe as a source of contrast with Kara in both forms of media, as well as an examination of emotion as the keystone character trait in adapting *Supergirl* to television.

Supergirl Begins

The television series *Supergirl* presents its titular character as a newly introduced hero to an existing fictional universe. While the nature of this universe is not explored overtly within the series, the opening moments of the pilot episode present audiences with the destruction of Krypton and the exodus of an infant Kal-El from the dying planet. While the opening implies that not only Superman but a range of other existing characters can be found in the series' setting, *Supergirl* is quick to add Kara as the emergent element of the narrative: a second child sent from Krypton to Earth. Kara in this sense is the unknown quantity of an already established universe and as the series progresses. Other characters drawn from DC's range of comic books are introduced into the series as established individuals within the setting but as first encounters for Kara; these include notable supporting cast members such as Martian Manhunter and Jimmy Olsen. Likewise, additional individuals are noted as present even if they do not directly appear in episodes, such as the much discussed but never seen Lex Luthor or a hinted at Lobo—the intergalactic bounty hunter mentioned in the first season episode "Trust, Justice and the American Way." It is not uncommon for a superhero narrative to introduce new, starring characters as part of an existing universe, and a similar process occurs for Supergirl's *New 52* comic book. What is distinctive in regard to the printed *Supergirl*, however, is that Kara Zor-El is one of a number of different versions of the character to exist within comic book continuities. Herein, the DC Comics universe has featured and repeatedly reintroduced vastly distinct versions of the character into their varied existing continuities. These include the familiar Kara Zor-El, who was introduced as a teenage Kryptonian that arrived on Earth after the destruction of her home planet, both respectively in 1959's *Action Comics* issue #252[1] and 2004's *Batman/Superman* issue #8.[2] This origin was most recently reproduced with 2011's *Supergirl* issue #1[3] as part of DC Comics' *New 52* relaunch of its entire comic line.

While Kara's status as the other survivor of Krypton is the current incarnation of the character, Supergirl has also been introduced in a number of diverse ways in mainstream DC Comics titles and storylines. These include Clare Kent, a Clark Kent transformed for a time into a woman by an adversary in *Superboy* #78,[4] a magic being created from Jimmy Olsen's wish in *Superman* #123,[5] Cin-El, the alleged daughter of Superman from *Superman 10-Cent Adventure*,[6] Linda Danvers and the symbiotic protoplasmic lifeform Matrix in *Superman* #16,[7] along with a variety of others. Yet each variation of *Supergirl* is introduced as a new character into an existing setting populated by established characters. The television series draws on the varied comic book history of Supergirl. Kara's name and origin are strikingly telling of this varied adaptation process. While the destruction of Krypton and subsequent arrival on Earth mirrors the *Action Comics* and *Batman/Superman* origins of the character, this aspect is married to the Danvers family and identity crafted in 1988's *Superman* comic books. The television origin is further interlinked to the Department of Extranormal Operations (DEO) originating from *Batman* issue #550[8] as the employer of Jeremiah Danvers. Jeremiah Danvers further links Kara's origins to another prominent DC Comics character, Martian Manhunter. As per Martian Manhunter's comic book origin in *Detective Comics* #255, there is a period of time between the character's arrival on Earth and his public action as a superhero. In the context of the *Supergirl* television series, during this time, Martian Manhunter is hunted by the DEO and Jeremiah Danvers. The television series thus is less an adaptation of a single comic book than a reworking of a broad series of characters, narratives, and events from the DC Universe into a television setting focused on the title character.

In terms of contrast, perhaps what makes the *New 52*—as the most recent comic book incarnation of *Supergirl*—the most pertinent for this essay is that it, like the television series, has at its disposal a long and varied history associated with the character on which it can draw. Naturally this extends to including characters from the wider series of *Superman* titles such as Superboy. Yet, the *New 52* series engages vicariously with the wider range of DC Comics franchises and characters, drawing on established titles beyond the *Superman* family with characters such as Red Hood from the *Batman* line-up and the Red Lanterns from the *Green Lantern* franchise playing major roles in the *Supergirl* series, along with liminal characters such as Lobo.

These pairings are highly thematic, with Kara herself presented as a less idealistic variant of Superman, arriving on Earth as a young adult and therefore having grown to near-maturity on Krypton. Thus, unlike Superman, Kara comes into her powers as an adult and suffers both trauma and culture shock over the death of her planet. In each case, Kara is contrasted with more conflicted variants of mainstream superheroes—Red Hood, a former Robin who was murdered by the Joker and returned to life without Batman's code of ethics, and the Red Lanterns, variants of the Green Lantern that tap into rage rather than willpower. In both the television series and *New 52* comic books, *Supergirl* thematically links to the wider DC Comics properties.

Danvers and Zor-El

With the television series drawing vicariously on content broadly associated with DC Comics, *Supergirl* is not a direct adaptation of comic book materials. Undertaking the same action, the *New 52* series does not act as a referent text for the television series. Rather, both texts—television and comic book—perform the same act of drawing on the character's pre-existing legacy along with materials from the wider setting. Many media franchises feature a central text that acts as their referent, with all other productions drawing from that central orientation.[9] Yet this is not the case with *Supergirl*, which instead draws from a varied quantity of select materials. The distinction between the way in which both the comic books of the *New 52* and television series draw on each other is both fluid and diverse.

In exemplary contrast, CW's *The Flash* television series, which—along with all of DC's CW programs—shares the developer talents of Greg Berlanti with *Supergirl*, is an example of a text with centrality. *The Flash* frequently directly adapts the comic book history of the title character with a developed mythos of legacy and inheritor characters such as Jay Garrick and Wally West. Both characters came to feature heavily in the second season of *The Flash*,[10] epitomized with the direct adaptation of comic book elements such as "The Flash of Two Worlds" cover from *Flash* issue #123[11] in the second season episode of the same title.[12] Thus, as a television counterpart to *Supergirl*, *The Flash* draws directly on its comic book antecedent in a manner that *Supergirl* does not.

The twin productions of *Supergirl* can thus best be understood as "parallel" texts,[13] that is, two individual productions occurring almost concurrently (2011 through 2015 for comic books, and 2015 and ongoing for television) that draw on the same productive history. However, while both texts draw on this same history, their renditions of Kara, her life and character are drastically distinct beyond the basic origin of the character and contrast with Superman as having grown up on Krypton. The television series presents Kara Danvers as a young woman on a steady journey of self-discovery. Kara's journey begins on television with her first public display of superpowers in the pilot episode and continues in the development of her public identity as Supergirl and professional identity as a reporter. In this sense, Kara does not know who she is at the onset of the television series, but continues to explore her sense of self as the narrative progresses.

In contrast, the *New 52*'s *Supergirl*, Kara Zor-El, knows firmly who she is: the heiress of the House of El, who is several days away from completing her final trials and becoming a leader of her planet. Kara's arrival on Earth in *Supergirl* issue #1[14] is a trauma heightened by the knowledge that her entire planet is destroyed, and she has missed decades of life, discovering her infant cousin, Kal-El, grown to adulthood as Superman. Inheriting the legacy of the House of El that survived Krypton's destruction, Kara Zor-El's journey contrasts sharply with that of Kara Danvers, as the former is weighed down by the lingering vestiges of her culture. Most notably, within the first seven issues of the series this takes the form of the World Killers (led by Reign, television's third season villain), genetically engineered Kryptonians created as super-soldiers by the House of El. While Kara Danvers is a young woman making her way in the world, Kara Zor-El is one grappling with a sudden and traumatic series of events.

The distinctions in characterization between Kara Danvers of television and Kara Zor-El of the *New 52* comics are far more than cosmetic. While Kara Danvers has emotions, Kara Zor-El is characterized as emotional. The contrast is sharply articulated, with Kara Danvers' training depicted in the season one episode "Stronger Together"[15] by the heroine working with small situations, such as stopping robberies and saving cats in trees, as well as undertaking exercises with the DEO. Kara Zor-El is not afforded the opportunity to train, however. The moment she arrives on Earth in issue #1,[16] her mind and body are overwhelmed by the heightened sensory perception she experiences on awakening with the sudden onset of her powers. In this state, Kara murders soldiers sent to investigate her vessel's crash landing with a sudden burst of heat vision and destroys part of the Great Wall of China.

As Kara Zor-El masters her powers, she engages them for indiscriminate destruction, such as destroying Simon Tycho's space station along with its population; on encountering Superman, he compares Kara to the World Killers. Positioning the legacy of the House of El and Krypton questionably, Kara Zor-El engages the role of the female superhero as an embodiment of emotion that Rebecca Davis frames as common to female characters in comic books,[17] that is to say, a figure who is a mixture of a "damsel in distress" and a counterpart "who needs to be put down gently."[18]

Indeed, despite her powers, Kara Zor-El's status as emotional and reactive often sees the character easily defeated, captured, and in need of rescuing. This occurs for the first time in issue #4,[19] with Supergirl is quickly incapacitated by Simon Tycho using Kryptonite, and then rescued by a sympathetic but wholly powerless henchman-turned-savior. Throughout the series, Kara is captured again multiple times and her status as an anti-hero in one moment and damsel in the next forms a recurring theme throughout the series. For example, in issue #6, Kara is captured by the World Killers but rescued by her father's spirit.[20] Kara is again captured in issue #10,[21] where she is devoured and trapped inside the Black Banshee, but is assisted in escaping by another trapped soul. In issue #28,[22] she is rescued from the blinding rage of the Red Lantern Ring by the intervention of the Green and Red Lantern Corps.

In contrast, Kara Danvers does not display the damsel in distress trope. While television's Supergirl is captured in episodes such as "Truth, Justice and the American Way,"[23] the emphasis is placed on supporting Kara, allowing her to rescue herself. In the case of the aforementioned episode, Alex Danvers shoots the ceiling of the Master Jailer's ship, causing sunlight to enter and recharge Kara.

Thus, while Kara Zor-El is incidentally rescued, Kara Danvers is supported by an expanded cast of family, co-workers and friends. In contrast, while Kara Zor-El acts without support, she also conducts herself without scrutiny. The comic book Supergirl does undergo initial inspection from Superman in the second and third issues of the *New 52* series, but Kara Zor-El is quickly left to her own devices after this point. In contrast, television's Kara Danvers is placed under constant scrutiny as Supergirl from multiple sources such as her DEO employers and the media, engaging the "'Hero on Trial'" trope also common to the portrayal of female superheroes.[24] That is to say, as a female superhero, Kara is expected to constantly prove herself.

In this sense, Kara Danvers is placed under a degree of inspection that is seldom depicted in regard to male characters. While there is an initial shock surrounding Hank Henshaw's reveal as Martian Manhunter, the character smoothly transitions into season two as the openly Martian leader of the DEO. Yet in season two, Kara's abilities and decisions are still deemed questionable. For example, much of the first season episode "Manhunter"[25] focuses on Kara's attempt to earn the trust of National City after her actions under the influence of Red Kryptonite. Likewise, throughout the second season—in particular the episode "Luthors"—Kara is questioned for her friendship with Lena Luthor, despite Lena's actions indicating no malicious intent regarding the character. While both variations of Supergirl are distinctive characterizations, each embodies the tropes and stereotypes of female superhero characterization.

The use of these tropes and stereotypes common to female superheroes sees anger as an integral part of Supergirl's character in both productive forms. While the *New 52*'s Kara Zor-El overflows with antagonism in using her powers, Kara Danvers often engages with her identity of Supergirl as an outlet for her sense of rage and frustration. While Kara's anger is a distinguishing feature from both text's rendition of Superman—each portraying the character as a stoic and moral figure—it is also a trait attributed to superheroes who fall into the male orphan trope. Lawrence C. Rubin suggests that male orphaned characters such as Superman present a reconciliatory narrative of loss and adoption in their origin stories.[26] Origins that both express the pain of loss and present the hero with a loving surrogate family, "who nurtured both his mortal and super soul as he experimented with his emerging God-like powers."[27] While the hero's journey thus begins with tragedy, for the male orphan it is one "shaped by the experiences of their early lives, most prominently adoption."[28]

But if the masculine story is one of loss nurtured into goodness, it is not one mirrored in either incarnation of *Supergirl* discussed here. While Kara Danvers begins her life on Earth with an adoptive family, the idealist home life of the Danvers household is shattered shortly after her arrival. When the DEO uncovers Kara's existence, Jeremiah is blackmailed into their employ, eventually resulting in his alleged death, kidnapping, and years-long capture. In contrast, Kara Zor-El is presented in the flashback issue #0 of *Supergirl* as a young woman on the cusp of graduation whose life is overturned by the cataclysmic destruction of her planet.[29] In this sense, *Supergirl* is denied the stable, adoptive family life of Superman and as a result, is characterized as lacking the moral and emotional stability of a masculine superhero.

While feelings of anger or frustration are common to male superheroes' as well as female, Stephanie R. deLusé argues that characters like Batman are portrayed as channeling their rage into productive outlets such as the array of gadgets or training regimes that Bruce Wayne uses in his fight against crime, or even Superman's fortress of solitude and curative collection of Kryptonian relics.[30] Framed by deLusé as a "proactive form of coping," the male hero's actions take the energy of frustration and shift it into functional form.[31]

Supergirl, however, is not depicted with a clear outlet for her anger. Kara Zor-El of the comic book series never develops a public identity in the manner of Batman's Bruce Wayne, Superman's Clark Kent, or television's Kara Danvers. Instead, Kara remains Supergirl throughout the series and is characterized by rage throughout, shown regularly struggling to control her powers. This culminates in issue #28,[32] when a Red Lantern ring seeking the emotion of rage latches onto Kara's anger, transforming her at one point into a rage-powered Red Lantern. Similarly, in the television series, Kara Danvers is shown to undertake anger-management exercises with James in "Red Faced."[33] Yet in later episodes, Kara struggles to restrain her actions. In the second season episode "Alex,"[34] for instance, Kara's solution to a bank-robbery-turned-hostage negotiation is to plummet through the ceiling of the building, violently confronting the criminals. Likewise, in the first season episode, "For the Girl Who Has Everything,"[35] Kara violently rushes into a confrontation with season one villain and fellow Kryptonian, Non, after recovering from the Black Mercy. While Kara Danvers is not characterized by the uncontrolled rage of Kara Zor-El, there is nonetheless an underlying recklessness associated with television's Supergirl. In both incarnations of *Supergirl*, the title protagonist is characterized by anger.

Emotion and Identity

Supergirl presents a derivative character in the manner of posing a hypothetical series of rearrangements or alterations to an existing character. And in this sense, Supergirl's anger comes to be evoked as a symptom of a series of distinctions between herself and Superman, providing distinguishing reinterpretations of the former's key background elements: What if Superman remembered Krypton? What if Superman suffered Post-Traumatic Stress? What if Superman had no parents on Earth (*New 52*) or an older, human sibling (television)? What if Superman was female? Allegorical and derivative characters represent a style of "mythic thinking" that engages the figure of the superhero as a series of signs and symbols, able to be reordered and reorientated.[36]

The reordering process questions the underlying problems and solutions encountered by the superhero. This style of characterization allows the ideological significance of the character to change or take on alternative forms, even as it develops and grows with the mainstream thought of the time.[37] Herein, Sean Carney offers the example of Superman's transformation from a champion of the people to a defender of the state from the 1930s through to the late twentieth century.

Supergirl, as a reinterpretation of the existing character and reconfiguration of a familiar narrative, offers an alternative to Superman's ideology. But much like Jennifer A. Swartz-Levine's assessment of *She-Hulk*, Supergirl exists as something of an antithesis of Superman.[38] Where Superman's powers and emotions are detached, presenting a character of stoic morality, Supergirl's are firmly interlocked. In regard to the contrast of the two characters, Supergirl acts in both the comic books and the television series with a much firmer and more militaristic orientation than Superman. Where Kal-El is horrified in season two of the television series by the prospect of the DEO retaining a Kryptonite arsenal, Supergirl understands its necessity.[39] Where Superman in the *New 52* regards Kryptonian culture in an idealistic light, Supergirl is intimately aware of the planet's warmongering nature through the work of her parents in developing weapons. Thus, while Supergirl begins with this contrast, the character has since been expanded on by successive volumes of publication and adaptive productions to take on a detailed alternative "Superman" mythology of her own,[40] one in which Kara is rendered distinct from male notions of super heroics.

The male superheroes presented alongside Supergirl come to represent various pinnacles of the United States: Martian Manhunter, the immigrant made good, or Guy Gardner, the Red Lantern who channels his anger into the fight for democracy and freedom on a galactic scale.[41] But in contrast as an antithesis to Superman, Supergirl can no longer be framed as embodying those ideals. In the television series, Kara Danvers acts as a public vigilante and employee of a clandestine government task force. In the New 52 series, she is disenfranchised and homeless, dwelling for a brief period informally in a friend's apartment and later aboard the Red Lantern's ship. The ideals Supergirl stands for are thus not clearly articulated in a similar manner to Superman's "Truth, Justice and the American Way." Rather, the ideals associated with Supergirl are abstract and redefined with each production.

Where Superman is portrayed as a paragon of idealism, Supergirl is a deeply flawed character. Mike Madrid argues that the flaws associated with the character render Supergirl significantly more believable.[42] Yet, Madrid additionally criticizes Supergirl for her lack of overt heroism in the New 52 series.[43] Indeed, while the New 52 Kara Zor-El does engage in superpowered battles, these fights are not the result of an ideological outlook or a particular abstract quest for justice. Rather, the foes Supergirl engages are largely incidental. Kara only stops Tycho's plans for Earth parenthetically after he attempts to kidnap her. Likewise, Supergirl only confronts Cyborg Superman in the New 52 because he is a fellow Kryptonian survivor, later revealed to be her father. Contrasting the New 52 with the television series depiction of Kara, Madrid further argues that the television version presents a Supergirl who is "adorably goofy" and "true" to the source material.[44]

However, as we have discussed, the comic books themselves are varied in their content and presentation of the character. Likewise, what Madrid does not address is that Kara Danver's actions are, much like the New 52 characters, not motivated by ideology or altruism. Rather, Kara acts publicly as a vigilante with the endorsement of the government of whom she is an employee and operative through the DEO. While Kara Danvers is a much more proactive figure and a closer fit to the heroic archetype than Kara Zor-El, much like her New 52 counterparts, the mission she embodies remains not one of peace or social justice. Rather, the lack of a clearly defined mission with objectives and an abstract morality helps further render Supergirl a relatable figure. In this capacity, Kara Zor-El is another young woman dealing with the legacy of a failed system and an idealistic but flawed society. Likewise, Kara Danvers is more akin to a police officer or soldier than a costumed vigilante. In this sense, the character articulates a relationship to society, its processes and problems in a similar manner to which she is also engaged with her emotional state. Power, emotion, and identity all flow together for Supergirl in a manner that avoids the traditional divisions of a male superhero.

The interplay of power and identity is underscored by the treatment of Kara's public self. Many characters within the television series are aware that Kara is Supergirl, ranging from known figures such as her employer Cat Grant and her sister's partner, police detective Maggie Sawyer, to unknown individuals such as former classmates that observed Kara's emerging powers during high school. Yet, the problems typically attributed to the need for a secret identity—enemies targeting family members, a lack of private or personal existence—are largely absent from television's *Supergirl*. The series details few such incidents, with the second season episode "Alex" marking a notable exception.

Likewise, Kara Zor-El simply does not attain a secret or alternative identity, existing permanently as Supergirl. Through avoiding the "secret identity" trope, Supergirl in both incarnations presents a unified identity when contrasted with male characters. Martian Manhunter in the television series, for instance, maintained multiple identities as Hank Henshaw and J'onn J'onzz. Likewise, Superman is forced to undertake an elaborate act and series of deceptions in order to maintain his identity, such as faux clumsiness. A similar action is undertaken by Superman in the *New 52* comics. Likewise, when Kara Zor-El joins the Red Lantern Corps, she encounters equally conflicted figures torn between their status as avatars of rage that sees them blindly lash out at their surrounding environment and role as the protectors of Space Sector 2814. Judge, an emergent Red Lantern in the series, demonstrates this aspect, compulsively lashing out at the society he deems immoral around him.

It is not uncommon for female protagonists within popular culture to have their actions directed by male mentor or employer figures.[45] In doing so, this mentorship allows male characters to direct or take partial ownership of the female protagonist's actions.[46] But in contrast, Supergirl's holistic identity defies male ownership of her actions. Kara Danvers' direct superiors in season two might be Martian Manhunter and James Olsen, for example, but her employers are President Olivia Marsdin and Cat Grant, both of whom are aware of Kara's total identity. Likewise, Kara Zor-El repeatedly and furiously rejects Superman's offers of mentorship in the *New 52* series, just as she eventually abandons the Red Lantern Corps, operating without tethers to other superheroes. Supergirl is a flawed, yet relatable character that engages existing tropes in an innovative manner.

Supergirl is not negatively portrayed for her characterization as emotional. Rather, the character's anger is the lynchpin on which a holistic rejection of commonplace superhero tropes is based. In this sense, Supergirl uses her anger as a positive force, a catalyst for action. Both renditions of Supergirl mirrors Gladys L. Knight's assessment of the female action heroine.[47] Knight further suggests that the use of anger as a transformative emotion sees the female action heroine transcend her status as an object of sex to become an avatar of power in her own right.[48] Supergirl's status as a figure of power sees her alternately heralded as a hero in the *New 52* comics and as a figure of fear, much as she was in the first television season via the media campaigning of Maxwell Lord and as a result of her behavior under the influence of Red Kryptonite in the first season episode "Falling."[49] However, in the television series, Kara Danvers' powers and their use sees Superman cede to her the title "champion of Earth" in the second season finale. The contrast highlights that it is less important how Supergirl is perceived by the surrounding inhabitants of the diegetic world around her but rather, much like other anger-driven comic book characters such as the *Hulk* or *Lobo*, that Kara can be and is treated questionably. But what is important for Supergirl is that she breaks the image of the female superhero as a sidekick, derivative or subordinate, yet is never also a wild and out-of-control monster.[50] Still, there remains between both renditions of Supergirl an alternating portrayal of Kara Danvers versus that of Kara Zor-El.

In their respective presentations of *Supergirl*, the television series and *New 52* comic books offer competing, rather holistic visions of the character. Each production's respective reorientation of Supergirl and her legacy continues throughout with the use of a wider cast of characters and expanded DC Universe. Silver Banshee, for example, is presented in both the television series and *New 52* comic books. Unlike the differences in how Supergirl herself is presented, those surrounding Silver Banshee are less extreme with both renditions of the character entering a period of disenfranchisement as the result of a family curse. While Silver Banshee is a victim of biology and circumstance, for Kara Danvers, Banshee's destructive nature and cynical worldview renders the character a foe. Yet, Kara Zor-El finds a kindred spirit in Silver Banshee and while the character may not necessarily live within the confines of law and order, neither does Kara, whose outbursts quickly see her branded a public menace.

Similar events follow for Kara Zor-El with the World Killers, who retreat and parlay after one of their number suffers a grievous injury battling Supergirl. Rather than engaging in a series of never-ending battles, Kara Zor-El establishes a rhetoric of accord with characters traditionally framed as villains, rivals, or foes. Unlike Kara Danvers, who battles and defeats all challengers, Kara Zor-El only violently engages those foes who are directly threatening her physically, such as the robot assassin Nanotech or Cyborg Superman. Villains in superhero literature typically represent some alternate, non-mainstream, ideology, physicality, or outlook.[51] Yet for the *New 52*'s *Supergirl* this difference does not equate, innately, to rivalry or criminality.

In this sense, Kara Danvers is locked in the perpetual, never-ending cycle of "villain-bashing exploits" to borrow Richard Reynolds' term.[52] Herein, Reynolds refers to a narrative formula of villainous plot or criminal activity, thwarted time and again by the hero. Indeed, the television series presents a number of villains that are utilized for multiple episodes and wider storylines, such as the White Martians and Cadmus, while others—such as T.O. Morrow,

Maxima, or Master Jailer—are simply abandoned after a single appearance. Thus, in contrast to the *New 52*'s Supergirl, Kara Danvers presents a more traditional mode of Superhero storytelling, with the television formula adopting a villain-of-the-week format.

Yet, the *New 52* breaks this cycle in a manner that raises questions of who, precisely, is the villain? As a result, Kara Zor-El has no nemesis and, at times the contrasting lines of allegiance see Kara Zor-El herself become the adversary. For example, during the *H'El on Earth* crossover event, Kara Zor-El allies with H'El, endangering the Earth to recreate Krypton. Where television presents a rendition of Supergirl that in many ways fits the traditional archetype of superhero narratives, the *New 52* engages a mixture of allegiances and goals that blurs traditional boundaries between notions of heroism and villainy.

In contrast to the linear, episodic adventures of Kara Danvers, the *New 52*'s Kara Zor-El presents a nuanced exploration of Supergirl's literary lineage. Zor-El, Kara's father, is perhaps the most notable of this aspect of the series. At one time, alive and well in Kara's memories as a loving father, the comic book engages a complex series of deconstructions of Zor-El's image. At one time exposed to be the manufacturer of the living weapons known as the World Killers, Zor-El is later revealed to have survived the destruction of Krypton as the Cyborg Superman, transformed into Brainiac's henchman in a bid to save Argo City from falling with the rest of the planet.

The pre–*New 52 Supergirl* storylines presented elements such as Cyborg Superman (then identified as Hank Henshaw as in the television series) and Zor-El with clearly distinct boundaries or moments of narrative. Yet, the *New 52* blends all elements of *Supergirl* together in an overarching master narrative that incorporates distinct genre-elements—superhero, science fiction and coming of age story—together. The effect is a series of "cross-genre or borderline-genre" thresholds that lack the distinct identity of being only one type of narrative or another,[53] but one that nonetheless shifts statuses from one thing to another, never wholly presenting the conventions and defying the anticipations of readers.[54] Due to this shifting status, Zor-El, for instance, never at once becomes a soulless menace or retains his status as a loving father. He is both Kara Zor-El's key parental figure and the mad scientist who threatens her world with monstrosities.

In contrast, Kara Danvers and the television series offer a much further singular association that sits closer to the blend of superheroics and science fiction familiar to the broader *Superman* family of narratives. Herein, characters are compartmentalized into singular roles better suited to the episodic storytelling of the series. Lena Luthor is a steward friend of Kara, at least as far as the second season is concerned, with the villainous Luthor role undertaken by her mother. Hank Henshaw is Cyborg Superman, distinct from a dead Zor-El. While a character such as Jeremiah Danvers is presented as duplicitous within the series, his motivation is enshrined as a love for his daughters. In this sense, Kara Danvers is characterized with a degree of equilibrium absent from Kara Zor-El. Where Kara Zor-El's role as *Supergirl* is an imposed identity, occupied by Kara herself only incidentally, Kara Danvers is squarely focused on the title and role itself. Though both characters are considered with a coupling of emotion and superpowers, television presents Kara Danvers as an established individual by the onset of season two, distinct from the coming of age story of Kara Zor-El. Indeed, by the end of the *New 52* series, Kara Zor-El has both found herself on Earth and lost her powers, her emotional turmoil and trauma disappearing with her Kryptonian abilities. Thus, while by season two, Kara Danvers is an established individual in the role of Supergirl, she is not deprived of any special or distinct quality in achieving a sense of self.

The *New 52* and television adaptations of *Supergirl* present distinct, contrasting reconfigurations of the character. In the television series, Kara Danvers presents audiences with a clearly defined mission statement, government sanction and positive outlook, features absent from comic book Kara Zor-El's traumatic landing on Earth, complex homeless status, and struggles to integrate into human society. Herein, consumers are confronted with twin, competing images of Kara—Danvers and Zor-El, television and comic book—offering contending ideologies concurrently. Most notably, where television presents a rendition of Supergirl that in many ways fits the traditional archetype of superhero narratives, the *New 52* engages a mixture of allegiances and goals that blurs traditional boundaries between notions of heroism and villainy. Yet, each variation of *Supergirl* is introduced as a new character into an existing setting populated by established characters. And in both the television series and *New 52* comic books, Supergirl engages in thematic linkings to the wider DC Comics properties, from Martian Manhunter on television to the Green Lantern comic books of the *New 52*. While the characterization of Kara and the construction of the wider cast of characters (with the exception of Superman and Cyborg Superman) remain distinct for each production, both comic books and television are essentially undertaking the same adaptive action. Thus, while both variations of Supergirl are highly distinct characterizations, each embodies the tropes and stereotypes of female superhero characterization. Most of all, in both incarnations of *Supergirl*, the title protagonist is characterized by anger, rendering Supergirl as a flawed, yet relatable character that avoids the tropes commonly associated with male superheroes. Power, emotion, and identity all flow together for Supergirl in a manner that avoids the traditional tropes of a male superhero.

Notes

1. Robert Bernstein, "The Menace of Metallo," *Action Comics*, 1, no. 252 (1959).
2. Jeph Loeb, "The Supergirl from Krypton, Part 1," *Batman/Superman*, 1, no. 8 (2004).
3. Mike Johnson and Michael Green. *Supergirl*, vol. 1 (New York: DC Comics, 2012).
4. Otto Binder, "Claire Kent, Alias Super-Sister!" *Superboy*, 1, no. 78 (1960).
5. Otto Binder, "The Three Magic Wishes," *Superman*, 1, no. 123 (1958).
6. Steven T. Seagle. "Truth," *Superman 10-Cent Adventure*, 1, no. 1 (2003).
7. John Byrne, "He Only Laughs When I Hurt," *Superman*, 2, no. 16 (1988).
8. Doug Monech, "Chasing Clay," *Batman*, 1, no. 550 (1998).
9. Carlos Albert Scolari, "Transmedia Storytelling: Implicit Consumers, Narrative Worlds, and Branding in Contemporary Media Production," *International Journal of Communication* 3 (2000): 586.
10. *The Flash*, various, aired 2014, on The CW.
11. Gardner Fox, "The Flash of Two Worlds," *The Flash*. 1, no. 123 (1961).
12. *The Flash*, "Flash of Two Worlds," season 2, episode 2, directed by Jesse Warn, written by Aaron Helbing and Todd Helbing, aired October 13, 2015, on The CW.
13. Scolari, "Transmedia Storytelling," 586.
14. Johnson and Green, *Supergirl*, vol. 1.
15. *Supergirl*, "Stronger Together," season 1, episode 2, directed by Glen Winter, story by Greg Berlanti and Andrew Kreisberg, teleplay by Andrew Kreisberg and Ali Adler, aired November 2, 2015, on CBS.
16. *Supergirl*, "Stronger Together," season 1, episode 2.
17. Rebecca Davis, "Fighting Like a Girl: Gendered Language in Superhero Comics," *Griffith Working Papers in Pragmatics and Intercultural Communication* 6 (2013): 29.
18. Davis, "Fighting Like a Girl," 29.
19. Johnson and Green, *Supergirl*, vol. 1.
20. Johnson and Green, *Supergirl*, vol. 1.
21. Mike Johnson and Michael Green, *Supergirl*, vol. 2 (New York: DC Comics, 2013).
22. Michael Alan Nelson, *Supergirl*, vol. 5 (New York: DC Comics, 2015).
23. *Supergirl*, "Truth, Justice and the American Way," season 1, episode 14, directed by Lexi Alexander, written by Michael Grassi, Yahlin Chang, and Caitlin Parrish, aired February 22, 2016, on CBS.
24. Davis, "Fighting Like a Girl," 29.
25. *Supergirl*, "Manhunter," season 1, episode 17, directed by Chris Fisher, story by Derek Simon, teleplay by Cindy Lichtman and Rachel Shukert, aired March 21, 2016, on CBS.
26. Lawrence C. Rubin, "Superheroes & Heroic Journeys: Reclaiming Loss in Adoption," *Creative Interventions in Grief and Loss Therapy: When the Music Stops, a Dream Dies* (New York: Routledge, 2005), 245.
27. Rubin, "Superheroes & Heroic Journeys," 245.
28. Rubin, "Superheroes & Heroic Journeys," 246.
29. Johnson and Green, *Supergirl*, vol. 2.
30. Stephanie R. deLusé, "Coping with Stress ... the Superhero Way," *The Psychology of Superheroes: An Unauthorized Exploration* (Dallas: BellaBooks, 2008), 194.
31. deLusé, "Coping with Stress," 194.
32. Nelson, *Supergirl*, vol. 5.
33. *Supergirl*, "Red Faced," season 1, episode 6, directed by Jesse Warn, written by Michael Grassi and Rachel Shukert, aired November 30, 2015, on CBS.
34. *Supergirl*, "Alex," season 2, episode 19, directed by Rob Greenlea, written by Eric Carrasco and Greg Baldwin, aired May 1, 2017, on The CW.
35. *Supergirl*, "For the Girl Who Has Everything," season 1, episode 13, directed by Dermott Downs, written by Ted Sullivan, Derek Simon, and Andrew Kreisberg, aired February 8, 2016, on CBS.
36. Sean Carney, "The Function of the Superhero at the Present Time," *Iowa Journal of Cultural Studies* 6 (2005).
37. Carney, "The Function of the Superhero."

38. Jennifer A. Swartz-Levine, "She-Hulk Crash! The Evolution of Jen Walters or How Marvel Comics Learnt to Stop Worrying About Feminism and Love the Gamma Bomb," *The Ages of the Incredible Hulk: Essays on the Green Goliath in Changing Times* (Jefferson: McFarland, 2016), 80–81.
39. *Supergirl*, "The Adventures of Supergirl," season 2, episode 1, directed by Glen Winter, story by Greg Berlanti and Andrew Kreisberg, teleplay by Andrew Kreisberg and Jessica Queller, aired October 10, 2016, on The CW.
40. *Supergirl*, "The Adventures of Supergirl," season 2, episode 1.
41. Though Gardner started as a Green Lantern, and is currently back to being one.
42. Mike Madrid, *The Supergirls: The Fashion, Feminism, Fantasy and the History of Comic Book Heroines* (Exterminating Angel Press, 2009), 100.
43. Madrid, *The Supergirls*, 101.
44. Madrid, *The Supergirls*, 101.
45. Gladys L. Knight, *Female Action Heroes: A Guide to Women in Comics, Video Games, Film, and Television* (Santa Barbara, CA: Greenwood, 2010), 286.
46. Knight, *Female Action Heroes*, 286.
47. Knight, *Female Action Heroes*, 130.
48. Knight, *Female Action Heroes*, 130.
49. *Supergirl*, "Falling," season 1, episode 16, directed by Larry Teng, written by Robert Rovner and Jessica Queller, aired March 14, 2016, on CBS.
50. Knight, *Female Action Heroes*, 132.
51. Richard Reynolds, *Superheroes: A Modern Mythology* (Jackson: University Press of Mississippi, 1992), 24.
52. Reynolds, *Superheroes*, 34.
53. Peter Coogan, "The Definition of the Superhero," *A Comics Studies Reader* (Jackson: University of Mississippi Press: 2009), 88.
54. Coogan, "The Definition of the Superhero," 89.

SELECTED BIBLIOGRAPHY

Bedard, Tony, Justin Jordan, Scot Lobdell, and Michael Alan Nelson. *Supergirl*, vol. 4. New York: DC Comics, 2014.
Bernstein, Robert. "The Menace of Metallo." *Action Comics*. 1, no. 252 (1959).
Binder, Otto. "Claire Kent, Alias Super-Sister!" *Superboy*. 1, no. 78 (1960).
_____. "The Three Magic Wishes." *Superman*. 1, no. 123 (1958).
Byrne, John. "He Only Laughs When I Hurt." *Superman*. 2, no. 16 (1988).
Carney, Sean. "The Function of the Superhero at the Present Time." *Iowa Journal of Cultural Studies* 6 (2005), 100–117.
Coogan, Peter. "The Definition of the Superhero." *A Comics Studies Reader*. Jackson: University of Mississippi Press: 2009.
Davis, Rebecca. "Fighting Like a Girl: Gendered Language in Superhero Comics." *Griffith Working Papers in Pragmatics and Intercultural Communication*. 6 (2013): 28–36.
deLusé, Stephanie R. "Coping with Stress ... the Superhero Way." In *The Psychology of Superheroes: An Unauthorized Exploration*. Edited by Robin S. Rosenberg, 187–200. Dallas: BellaBooks, 2008.
Fox, Gardner. "The Flash of Two Worlds." *The Flash*. 1, no. 123 (1961).
Knight, Gladys L. *Female Action Heroes: A Guide to Women in Comics, Video Games, Film, and Television*. Santa Barbara: Greenwood, 2010.
Loeb, Jeph. "The Supergirl from Krypton, Part 1." *Batman/Superman*. 1, no. 8 (2004).
Hannah, Frank, and Mike Johnson. *Supergirl*, vol. 3 (New York: DC Comics, 2014).
Johnson, Mike, K. Perkins and Tony Bedad. *Supergirl*, vol. 6. New York: DC Comics, 2015.
Johnson, Mike, and Michael Green. *Supergirl*, vol. 1. New York: DC Comics, 2012.
_____. *Supergirl*, vol. 2. New York: DC Comics, 2013.
Madrid, Mike. *The Supergirls: The Fashion, Feminism, Fantasy and the History of Comic Book Heroines*. Exterminating Angel Press, 2009.
Monech, Doug. "Chasing Clay." *Batman*. 1, no. 550 (1998).

Nelson, Michael Alan. *Supergirl*, vol. 5 New York: DC Comics, 2015.
Reynolds, Richard. *Superheroes: A Modern Mythology*. Jackson: University Press of Mississippi, 1992.
Rubin, Lawrence C. "Superheroes & Heroic Journeys: Reclaiming Loss in Adoption." In *Creative Interventions in Grief and Loss Therapy: When the Music Stops, a Dream Dies*. Edited by Thelma Duffey, 237–252. New York: Routledge, 2005.
Seagle, Steven T. "Truth." *Superman 10-Cent Adventure* 1, no. 1 (2003).
Scolari, Carlos Albert. "Transmedia Storytelling: Implicit Consumers, Narrative Worlds, and Branding in Contemporary Media Production." *International Journal Of Communication* 3 (2000): 586–606.
Swartz-Levine, Jennifer A. "She-Hulk Crash! The Evolution of Jen Walters or How Marvel Comics Learnt to Stop Worrying About Feminism and Love the Gamma Bomb." In *The Ages of the Incredible Hulk: Essays on the Green Goliath in Changing Times*. Edited by Joseph J. Darowski, 78–92. Jefferson, NC: McFarland, 2016.

"I embraced who I am and I don't want to stop"
Queering Supergirl

JAIME CHRIS WEIDA

In the ongoing "war" between the two major names in comics—DC and Marvel—both companies have developed several live-action television shows geared towards adult audiences. These include *Jessica Jones*, *Iron Fist*, and *Runaways* (from Marvel); and *Arrow*, *The Flash*, and *Supergirl* (from DC). While critical and fan reaction has been mixed, these shows, including *Supergirl*, have been successful enough to garner multiple seasons. For example, *Arrow*, focused on the DC hero Green Arrow, is now in its sixth season (it has been on the air since 2012), and as of early January 2018 has received a 94 percent on the popular media rating website *Rotten Tomatoes*.[1] Like Marvel, DC has extended their superhero brand past comic books, action figures and collectables, and films into television. DC has also moved into streaming-only content with *Netflix*-exclusive shows. According to *The Washington Post* in the article "Superhero and Sci-Fi Fans Are Going to Need a Lot of Streaming Apps—And That's Not Cheap," DC is starting its "own streaming service, which arrives in 2018."[2]

Comic narratives and comic heroes are a hot commodity. Especially in the present moment, television shows have the potential to seriously shape and impact the cultural consciousness. Overall, movie ticket sales are down while subscriptions to online streaming services are up. A television series, because of its length, contains a potential for plot and character development not necessarily shared by films. A brief glance at television fandoms like *Game of Thrones* and *The Walking Dead* demonstrates to what extent fans are willing to devote themselves to a television show.[3] In spring 2017, fans waited with bated breath—and happily shelled out money for *Showtime* subscriptions—

to watch the long-awaited next season of *Twin Peaks*.[4] The U.S. is rapidly moving to the point where television shows are even more anticipated than major studio movies.

This brings me to *Supergirl*. While Supergirl is not herself an "A-list" superhero, she has more name recognition than many other heroes because of her connection to Superman. *Supergirl* as a television show is also unique because it focuses on a female main hero and a diverse supporting cast that contains a number of female characters. Among the few similarly gender-diverse SF (Speculative Fiction)[5] adult shows are *Xena: Warrior Princess, Buffy the Vampire Slayer, Charmed*, and—debatably—the fairytale retellings of *Once Upon a Time*. I maintain that *Supergirl* is also "Queer" in multiple ways. It explicitly introduces a Queer main character; in season 2, Alex Danvers, Supergirl's adoptive sister, comes out as Queer. However, *Supergirl* also Queers traditional superhero tropes and narratives. The show reverses the "male superhero/female sidekick or assistant" trope, repeatedly shows women in positions of power, and even passes the Bechdel Test[6] in every episode. I propose that *Supergirl* not only adds Queer visibility to the superhero genre, but also offers a much-needed opportunity to Queer the entire genre as a whole.

In this work, I am using the word "Queer" as it has been used by theorists such as Eve Sedgwick, Julia Scheele, and J. Halberstam.[7] I use it as an "umbrella" terms that covers many different non-heteronormative sex and gender identities, such as gay, lesbian, bi/pan/omnisexual, Trans*,[8] asexual/ace, intersex, etc. It is in no way used in the archaic pejorative sense.

"Truth, justice, and the American way": Superheroes and the Politics of Normalization

For such an imaginative and creative genre and art form, superhero comics have historically been surprisingly conservative and normalizing.[9] Since this essay is about the DC show *Supergirl*, I am primarily focusing on DC characters and storylines. I am aware that these characters have been re-envisioned and "ret-conned" since their inceptions; however, I think it is important to look at how their initial identity was far from liberatory, which is an ideology I contend still informs contemporary superhero narratives.

The "big three" main DC heroes are Superman, Batman, and Wonder Woman. Superman was created by Jerry Siegel and Joe Schuster; his first appearance was in *Action Comics #1* in 1938. Superman may be seen as the "model" for all subsequent male superheroes; as Umberto Eco wrote, "he can be seen as the representative of all his similars."[10] What, then, does Superman represent? Famously: "truth, justice, and the American way."[11] During World War II, there were several *Superman* story arcs that depicted Superman fighting America's enemies, including him "duking it out" with Hitler and Stalin. Superman's strong—and American-European specific—sense of morality has led to many characters in his narratives to call him a "Big Blue Boy Scout."[12] Superman represents a very traditional incarnation of the so-called American Dream; despite having superpowers, he toils as a reporter for the newspaper *The Daily Planet*. While there have been different and continually revised Superman origin stories over the years, most of these stories say that he was raised on a farm in the Midwest by the Kents, a heteronormative husband and wife. The Kents are not only heteronormative; they are almost a pastiche of the traditional "American family." Pa Kent (as Superman calls him) is a hard-working farmer, while Ma Kent is a housewife who devotes herself to raising Superman as Clark Kent. Superman himself has a long-running, mostly monogamous relationship with Lois Lane. Also, in his costume as Superman, he represents the ultimate image of "respectable" American hetero-masculinity.

Batman is slightly more problematic as he is often cast as the dark "anti-hero" foil to Superman's "Boy Scout." However, most of the violent and gritty depictions of Batman come from the "grimdark" period in comics during the 1980s, when Alan Moore and Dave Gibbon's explicitly brutal *Watchman* was released. Frank Miller's famous *The Dark Knight Returns* presented an angry, violent, vigilante Batman. Originally, while still functioning as a foil to Superman when he was introduced in *Detective Comics #27* in 1939, Batman was still devoted to law and order and the status quo. Since his parents were killed by a mugger, he pledged to rid society of crime by becoming a kind of "super-cop." During the "Silver Age" of comics in the 1970s, the Gotham City police department deputized Batman. Certainly, Batman's secret identity, millionaire Bruce Wayne, reinforces the American narrative of the meritocracy where the wealthiest people are benevolent and praiseworthy citizens.

Wonder Woman has the latest origin date of the trio; she was created by William Moulton Marston in 1941. She was and is arguably the most easily-recognizable female comic-book superhero[13] and may be seen as a liberatory figure; she leaves her female Amazon paradise of Themyscira to fight oppression in "man's world." Gloria Steinem put Wonder Woman on the cover of *Ms.* magazine in the 1970s and Wonder Woman has been praised as a feminist icon. However, Wonder Woman's first appearance on the big screen was not until *The Lego Movie* in 2014. Her first live-action film appearance was in a secondary role in *Superman vs. Batman: Dawn of Justice* in 2016. A feature Wonder Woman film, starring Gal Gadot, was finally released in summer 2017. According to *Box Office Mojo*, *Wonder Woman* was the third highest-grossing film of 2017 with a total worldwide gross of over $800,000,00,[14] which was a long-awaited triumph for Wonder Woman fans.

What does any of this have to do with Supergirl? Currently, Supergirl and Wonder Woman are somewhat equal in terms of brand and character exposure (although the recent *Justice League* film and the upcoming *Wonder Woman 1984* film arguably might give Wonder Woman an edge); while *Supergirl* is the character's first television series, there was a *Supergirl* film released in 1984 that was universally considered a disaster. The film currently has a 10 percent ranking on *Rotten Tomatoes*.[15] It has only 4.3 out of ten stars on *IMDb*, as well as a comments thread with some brutally negative comments: "Genuine contender for the worst film ever made. End of story."[16]

One might argue that Superman and Batman are more compellingly-written characters or that the visual media versions of their stories are of better quality. However, that is a facile argument that does not explain critical and commercial disasters like *Superman IV: The Quest for Peace* or *Batman and Robin*. These "flops" did not kill the Superman and Batman franchises, nor did they delay upcoming future films for decades (according to the Warner Brothers Studio, a Wonder Woman feature film was in some degree of production since 1996—her fans had to wait until summer 2017).[17] Like Wonder Woman, Supergirl has the potential to Queer the superhero narrative in a way that frightens those who turn to these narratives in order to see their heroes uphold their preferred conservative values, which I believe ultimately makes her a far more powerful and inspiring superhero.

"People should just be allowed to look in the mirror and see all kinds of possibilities": Overtly Queer Themes in Supergirl

The quote that headlines this section is from the young adult author M-E Girard, who recently wrote the successful and award-winning YA novel *Girl Mans Up*, focused around a Queer teenage girl who does not fit into heteronormative conceptions of female identity. Girard herself identifies as Queer. Her words speak to the idea that television is, for many viewers, a mirror in which they try to see themselves. In fact, the television screen in contemporary technology is, *literally*, a mirror. The viewer may choose to watch *Supergirl* or any other show on their smartphone, tablet, laptop, or flat-screen television. Unlike some old cathode-ray television sets, these modern electronics often have reflective screens. Once the viewer turns off their device, they see themselves reflected on that screen in a way they may not have seen themselves reflected in contemporary visual media.

Representation is essential; any television show that engages with but does not represent Queer characters and themes in a respectful manner does a disservice to its many Queer viewers. Unfortunately, there is no dearth of such disrespectful shows. For example, consider Jack from the original *Will and Grace*, Titus Andromedon from *The Unbreakable Kimmy Schmidt*, or Kenny from *The Real O'Neals* (which has since been cancelled). While each of these shows was praised for its sexual diversity, they all helped to reinforce heteronormative preconceptions about Queer identity. For example, in *The Unbreakable Kimmy Schmidt*, Titus is a "flamboyantly" gay man who, after he separates from his male partner in season three of the show, performs an over-the-top satire of Beyoncé's "Lemonade" while dancing through the streets of New York City in a feathered yellow dress. Jack in the original *Will and Grace*, as well as the current follow-up series, seems to epitomize heteronormative ideas about gay male behavior, even down to his "jazz hands" and "limp wrists," which are coded as "feminine" by the show. In *The Real O'Neals*, teen-age Kenny's admission that he is gay shakes his conservative family to the core. Television characters' Queerness is often presented for drama or for laughs.

As a major network television show that depends upon ratings and viewership, *Supergirl* cannot entirely disengage with this ongoing phenomenon. However, I maintain it more effectively holds up a non-distorted mirror to Queer viewers than many other shows containing Queer characters and themes. Most Queer discussions of *Supergirl* focus on Alex Danvers coming out as Queer. Before I discuss that specifically, I would like to turn to some other, lesser-discussed "Queer" elements in the series as a whole.

In the early episodes of the first season, Supergirl is faced with the challenge of whether or not she should let people know about her superhero identity. To most of the people in her life, including her adopted mother and father, she is simply "Kara Danvers." She has spent her adolescent and adult life trying to fit in and normalize herself to the human world. This is especially important because many Queer people begin to realize their identity around adolescence. While her adoptive parents, the Danvers, know she is superpowered, they encourage her to try to live as "normal" a life as possible. Early in season 2 during a flashback to her adolescent years, viewers discover that Supergirl's adoptive father, Jeremiah Danvers, made her a pair of glasses with lead frames to block her super-vision after she nearly exposes her superpowers by trying to stop a car accident. While Jeremiah insists he only wants to keep Supergirl safe, his action mirrors parents who counsel a Queer child to hide who they are for their own safety. Jeremiah gives Supergirl the glasses so that she can see the world differently, analogous to the way that well-meaning but bigoted parents of Queer children often try to impose their own "vision" of a heteronormative identity upon their children. Kara never stops wearing the glasses and later asks Alex to let their father know that she has always worn them. Despite her achievements as Supergirl, Kara has internalized the idea that she needs to "see" herself and the world the same way as her conservative adoptive parents see it. Throughout the course of the series, she continues to struggle with this internal normalization.

At the very beginning of the series her normalization seems total, until Supergirl uses her powers for the first time in years when her sister Alex's plane is about to crash. This is the point at which Supergirl "becomes" Supergirl and acknowledges her superhero identity to herself. In the "Livewire" episode,[18] Supergirl faces the challenge of "coming out" as Supergirl to her adoptive mother Eliza Danvers. Winn, her male friend and collaborator/sidekick flat-out says, "Isn't that dangerous?" echoing the cautions and fears surrounding many Queer people who consider coming out.[19] Supergirl's sister Alex is also fearful of their mother's reaction to Supergirl's disclosure, to which Supergirl responds by saying that Alex herself should "come out" as a member of the DEO (Department of Extranormal Operations), a secret Alex has kept from their mother and which foreshadows Alex coming out as Queer in the next season. It is clear this is not an accidental metaphor; early in the episode a newscaster, Leslie Willis, reports, "[Supergirl] does kind of give off a Sapphic vibe, with that big ol' butch 'S' chest plate."

The theme of Supergirl being "outed" pervades the entire first season of the show. For example, in the episode "Bizzaro,"[20] after planting a hidden camera in Alex's handbag, the male antagonist Maxwell Lord says that he know about the "relationship" between Alex and Supergirl. While in the narrative of the show, Alex correctly assumes it means he knows they are sisters, I "read" that statement as Lord assuming they were a Queer couple. A major plot point in season 1 is Supergirl's boss, Cat Grant, being determined to "out" Kara as Supergirl. Cat is otherwise a fairly sympathetic figure; she is a powerful female character who becomes one of Supergirl's most ardent defenders. She is the head of the media conglomerate CatCo and uses her status to aid Supergirl's heroic endeavors. However, her insistence on outing Kara as Supergirl recalls the manner in which the supposedly-liberal *New York Times* outed Queer people during the Stonewall Resistance. Michelangelo Signorile discusses how the *Times* did not quail to "name names" of Queer people; on December 16, 1963, the front-page headline was "Growth of Overt Homosexuality in City Provokes Wild Concern."[21] The *Times*' irresponsible reporting practices endangered the lives and livelihoods of many, just as Cat's insistence upon outing Kara as Supergirl endangers Kara's "human" livelihood, as well as her physical life and the lives of those in whom she has confided.

One area in which *Supergirl* initially seems less liberatory is in the lack of any Trans* characters in the current seasons of the show. At the time of this writing, Trans* rights are under attack in the United States. In February 2017, President Trump repealed former President Obama's bill allowing K–12 public school students to use the bathroom corresponding to their gender identity. The Republican attacks on the Affordable Care Act will mean that many Trans* people may lose important medical services, such as affordable access to necessary hormones. President Trump has also instituted the Trans* military ban, which could prevent Trans* people from joining the U.S. military and may negatively affect many Trans* people who are currently serving. While *Supergirl* should tackle these issues head-on, I maintain that the show has addressed them metaphorically in the character of J'onn J'onzz, the Martian Manhunter, and M'gann, a White Martian.

J'onn is a shapeshifter; he is a Green Martian who is, seemingly, the last survivor of his race. He is played by the Black actor David Harewood. In the course of the series' narrative, J'onn takes on the identity of Hank Henshaw. J'onn was being hunted by the real Hank Henshaw and by Jeremiah Danvers. After J'onn meets Jeremiah, they form an alliance and J'onn vows to protect Alex and Kara by taking on Henshaw's form after Henshaw dies. He has worked at the DEO for years while "passing" for the actual Hank Henshaw. My use of the term "passing" here is not accidental. Some members of the Trans* community seek to "pass" as their actual gender rather than the gender assigned to them at birth. The extent to which someone who wants to pass is able to do so can be a determining factor in their self-image and how they are treated in a heteronormative society.

For example, in the episode "Childish Things,"[22] after J'onn has revealed his alien identity to Alex, she essentially says he does not need to hide it because Supergirl is accepted as an alien. J'onn's response to Alex in the same episode is: "Your sister looks like a pretty blonde cheerleader. I look like a monster." He says that he will not be accepted by humans unless he "transforms" into a less "threatening" form. So might Trans* people say who fail to "pass" as their gender and who challenge heteronormative societal ideas about what a man or a woman should "look like." There are other hints towards this Trans* subtext; in the previously-referenced "Bizzaro" episode, J'onn makes a joke about wearing a skirt. In "For the Girl Who Has Everything,"[23] J'onn transforms into Kara's form in order to keep Cat from "outing" her as Supergirl.

Once J'onn reveals himself in order to save Kara and Alex, he is attacked, detained, and tortured by the DEO. While he is in custody, he is placed in a "stasis field" that prevents him from transforming out of the Hank Henshaw form in the episode "Manhunter."[24] One of his captors even quips that he hopes J'onn likes that form because he will be "stuck" in it. This recalls not only the torturous so-called "pray the gay away" conversion camps that have been outlawed in many states in the U.S., but also a Trans*phobic insistence that one's physical body defines one's identity. Like many Trans* people, for a large portion of the show's narrative, J'onn is scared of revealing himself as an alien because he believes that others will react negatively to his nonnormative identity. And, despite the reassurances of Alex and Supergirl (who, as J'onn notes, can easily "pass" for human), he is proved entirely right.

The themes of passing, discrimination, and Trans* identity are further complicated by M'gann. She is an expatriate Martian and an immigrant to Earth, like J'onn. She is wearing several layers of masks; a point to which I will return shortly in my discussion of Alex Danvers. In her human form, M'gann is a woman of color. When she meets J'onn and strikes up an acquaintanceship, she seemingly "reveals" herself as a Green Martian, just like J'onn. However, in the "The Darkest Place" episode,[25] M'gann is revealed as a *White* Martian: a member of the race that enslaved and committed genocide against J'onn's people, the Green Martians.

The oppression of the Green Martians by the White Martians is DC comic book canon. However, *Supergirl* problematizes it on several levels of gender and sexual politics. While the Martins have different genders, in their "natural" form, both J'onn and M'gann appear somewhat physically androgynous. Their chosen human forms, however, visually conform to physical gender norms. In the episode "Survivors," J'onn says to M'gann, "Everything we do is under a microscope.... All it takes is [one] to ruin it for the rest of us."[26] This sounds very similar to what a member of an oppressed group, such as someone who is Trans*, might say; it is sadly true that single members of such marginalized groups are often "expected" to represent all those who share the same identity, and that whole groups are judged and demonized based on the actions of a few. M'gann responds during the same episode by saying, "I'm whatever I need to be in order to survive," rejecting that narrative and putting her own identity above that of the biological group to which she belongs. In the episode "The Darkest Places,"[27] when J'onn and M'gann are locked in lethal combat in their human forms, J'onn orders her to "show me your true self," i.e., demanding she transform into her White Martian form. M'gann responds: "Kill me, if that's what you want. But not like that. This is who I want to be."

M'gann is willing to die for her identity; she is asserting agency to live and die in the body that defines her, no matter what outside forces (J'onn) demand. There are several layers of subtext here. Despite his previous experience of being shunned for his bodily form, and his adoption of the human form, J'onn insists that M'gann's White Martian form is her "true" self. He is re-inscribing the bigotry he himself has faced. There is much to parse out here, especially because, when J'onn is on the verge of death, M'gann reluctantly agrees to a blood transfusion to save him. J'onn is initially furious that her White Martian blood has "tainted" him, even though it kept him from death.

While a full discussion of the racial implications is outside the scope of this essay, the fact that J'onn chooses to take on the form of a Black man (when he can literally assume any form he desires) is significant. Canonically the character of the Martian Manhunter is one of the most powerful in the DC Universe. J'onn has some powers that exceed even Superman's (for example, Superman cannot usually change form, nor can he usually read minds). Yet J'onn takes on a form that visually marks him as a member of a racial/cultural group that has historically and currently experienced severe discrimination and violence. I previously spoke of "passing" in terms of Trans* identity. However, the earlier use of the word was in relation to someone of Black heritage who had light skin "passing" for white. (The novels *The Human Stain* by Phillip Roth and, arguably, *The Great Gatsby* by F. Scott Fitzgerald address the theme of light-skinned characters "passing" as white in order to benefit from the white privilege so prevalent in the U.S.) J'onn passes as human, but he does *not* pass as white. On one level, this may be seen as a casting choice because Harewood is a skilled and popular actor. On another level, the war between the Green Martians and the White Martians can be deconstructed in terms of real-life racial tensions, even down to the idea of "tainted blood" predicated on skin color. J'onn's race has been killed and enslaved by the White Martians and he has chosen a Black human form. In the U.S. as well as elsewhere, white people have enslaved and killed Black people, so J'onn's human form mirrors the racial politics and history associated with his Green Martian form. M'gann's human form further problematizes the issue of race because, while she is a White Martian, she chooses to appear as a woman of color (the actor who plays M'gann, Sharon Leal, has a Filipina mother and a Black father, so she is of mixed heritage). Again, this may be a casting choice, but it also may speak to the complex nuances of race and culture in the U.S. While Leal is visibly identifiable as a person of color, she has lighter skin than Harewood does. Relatively darker or lighter skin has long been a sign of status in the U.S. For example, consider the infamous historical "paper bag" test, in which someone whose skin was the same color or lighter than a brown paper bag might be accorded privileges that a darker-skinned person would not be, such as admission to churches or social clubs. Even now, it is common for stores in U.S. neighborhoods with significant Black populations to sell "bleaching" lotions designed to lighten dark skin. The contemporary television show *Blackish* has tackled this issue with episodes that examine discrimination and treatment based upon skin color; for example, one of the daughters on the show (played by Marsai Martin) has darker skin than her parents and siblings, including her twin brother. In one episode, she is barely visible in the prints of her class photo because the photographer was not aware of how to light people with dark skin. The mother on the show, played by Tracee Ellis Ross, is, like her character Dr. Rainbow

Johnson, of mixed race. She is lighter-skinned than many other members of the main cast and the show has addressed the privilege she experiences as a lighter-skinned Black woman. While both J'onn and M'gann are marginalized within the world of the *Supergirl* television show, which is why they have to "pass" as human, it is also possible to say that they both have chosen human forms that racially re-inscribe the privilege or lack thereof that they each have experienced in their Martian identity.

As I previously stated, a full unpacking of the racial implications in J'onn's and M'gann's human forms is beyond the scope of my discussion here. However, the gender and sexual implications are also quite provocative. Despite his androgynous Martian body, J'onn is coded as male, not only due to his male human form but also because of his name. J'onn is an obvious alternate version of the traditional male name "John." M'gann is similarly coded as female with her female human body and name, which is a version of "Megan." As a male, J'onn has experienced revulsion, fear, and even threats to his life from others due to his "transition" to human. M'gann has experienced the exact same thing, with an added dimension; her birth identity was that of a race with a history of genocide and war against other Martians.

The reason M'gann is an expatriate from Mars and living on Earth in human/Green Martian form is because she helped save Green Martians from her peoples' persecution. Similarly, J'onn initially took human form in order to protect Alex and Kara. Ironically, he attacks M'gann for essentially undergoing the same "transition" he did. While I am using the umbrella term "Queer" throughout this essay, it is disingenuous to assume that all people who identify with the term Queer see each other as comrades or allies, as I believe the aggression between J'onn and M'gann illustrates. As Emma Lindsay wrote in "The Whole 'Are Trans Women Real Women?' Thing is Gross": "Often, the question around trans people—especially trans women—is phrased as are they 'real.' Is a trans woman 'a real woman?'" She continues, "As far as I can tell, the only common trait that differentiates 'real' women from 'fake' women is that *all the 'real' women had their gender imposed upon them by society*. They had no *autonomy* when it came to their gender."[28] White cisgender heteronormativity, sadly, often seeks to deprive "non-normative" people of their *autonomy* and *agency* when it comes to their lived experience of their identity. I continue to maintain that *Supergirl* subverts this conservative ideology.

M'gann exercises autonomy and personal agency in terms of both her culture and her gender. She chooses her path among the White Martians by rebelling. She chooses to "transition" into a physical form that fits her identity. She chooses to try to befriend J'onn, even though she knows he would hate her if he knew she was previously a White Martian. She chooses to sacrifice what she sees as any connection between them to save his life. And most tellingly, she chooses to die in her chosen body rather than be forced into an identity that is not hers. She does not allow society to "impose" an identity upon her. Happily, in later episodes in season 2, J'onn reevaluates his attitude towards M'gann. However, the tension between them illustrates a sad truth about acceptance and tolerance, both within and without the Queer community.

"I'm Not Ashamed of It, There's No Shame in Me": Alex Danvers' "Coming Out"

This brings me to Alex Danvers. The quote above is from the Queer literature classic, *The Well of Loneliness* by Radclyffe Hall, written in the early twentieth century. Those words are spoken by the main character Stephen while coming out to her mother as a lesbian. A modern reader of Hall's books might well wish that Stephen's mother was as sympathetic as Alex's family or that Stephen lived in a world with the potential for acceptance and tolerance that Alex happily seems to experience in *Supergirl*.

While a great deal of the Queer analysis of *Supergirl* focuses on Alex, her Queer narrative did not emerge until season 2. In season 1, Alex is never linked romantically to anyone, nor does she show any apparent interest in dating. However, in season 2, *Supergirl* moved from the CBS network to the CW network. Elizabeth Wagmeister of *Variety* magazine reports that CBS's president cited *Supergirl's* decreasing ratings over the course of the season as one motivating factor for the move. Wagmeister also notes that the CW network (which is co-owned by CBS) is also geared towards younger viewers. She writes, "*Supergirl*, starring Melissa Benoist, averaged a 2.5 rating in adults 18–49 and 10.03 million viewers overall on CBS in Nielsen's 'live plus-7 estimates. The superhero series was CBS' top-rated freshman drama in the demo and its youngest-skewing drama with a median age of 55.6."[29]

On one hand, the move to the CW may seem conservative; CBS is a more "major" television network than the CW. One could argue that the shows that succeed—and the ones that fail—on the three major networks (ABC, NBC, and CBS) represent the cultural ideology of the United States as a whole. On the other hand, the CW *is* skewed towards younger viewers who may be more likely to be open-minded about the identities of television characters. The future of Queer rights in the U.S. will be determined by the younger generation: the generation of viewers who watch shows like *Supergirl* on the CW network. The network has also carried other shows with openly Queer recurring characters, including *Supernatural, The 100, The Vampire Diaries, Jane the Virgin,* and *Arrow* (another DC show).

In season 2, Maggie Sawyer, a member of the Science Force who is investigating aliens, takes Alex to an underground club that is a "safe haven" for aliens. The comparison to underground gay clubs in the early and mid-twentieth century is inescapable. For example, the Stonewall Inn in Greenwich Village in New York City was, for a long time, one of the few "safe havens" for Queer people who felt "alien" in a violently heteronormative culture. Like the aliens in *Supergirl*, Queer people faced persecution, physical violence, and even death if they "outed" themselves to a society that refused to accept them. While at the underground club in the episode "Survivors,"[30] Maggie "comes out" to Alex. She says, "Growing up a non-straight, non-white girl, in Blue Spring Nebraska, I might as well have been from Mars." Not only does this highlight the "otherness" of Queer identity, but it also reinforces my idea that J'onn and M'gann symbolically represents Trans* identity.

Returning to the previously-referenced episode "Survivors," Maggie brings Alex to an alien "fight club." Maggie and Alex both arrive in evening dress and wearing masks; they non-platonically praise each other's appearance and hold hands as they enter the club. I contend the masks are significant for more than the obvious reasons. Within the narrative of *Supergirl*, this is a "secret" club so the attendees keep their identities unknown. Yet, in her life, Alex *does* wear a mask. Queer people are often forced to "wear a mask" as well to protect themselves from a hostile societal environment. I have previously discussed how J'onn and M'gann both wear "masks"—often multiple layers of masks—in order to survive. Also, sometimes a "mask" can reveal one's fundamental self: as Oscar Wilde famously said, "Give [someone] a mask, and [they] will tell you [the] truth."[31] This seems especially true in the case of both M'gann and J'onn. It is also debatable to what extent their "transition" into human form is a mask, any more than a Trans* person transitioning to their true identity is a "mask." The concept of "masking/unmasking" oneself is slippery. If one, like J'onn or M'gann, has been wearing multiple layers of masks for an extended time, what does "unmasking" really mean? I contend that choosing a mask can be a profound form of unmasking.

However, this is not necessarily true in all cases, especially for Alex Danvers. It is notable that Alex and Maggie wear masks in "Survivors," as Supergirl *never* does. Superheroes in masks are a common trope of the genre. I previously mentioned that J'onn says Supergirl can "pass" for human because of her normative appearance. Supergirl also displays heterosexual behavior in her flirtations/relationships with various men in the show such as Winn, James, and Mon-El. While Supergirl feels the need to hide her superhero identity to protect the people in her life, she never wears a mask to do so. In fact, in the first season, there are more than a few jokes about her boss Cat Grant eventually disbelieving that her assistant Kara and Supergirl are the same person. In her blonde white heteronormativity, Supergirl does not require a mask because her appearance (unlike J'onn's natural form) is in line with what is considered "acceptable." She "passes" for human. Meanwhile, in "Survivors," Alex literally wears the mask that many Queer people metaphorically must wear every day just to survive. Alex must stay masked, and masks her identity even from herself.

While the show sets up an immediate attraction between Alex and Maggie, Alex is initially defensive about her feelings. In the episode "Crossfire," Maggie responds to Alex's ambivalence by saying, "I get it. You're not gay. You'd be surprised how many gay women I've heard that from."[32] Later in the same episode, Alex confesses that her "whole life has been about being perfect" and that while she "tried" to date men, she "never liked being intimate [with men] ... I thought maybe that's just not the way I was built." This is a nice acknowledgment of the reality that being gay is not a choice. It also links well to Supergirl's own identity. While she may wish to live a normal life and has tried to deny her superpowers, she was "born that way." She was born to be a superhero. A good portion of her narrative focuses on her acceptance of her superhero identity, just as season 2 of the show focuses on Alex's acceptance of her sexual identity. She finally confesses to Maggie in "Crossfire," "Now I can't stop thinking about ... that maybe there's some truth to what you said."

Both Alex and Kara have repressed who they are. In the episode "Changing,"[33] Alex comes out to Kara in an initially awkward scene. She tells Kara that Maggie encouraged her to come out to her family and recalls an incident in high school when she was attracted to a female friend but "shoved that memory down, so deep inside, that it's like it never happened." Kara has insisted on trying to live a "normal"—i.e., normalized—life and is even willing to accept sarcasm, criticism, and borderline abuse from her new boss in the service of preserving her public, human self. Initially, Kara is flummoxed by Alex's confession: partially, I maintain, because she herself is still negotiating her own "coming out" as Supergirl.

However, Kara's subsequent reaction later in this episode redeems her initial awkwardness. She begins by apologizing for "not creating an environment where you felt like you could talk about this with me," declares her unconditional acceptance of Alex, and says, "I know this is not the same at all, but I *do* know how it feels to keep a part of yourself shut off." In the next episode ("Medusa"),[34] Alex comes out to her mother. She says that she feels she is "letting her down" by being gay. Her mother responds: "Why would you being gay ever let me down?" and continues, "I love you, however you are."

I contend that Alex's coming-out experience represents *Supergirl's* most Queer-positive and liberatory moment. On one level, it is modeling appropriate behavior for the friends or family of someone coming out as Queer. Once over her surprise, Kara apologizes for not fully facilitating a "safe space" within her relationship with Alex. Their mother voices her unconditional love and acceptance. On another level, these interactions serve as an alternate narrative for Queer viewers whose own coming-out experiences may not have been nearly as positive. *The Human Rights Campaign* website reports that 42 percent of Queer youth say that the communities in which they live are not accepting of Queer people. They also report that 26 percent of Queer youth list as, among their biggest problems, not being out to their families and/or a fear of coming out.[35] *PFLAG NYC* reports that 26 percent of gay men are thrown out of their home as a result of coming out to their family and between 25 percent and 50 percent of homeless Queer youths are homeless because they were open about their sexual or gender identity.[36] Alex's experience shows viewers, especially young viewers (who are the target audience for The CW Network) that there *is* a possible alternate narrative of coming out. Their negative experience need not be the only possibility. Ultimately, in "Changing," Alex declares, "[Being gay] is my new normal. And I finally get me." With the support of her family, Alex is finally able to internally "normalize" her identity and take off her mask. She takes a further step towards personal agency and acceptance as she enters into a romantic and sexual relationship with Maggie in subsequent episodes.

As a final note in this section, I would like to examine Alex and Maggie's terminology regarding their sexual identities. Both characters use the word "gay" to describe themselves and each other. One of the main tenets of Queer theory is an individual's right to name themselves as they feel comfortable and to reject the "names" others have assigned to them. In fact, the very word "Queer" came from a movement to reclaim a name that had once been used as an insult against non-heteronormative people. That being said, the term "gay" is often used to refer to men who are attracted romantically and/or sexually to other men. In contrast, the term "lesbian" is almost always used exclusively to refer to women who are attracted romantically and/or sexually to other women. Alex and Maggie, both women who are attracted to other women, identify as gay, not lesbian. In the next and last section of this essay, I discuss the manner in which *Supergirl* Queers some traditional gender roles and expectations of the superhero genre as a whole. When Alex and Maggie, as women, claim the word "gay" they are symbolically claiming the right to occupy a space not bound by traditionally gendered terminology and expectations.

The Hero We Need and the Hero We Deserve: Queering Superhero Gender Politics

The term "Queer" can function as both a noun and a verb. In most of this essay, I have used it as an umbrella term to describe someone who, to a greater or lesser degree, does not identify with traditional heteronormative sexual or gender identities. However, a narrative may also "Queer" heteronormative themes, tropes, and/or characters. Not only does *Supergirl* contain literally and symbolically Queer characters, it also Queers traditional superhero gender politics.

In an earlier section of this essay, I discussed how Wonder Woman and Supergirl both can be seen as complicating the essentially conservative traditional superhero narrative. To a great extent, the superhero genre is based on wish-fulfillment and escapism. There is a preponderance of the male gaze in the visual representations of superheroes. Superman and Batman both wear skin-tight costumes, but not necessarily to titillate their male readers/viewers. Rather, they visually present a masculine bodily ideal to which men and boys might aspire. In contrast, Wonder Woman's skimpy costume, especially combined with the repeated theme of bondage in the early comics, *is* specifically designed for to titillate the male gaze. One could say the same about Supergirl's traditional costume of mini-skirt and high-heeled boots, or Power Girl's[37] so-called "viewing window"—a cut-out section of her skin-tight leotard that reveals a substantial amount of cleavage.

Currently, more girls and women are consuming superhero media than in the early days of the genre. According to "The Rise of the Woman Comic Buyer" by Jose Fermoso, in 2015, 53 percent of comic readers were women.[38] Yet Laura Mulvey's male gaze and heteronormativity are still common in the genre. DC in particular has a problematic relationship with the representation of female superheroes. For example, they recently faced criticism from readers, particularly female readers, who objected to extremely sexualized rebooted versions of DC female superheroes like Starfire and Catwoman. As Laura Hudson writes in "The Big Sexy Problem with Superheroines and Their 'Liberated Sexuality'":

> I keep coming back to is that superhero comics are nothing if not aspirational. They are full of heroes that inspire us to be better, to think more things are possible, to imagine a world where we can become something amazing. But this is what comics like this tell me about myself, as a lady: They tell me that I can be beautiful and powerful, but only if I wear as few clothes as possible ... as long as I have enormous breasts ... as long as I do it in ways that feel inauthentic and contrived to appeal to men.... I'm so, so tired of hearing those messages from comics because they aren't the dreams or the escapist fantasies or the aspirations that I want to have.[39]

Supergirl is a refreshing alternative to the male-centric gender politics of superhero representation. It is far from perfect. One might very well wish that Supergirl wore pants instead of a skirt, that she was played by a woman of color, or that Supergirl *herself* came out as Queer. At the end of the day, Supergirl the character is a brand and the show is inevitably going to reflect that. Part of the "Supergirl brand" involves portraying Kara/Supergirl as the white, blonde-haired, blue-eyed "All-American Girl" analogue to her cousin Superman. It involves an already-existing cast of heroes and villains. It involves character details such as Supergirl feeling inferior to her more-famous cousin and to an extent, falling into a "little sister" role. To a greater or lesser degree, the show preserves these aspects of the Supergirl brand because Supergirl, like other superheroes, is a product and a commodity. That commodity has no value if viewers and fans don't "buy" it.

Yet, within the constraints of the brand, *Supergirl* pushes back against—i.e., Queers—the brand expectations. The actor who plays Supergirl, Melissa Benoist, has realistic physical proportions for a woman of her body type and is visibly muscled. She rarely appears in very revealing outfits as either Kara or Supergirl. While the Supergirl costume does include the character's iconic skirt, in the show, it is slightly longer than the traditional miniskirt. The top of her costume is relatively high-necked, without a "viewing window" or bare midriff—the latter has appeared in several versions of Supergirl's character—and she wears boots with chunky, not stiletto, heels. Nor does she appear overly made-up or coiffed in either of her identities. The end result is that of a realistically-represented female superhero. It is not a perfectly diverse or liberating representation, but it is one that is not dependent upon male fantasies. It is a representation with which at least some non-supermodel female viewers may be able to identify. As the *Vanity Fair* article "See the Tasteful Supergirl Costume Created by Oscar-Winning Designer Colleen Atwood" intelligently points out, "*this* is what an elegant superheroine costume looks like" and "Benoist's Supergirl will hopefully prove that you don't have to flash T&A or be vacuum-packed into a latex pantsuit to fight crime as a female."[40] That is a refreshing and empowering image for women in an era when Harley Quinn and Black Widow sometimes seem to dominate the silver screen.

Moreover, in several episodes, *Supergirl* also Queers the traditional "female heroes fight female villains and male heroes fight male villains" trope. A quick look at DC's roster of main female superheroes reveals that many of their primary antagonists are female. For example, some of Wonder Woman's main villains are Cheetah, Baroness von Gunther, and Circe. One of Black Canary's major foes is White Canary, and she is often paired up with the male character Green Arrow when fighting male opponents. In the comics, Supergirl's enemies include Superwoman, Nasthalia Luthor, and Rachel Berkowitz as Blackstarr. In contrast, it is common for male superheroes to have ambiguous and/or sexualized relationships with female enemies, such as Batman does with Catwoman and Talia Al Ghul.

Yet in the *Supergirl* television series, Supergirl regularly takes on both male and female opponents. For example, in season 1, she goes head-to-head with multiple male antagonists, such as the Kryptonian Non. J'onn also inverts the same trope. In the episode "Better Angels,"[41] he literally rips the female villain Indigo in half. While Supergirl certainly takes on female antagonists as well, she is no way confined to fighting female villains any more than the male characters in the series fight only male villains. Not only does this establish Supergirl's strength and skill as a superhero (in the first season it is revealed that she can fly faster than Superman), it also refuses to pander to the sexist trope that women fighting each other is a titillating "catfight" and men fighting each other is "real" fighting.

Supergirl's male friends, James Olsen and Winn, also "Queer" traditional gender roles within superhero narratives. James Olsen, formerly known as Jimmy Olsen, is Superman's long-running friend and sidekick, dating back to the early days of the comics. He and Winn quickly become Supergirl's sidekicks and collaborators, helping her from "home base" while she is out on missions. Previously, this is a role that has often been filled by female characters, such as Oracle in some of the *Batman* comic arcs. In season 2, James assumes the role of the Guardian wearing a superpowered suit that Winn designed for him. Yet, the seemingly conservative trope of the male sidekick "stepping up" is not uncomplicated or totally conservative in this series. James says to Winn upon making the decision, "We're heroes. Just like Kara." Instead of a male hero inspiring a female sidekick to heroics (Batgirl, Huntress, Lois Lane as Superwoman), a female hero is doing the same for her male sidekicks. In the episode "We Can Be Heroes," Supergirl "unmasks" James as the Guardian after he unsuccessfully goes up against the female villain Livewire (yet another level of unmasking) and tells him in that episode, "you are never going to be strong enough for this." Livewire herself taunts James and Winn by saying, "You know what I love? Little boys who think they can do a better job than the woman who's an actual superhero."[42]

A final "super" character who is not superpowered yet helps subvert and Queer the traditional superhero narrative is Kara's boss in season 1, Cat Grant. Cat has an unfortunate symbolically homophobic story arc with her insistence upon "outing" Kara as Supergirl, as I have discussed previously. However, she also presents a liberatory feminist point of view. She "names" Supergirl as Supergirl early in the series, thus removing some of the anti-feminist bias of the moniker Super*girl*. In the season one episode "Red Faced," Cat acknowledges the double-standard against working women to Kara: "You cannot get angry at work, especially when you're a girl.... Girls are taught to smile and keep it on the inside."[43] Later, in the episode "Falling," when Cat is publicly honored for her work at CatCo, she pointedly responds, "No one is calling me the most powerful *woman* in National City. They are calling me the most powerful *person* in National City."[44] She is later referred to by Non as "the best of [the human] world." As a final note, Cat is not the only human woman in a position of power in the series; Lynda Carter (who played Wonder

Woman in the 1970s television show) has a cameo as the President of the United States.

The season 2 finale illustrates the series' liberatory reality and potential.[45] The episode is titled "Nevertheless, She Persisted"—an obvious reference to U.S. politician Elizabeth Warren's dedication during the confirmation hearing for the now-Attorney General Jeff Sessions, to speak against his confirmation, which included reading part of a letter written by Coretta Scott King. Warren "persisted" in speaking until she was formally "silenced" by various male senators, and the phrase has been adopted by some parts of the feminist movement. In this episode, Supergirl goes head-to-head with her cousin Superman and wins. Calista Flockhart reprises her role as Cat Grant and at one point in the episode says to Kara, "The thing that makes women strong is that we have the guts to be vulnerable.... We have the ability to feel the depths of our emotions and we know that we will walk through it to the other side." Cat's declaration of emotional strength is a nice bookend to Supergirl's demonstration of physical strength, illustrating how the series as a whole allows Supergirl and its many other heroes (whether superpowered or not) to Queer what it means to be a superhero. These various characters all battle with how they fit within the traditional superhero/heterosexist action narrative, or even if they fit within it at all. Finally, Alex proposes to Maggie, which completely inverts the conservative Disney-esque narrative of a heteronormative "happy ending" for a woman. Alex's love story doesn't depend upon a man and that makes her just as much of a "supergirl" as her sister.

Supergirl is a Queer-positive visual narrative that subverts ("Queers") many heterosexist tropes of the superhero genre. While not perfect, it stands as an example of how the genre, while retaining many of the features beloved by fans, can evolve into a more inclusive and tolerant art form. The phrase "game-changer" is often overused in media criticism. I contend that *Supergirl* truly *is* a game-changer and is changing the entire superhero game for the better. The viewing and critical audience seems to agree as *Supergirl* was nominated for a GLAAD award. I believe we are already seeing some of the positive effects of *Supergirl*. For example, consider the unexpected success of *Wonder Woman* movie. Before its release, nay-sayers predicted a dismal showing for the arguably first big-budget comic-book "superheroine" film since *Catwoman* in 2004. They were wrong. According to the article "Wonder Woman Passes 'Mama Mia' as Highest-Grossing Film by Female Director," *Wonder Woman* had "the best opening weekend [for a film directed by] a female director" and is "the highest-grossing film ever directed by a woman."[46] At the time of this writing, *Wonder Woman* has grossed over $800 million worldwide, as I have previously mentioned. It received mostly positive reviews from critics and fans alike; it has a 92 percent rating on *Rotten Tomatoes*.[47] While the Queer subtext of *Wonder Woman* remains *subtext* (the character is canonically bisexual in recent comic arcs), the film nevertheless contains the unprecedented exchange between Wonder Woman and her "love interest," Steve Trevor. Wonder Woman tells Steve that, while men are necessary for procreation, women can experience "erotic pleasure" without men.[48] In "Why Have Female Superhero Movies Failed (So Far)?," Kayleigh Donaldson writes, "We've waited long enough for women to save the day, and once won't be enough."[49] *Supergirl* has "saved the day" by paving the way for more liberatory portrayals of classic superhero archetypes. There is a *Wonder Woman* sequel planned for 2019 and *Supergirl* was renewed for a third season. Let's hope *Supergirl's* continued success is a harbinger of many more necessary changes to come.

Notes

1. "Arrow," *Rotten Tomatoes*, January 8, 2018 https://www.rottentomatoes.com/tv/arrow.

2. David Betancourt, "Superhero and Sci-Fi Fans Are Going to Need a Lot of Streaming Apps—And That's Not Cheap," *The Washington Post*, September 8, 2017: https://www.washingtonpost.com/news/comic-riffs/wp/2017/09/08/superhero-and-sci-fi-fans-are-going-to-need-a-lot-of-streaming-apps-and-thats-not-cheap/?utm_term=.15c95778694d.

3. For example, as of early 2018, the subreddit r/game of thrones has thousands of posts and over a million subscribers; it is one of only several *Game of Thrones* subreddits. The *Walking Dead* subreddit that focuses solely on deconstructing episodes of the television series has over 400,000 subscribers.

4. According to Michael O'Connell's article for *The Hollywood Reporter*, "The series is being chalked up as a win for the cable network ... from a financial perspective ... *Twin Peaks* has exceeded expectations."

5. "Speculative fiction" (SF) is a fairly recent designation that includes imaginative narratives, such as those that might fall within the genres of science fiction, horror, fantasy, dystopian fiction, futurism, and many more. I am using SF in a manner that includes superhero narratives, as do many others.

6. The Bechdel Test was explained by Alison Bechdel in her Queer comics series *Dykes to Watch Out For* and is a measure of female representation in any given work. To pass the Bechdel Test, a work must contain at least two women who (1) have names (2) talk to each other directly, and (3) talk about something *other* than a man.

7. For example, Sedgwick's website refers to her as a "pioneer of Queer theory"; Scheele has co-authored a popular educational graphic novel titled *Queer: A Graphic History* (London: Icon Books, 2005), and Halberstam has written the important book *In a Queer Time and Place: Transgender Bodies, Subcultural Lives* (New York: New York University Press, 2005).

8. The term Trans* is a fairly new designation that is more inclusive of all the many identities included within the Transgender spectrum. These include transgender, genderqueer, non-binary gender, non-gendered, and many more.

9. I use the term "normalizing" to refer to the process of something both engaging with and also becoming what is considered a social "norm" during any particular place and time. This is not necessarily negative; for example, normalizing Queer narratives is liberating. However, when I say, "superhero comics have historically been surprisingly conservative and normalizing," I mean that they have often served to reinforce ideas about white cissexualist patriarchy.

10. Umberto Eco, "The Myth of Superman," *Arguing Comics: Literary Masters on a Popular Medium*, Ed. Jeet Heer and Kent Worcester (Jackson: University Press of Mississippi, 2005), 31.

11. The specific origin of this phrase is discussed in Erik Lundegarde's *New York Times* article "Truth, Justice, and (Fill in the Blank)."

12. According to Brian Cronin of CBR.com, in a comic from 1951 Superman literally joined the Boy Scouts of America.
13. Donna Dickens, "DC Comics Almost Had Wonder Woman Right but Then They Did This…" *UpRoxx: The Culture of Now,* May 10, 2016: http://uproxx.com/hitfix/dc-comics-almost-had-wonder-woman-right-but-then-they-did-this.
14. "Yearly Box Office," *Box Office Mojo,* January 8, 2018: http://www.boxofficemojo.com/yearly/chart/?yr=2017.
15. "Supergirl," *Rotten Tomatoes: Movies, TV Shows, Movie Trailers, Reviews,* 8 January 2018: https://www.rottentomatoes.com/m/supergirl.
16. "Supergirl," *IMDb,* January 8, 2018: http://www.imdb.com/title/tt0088206/?ref_=nv_sr_2.
17. As of the time of this writing, there have been eight Superman movies since the 1951 film serial *Superman vs. the Mole Men,* including the recent reboot with Henry Cavill. There have been eleven Batman movies with multiple actors and conceptions of the character, from the Adam West film in 1966 to the contemporary Ben Affleck Batman.
18. *Supergirl,* "Livewire," season 1, episode 5, directed by Kevin Tancharoen, story by Roberto Aguirre-Sacasa and Caitlin Parrish, aired March 28, 2016, on CBS.
19. Michael C. LaSala, "Is It Okay Not to Come Out? For LGBT Youth, Staying in the Closet Is Sometimes the Smart Choice," *Psychology Today,* July 13, 2015: https://www.psychologytoday.com/blog/gay-and-lesbian-well-being/201507/is-it-ok-not-come-out.
20. *Supergirl,* "Bizarro," season 1, episode 12, directed by John Showalter, written by Roberto Aguirre-Sacasa and Rachel Shukert, aired February 1, 2016, on CBS.
21. Michelangelo Signorile, "Out at the New York Times: Gays, Lesbians, AIDS, and Homophobia Inside America's Paper of Record." *The Huffington Post.* 28 November 2012: http://www.huffingtonpost.com/2012/11/28/new-york-times-gays-lesbians-aids-homophobia_n_2200684.html.
22. *Supergirl,* "Childish Things," season 1, episode 10, directed by Jamie Babbit, written by Yahlin Chang, teleplay by Anna Musky-Goldwyn and James Dewille, aired January 18, 2016, on CBS.
23. *Supergirl,* "For the Girl Who Has Everything," season 1, episode 13, directed by Dermott Downs, written by Ted Sullivan, Derek Simon, and Andrew Kreisberg, aired February 8, 2016, on CBS.
24. *Supergirl,* "Manhunter," season 1, episode 17, directed by Chris Fisher, story by Derek Simon, teleplay by Cindy Lichtman and Rachel Shukert, aired March 21, 2016, on CBS.
25. *Supergirl,* "The Darkest Place," season 2, episode 7, directed by Glen Winter, written by Robert Rovner and Paula Yoo, aired November 21, 2016, on The CW.
26. *Supergirl,* "Survivors," season 2, episode 4, directed by James Marshall and James Bamford, written by Paula Yoo and Eric Carrasco, aired October 31, 2016, on The CW.
27. *Supergirl,* "The Darkest Place," season 2, episode 7.
28. Emma Lindsay, "The Whole 'Are Trans Women Real Women?' Thing Is Gross." *Medium.com,* March 23, 2017: https://medium.com/@emmalindsay/this-whole-are-trans-women-real-women-thing-is-gross-1b15f3d7ad41.
29. Elizabeth Wagmeister, "CBS President Explains 'Supergirl' Moving to the CW." *Variety.* 18 May 2016: http://variety.com/2016/tv/news/supergirl-cbs-president-reaction-cw-1201777795.
30. *Supergirl,* "Survivors," season 2, episode 4.
31. Oscar Wilde, *The Critic as Artist: Upon the Importance of Doing Nothing and Discussing Everything* (New York: Mondial, 1891) 2007.
32. *Supergirl,* "Crossfire," season 2, episode 5, directed by Glen Winter, written by Gabriel Llanas and Anna Musky-Goldwyn, aired November 7, 2016, on The CW.
33. *Supergirl,* "Changing," season 2, episode 6, directed by Larry Teng, story by Greg Berlanti, teleplay by Andrew Kreisberg and Caitlin Parrish, aired November 14, 2016, The CW.
34. *Supergirl,* "Medusa," season 2, episode 8, directed by Stefan Pleszczynnski, written by Jessica Queller and Derek Simon, aired November 28, 2016, on The CW.
35. "Growing Up LGBT in America," *Human Rights Campaign*: https://www.hrc.org/youth-report/view-and-share-statistics.

36. "Statistics You Should Know About Gay & Transgender Students," *PFLAG NYC*: http://www.pflagnyc.org/safeschools/statistics.
37. Power Girl is another Superman "spin-off." She debuted in 1976 and was originally conceived as a Kryptonian from an alternate universe ("Earth-Two") who traveled to the main DC Universe and met Superman and Supergirl. She is also described as Superman's cousin.
38. Jose Fermoso, "The Rise of the Woman Comic Buyer," *OZY: Stay Interesting*: http://www.ozy.com/acumen/the-rise-of-the-woman-comic-buyer/63314.
39. Laura Hudson, "The Big Sexy Problem with Superheroines and Their 'Liberated Sexuality,'" *Comics Alliance*, September 22, 2011: http://comicsalliance.com/starfire-catwoman-sex-superheroine.
40. Julie, Miller, "See the Tasteful Supergirl Costume Created by Oscar-Winning Designer Colleen Atwood," *Vanity Fair*, March 6, 2015: https://www.vanityfair.com/hollywood/2015/03/supergirl-melissa-benoist-costume.
41. *Supergirl*, "Better Angels," season 1, episode 20, directed by Larry Teng, written by Andrew Kreisberg and Ali Adler, teleplay by Robert Rovner and Jessica Queller, aired April 18, 2016, on CBS.
42. *Supergirl*, "We Can Be Heroes," season 2, episode 10, directed by Rebecca Johnson, written by Caitlin Parrish and Katie Rose Rogers, aired January 30, 2017, on The CW.
43. *Supergirl*, "Red Faced," season 1, episode 6, directed by Jesse Warn, written by Michael Grassi and Rachel Shukert, aired November 30, 2015, on CBS.
44. *Supergirl*, "Falling," season 1, episode 16, directed by Larry Teng, written by Robert Rovner and Jessica Queller, aired March 14, 2016, on CBS.
45. *Supergirl*, "Nevertheless, She Persisted," season 2, episode 22, directed by Glen Winter, story by Andrew Kreisberg and Jessica Queller, teleplay by Robert Rovner and Caitlin Parrish, aired May 22, 2017, on The CW.
46. Trey Williams, "Wonder Woman Passes 'Mama Mia' as Highest-Grossing Film by Female Director," *Market Watch*, June 24, 2017: http://www.marketwatch.com/story/wonder-woman-passes-mamma-mia-as-highest-grossing-film-by-female-director-2017-06-23.
47. "Wonder Woman," *Rotten Tomatoes: Movies, TV Shows, Movie Trailers, Reviews*. January 8, 2018: https://www.rottentomatoes.com/m/wonder_woman_2017.
48. *Wonder Woman*, directed by Patty Jenkins, 2017, Blu-ray.
49. Kayleigh, Donaldson, "Why Have Female Superhero Movies Failed (So Far?)," *ScreenRant*, March 15, 2017: http://screenrant.com/why-have-female-superhero-movies-failed-so-far.

SELECTED BIBLIOGRAPHY

"Arrow." *Rotten Tomatoes: Movies, TV Shows, Movie Trailers, Reviews*. January 8, 2018. https://www.rottentomatoes.com/tv/arrow.
Bechdel, Alison. *Dykes to Watch Out For*. New York: Harcourt Mifflin, 2008.
Betancourt, David, "Superhero and Sci-Fi Fans Are Going to Need a Lot of Streaming Apps— And That's Not Cheap." *The Washington Post*. September 8, 2017. https://www.washingtonpost.com/news/comic-riffs/wp/2017/09/08/superhero-and-sci-fi-fans-are-going-to-need-a-lot-of-streaming-apps-and-thats-not-cheap/?utm_term=.15c95778694d.
Cronin, Brian. "Comic Book Questions Answered: Was Superman, the "Big Blue Boy Scout," Ever an ACTUAL Boy Scout?" CBR.com. January 31, 2012: https://www.cbr.com/comic-book-questions-answered-was-superman-the-big-blue-boy-scout-ever-an-actual-boy-scout.
Dickens, Donna. "DC Comics Almost Had Wonder Woman Right but Then They Did This…" *UpRoxx: The Culture of Now*. May 10, 2016. http://uproxx.com/hitfix/dc-comics-almost-had-wonder-woman-right-but-then-they-did-this.
Donaldson, Kayleigh. "Why Have Female Superhero Movies Failed (So Far?)." *ScreenRant*. March 15, 2017: http://screenrant.com/why-have-female-superhero-movies-failed-so-far.
Eco, Umberto. "The Myth of Superman." *Arguing Comics: Literary Masters on a Popular Medium*. Edited by Jeet Heer and Kent Worcester, 146–64. Jackson: University Press of Mississippi, 200.

"Eve Kosofsky Sedgwick." *The Eve Kosofsky Sedgwick Foundation*. September 24, 2017. http://evekosofskysedgwick.net.
Fermoso, Jose. "The Rise of the Woman Comic Buyer." *OZY: Stay Interesting*. September 11, 2015. http://www.ozy.com/acumen/the-rise-of-the-woman-comic-buyer/63314.
Gadot, Gal. *Wonder Woman*. Directed by Patty Jenkins. 2017. Blu-ray.
"Game of Thrones: A Reddit of Ice and Fire." Reddit.com. January 8, 2018. https://www.reddit.com/r/gameofthrones.
Girard, M-E. *Girl Mans Up*. New York: Harper-Collins, 2016.
"Growing Up LGBT in America." *The Human Rights Campaign*. http://www.hrc.org/youth-report/view-and-share-statistics.
Halberstam, Judith. *In a Queer Time and Place: Transgender Bodies, Subcultural Lives*. NewYork: New York University Press, 2005.
Hall, Radclyffe. *The Well of Loneliness*. New York: Anchor Books, 1928, 1990.
Hudson, Laura. "The Big Sexy Problem with Superheroines and Their 'Liberated Sexuality.'" *Comics Alliance*. September 22, 2011. http://comicsalliance.com/starfire-catwoman-sex-superheroine.
LaSala, Michael C. "Is It Okay Not to Come Out? for LGBT Youth, Staying in the Closet IsSometimes the Smart Choice." *Psychology Today*. July 13, 2015. https://www.psychologytoday.com/blog/gay-and-lesbian-well-being/201507/is-it-ok-not-come-out.
Lindsay, Emma. "The Whole 'Are Trans Women Real Women?' Thing Is Gross." *Medium.com*. March 23, 2017. https://medium.com/@emmalindsay/this-whole-are-trans-women-real-women-thing-is-gross-1b15f3d7ad41.
Lundegaard, Erik. "Truth, Justice, and (fill in the Blank)." *New York Times*. June 30, 2006. http://www.nytimes.com/2006/06/30/opinion/30iht-ederik.2093103.html?_r=0.
Miller, Julie. "See the Tasteful Supergirl Costume Created by Oscar-Winning Designer Colleen Atwood." *Vanity Fair*. March 6, 2015. https://www.vanityfair.com/hollywood/2015/03/supergirl-melissa-benoist-costume.8 January 2018.
O'Connell, Michael. "Has 'Twin Peaks' Been a Hit for Showtime?" *Hollywood Reporter*. September 1, 2017. https://www.hollywoodreporter.com/live-feed/has-twin-peaks-been-a-hit-showtime-1034370.
Scheele, Julia, and Barker, Meg-John. *Queer: A Graphic History*. London: Icon Books Ltd., 2016.
Signorile, Michelangelo. "Out at the New York Times: Gays, Lesbians, AIDS, and Homophobia Inside America's Paper of Record." *The Huffington Post*. November 28, 2012. http://www.huffingtonpost.com/2012/11/28/new-york-times-gays-lesbians-aids-homophobia_n_2200684.html.
"Statistics You Should Know About Gay & Transgender Students." *PFLAG NYC*. http://www.pflagnyc.org/safeschools/statistics.
"Supergirl." *IMDb*. January 8, 2018. http://www.imdb.com/title/tt0088206/?ref_=nv_sr_2.
"*Supergirl*." *Rotten Tomatoes: Movies, TV Shows, Movie Trailers, Reviews*. January 8, 2018. https://www.rottentomatoes.com/m/supergirl.
Wagmeister, Elizabeth. "CBS President Explains 'Supergirl' Moving to the CW." *Variety*. May 18, 2016. http://variety.com/2016/tv/news/supergirl-cbs-president-reaction-cw-1201777795.
"The Walking Dead Reddit." Reddit.com. January 8, 2018. https://www.reddit.com/r/thewalkingdead.
Wilde, Oscar, *The Critic as Artist: Upon the Importance of Doing Nothing and Discussing Everything*. New York: Mondial, 1891, reprinted 2007.
Williams, Trey. "Wonder Woman Passes 'Mama Mia' as Highest-Grossing Film by Female Director." *Market Watch*. June 24, 2017. http://www.marketwatch.com/story/wonder-woman-passes-mamma-mia-as-highest-grossing-film-by-female-director-2017-06-23.
"Wonder Woman." *Rotten Tomatoes: Movies, TV Shows, Movie Trailers, Reviews*. January 8, 2018. https://www.rottentomatoes.com/m/wonder_woman_2017.
"Yearly Box Office," *Box Office Mojo*, January 8, 2018. http://www.boxofficemojo.com/yearly/chart/?yr=2017.

"It's real, you're real, and you deserve a full, happy life"

Supergirl's "Sanvers" as an Affirmation to Queer Tumblr Fangirls Everywhere

CHELSEA M. GIBBS

Every queer fangirl remembers her first "ship."

Perhaps she found it watching *The L Word* through her hands on Netflix when she was really too young for it and learned how to erase evidence of viewed media from her family's queue. Perhaps she escaped down a YouTube rabbit hole of lesbian clips people had isolated from shows, with characters she'd never heard of, sometimes subtitled or spoken in languages she did not understand. Most likely at some point in time she learned the art of projecting onto the dreaded no-homo "female friendship," leading her to "ship" two characters together, as in wishing they would enter a relation*ship*. Millisecond exchanges from films and TV shows are slowed down 200 percent to be made into sensual gifs where anything from a tiny smile to an arched eyebrow can be over-analyzed *ad nauseam*. Fan videos are set to romantic songs from multiple eras, fan art is drawn, and fan-fiction written depicting "things with those existing characters and worlds that their creators couldn't or wouldn't do."[1] Zines gave way to message boards, which gave way to fansites before the greatest fangirl site of them all emerged: Tumblr.

For the uninitiated, Tumblr defies easy categorization. Its users reject its label as social media, as the bulk of personal blogs present are intended to be a space devoted to passions or identities users either must or prefer to keep secret—a stark contrast to overt look-at-me sites like Instagram or Facebook. Though many Tumblr users choose to share their pictures and real names, the majority find comfort in the anonymity offered by the site. This privacy and the diverse fan communities offer users the opportunity to safely do things like explore their sexuality, which they may not be free to do openly "irl" (in real life). Although plenty of straight users frequent Tumblr, the site has a reputation for being a safe haven for like-minded queer folks, both in and out of the closet, essentially functioning as a privatized public space. They can be active creators of queer content, whether that is creating original works or fan works, and can be part of a larger community to fangirl with by following other queer blogs and seeing such posts on their "dash" (newsfeed). To paraphrase Anthony Freitas, "individuals and their attractions to others of the same sex existed before [Tumblr], as did the community itself. But the [site] pulls them together again as queers [...] reinforcing that the community exists."[2] Tumblr serves as a great vehicle for spreading the word about queer content in movies and television shows, both well-known and not, as summed up in this post by this user:

> SOMEONE: Hey do you know what's happening on [insert gay/lesbian show]?
> ME, who has never watched the show but whose tumblr [sic] dash does the Great Gay Migration™ anyway: Yes.[3]

To that end, it was Tumblr which first alerted my attention to CBS's show *Supergirl* in 2015.

To understand this, it's important to contextualize *Supergirl* in an era when queerbaiting has reached an all-time high. Queerbaiting is what occurs when a show or network wants to accrue the revenue of LGBTQ viewers without the risk of offending the perceived (straight, cis, conservative) majority. In a twisted way, this could be construed as something of a step forward from the 1970s, when homosexuality first began being openly addressed on narrative television and generating a fair amount of controversy and ratings.[4] To avoid alienating conservative audiences or sponsors and getting accused of promoting a gay rights agenda, these storylines most often concluded in a DeMillian manner, wherein the scandalous lives of queer characters could be put on display so long as they were properly punished or corrected by the episode's end (or an episode might reveal a situation wherein a character had been assumed to be gay, only to have the comical misunderstanding corrected). Today, gay male viewership is considered highly valuable, as they are perceived as a consumer-friendly demographic. Furthermore, pandering to gay men "endorses the adage that [they] are women's best friends," meaning straight women are drawn to the product as well, whereas catering to lesbians would seem to alienate those consumer-friendly straight women.[5]

Thus, media producers must learn to walk a fine line: one that is heterosexual enough to appease straight viewers, but offers enough subtext to appeal to queer women. Condition queer women to expect nothing, and the least little something gets them all excited. There are several examples of this, but one particularly pertinent to this essay involves Lily Reinhart, the actor who portrays Betty on *Riverdale*, The CW's 2017 update of the *Archie* comic books. After an ad dropped that showed Betty and Veronica kissing, the Internet exploded with anticipation that this meant the girls would be romantically involved. In response to this, Reinhart told Hollywood Life, "there's a group that very, very much wants [this relationship], but [Betty and Veronica] are soul mates in a friends' way. Our show is not meant to be fan fiction. We give them a taste of it when they kiss, but that's all it is [...] that's just not our show."[6] Comments like these reinforce two ideas: first of all, two women being together belongs in works by fans, *not* in popular culture; second of all, bait like Betty and Veronica kissing in an ad—highly sexualized and ripped from context[7]—hooks straight male viewers as well, and Reinhart's remarks reassure the boys that the girls who kissed each other are, to be certain, one-hundred-percent into guys so worry not, your masculinity should not feel threatened. Betty and Veronica *are* soul mates, but not in a "gay way"!

Queer viewers are all too familiar with being accused of reading too much into relationships between characters of the same gender. As Yvonne Tasker puts it, "while friendship between women is a source of strength in contemporary [media], the question of the closeness of that friendship to lesbian desire is in constant negotiation."[8] Content creators can wink and nudge their queer viewers, teasing the possibility of a canonical queer character or relationship, especially when speaking to queer publications such as *AfterEllen* or *The Advocate*. However, when addressing broader audiences on talk shows or in non-niche publications, they can validate straight viewers by insisting the characters are straight and dismissing fangirls to do actual queering in fan fiction and fan art. In this too-common scenario, queer women viewers almost always lose the negotiation.[9]

What leads to this negotiating in the first place? Consciously or not, queer women in spaces like Tumblr are building on what Patricia White deems a "legacy of absence."[10] After decades of being denied overt onscreen representation in film and in television, queer women learned to read cues into depictions of female friendship. Jay Belle, onetime president of the early lesbian organization Daughters of Bilitis, argued, "there is a greater stigma attached to male homosexuality because the public is ignorant, or in denial, that lesbianism actually exists."[11] This translates to more representation for gay men over time, as well as more distinct codes for when overt representation was not permitted or was at least discouraged.

Thus, queer women have inherited what Julie Levin Russo calls an "interpretive heritage": parsing media for subtext. Russo explains the difference in fans reading into "male slash" (wanting two male characters to be a couple) versus femslash (wanting two female characters to be a couple):

Because affectionate gestures between men are taboo, onscreen instances of intimate male-male relationships appear charged with romance and eroticism. In the rarer cases where two female characters have a close relationship, their attachment may be expressed more freely but thus read less clearly as homoerotic. These factors—the particular inflection of women's engagement with televised women, the underrepresentation of female characters in the mass media, and the unique interpretive strategies involved in investing in femslash pairings—point to specificities of queer female fandom.[12]

This whole notion of parsing for subtext—a queer girl's bread and butter—can be explained by David Bordwell's cognitive viewing theory. He contends that viewers draw their own understandings of a text based on given cinematic cues and schemas, which he defines as "knowledge structures [that] enable the perceiver to extrapolate beyond the information given" in a scene.[13] These knowledge structures allow viewers to understand subtext by drawing conclusions based on past personal experiences and more significantly, recollections of cues they have seen in other movies and television shows.

A good example of this is the scene in which detective Maggie Sawyer (Floriana Lima) and agent Alex Danvers (Chyler Leigh) are introduced to each other on *Supergirl*, culminating in a Hollywood-style meet-cute: Alex stalks across the pavement and barks at Maggie, crouching near some evidence, "What the hell are you doing at *my* crime scene?" What follows is not the kind of catty argument many writers fall back on when trying to write empowered women, simply transferring sexist ideas about competitive women from romance to the workplace; in fact, more than a catfight, the scene resembles a pissing contest two men would have on the job. At least, it does until Maggie shows Alex her badge upon Alex's demand and then says, "I showed you mine; now you show me yours."[14] This is a tried and true flirtatious cue most viewers would recognize as such if one of the participants had been a man. The scene ends with Maggie smilingly conceding to Alex's jurisdiction and Alex fighting a happy—not smug—grin before repressing it and telling off an inferior, a second brief flirty *schema* that has been fleshed out.

Dialogue delivery and editing are critical in conveying these cues. The first time I saw Alex and Maggie interact was not by watching the show but by seeing gifs on Tumblr. It is impossible to follow as many queer women on there as I do and *not* learn about a mainstream show or movie that delves into maintext or subtext exploration of lesbians, and "Sanvers" (the portmanteau ship name of Maggie Sawyer and Alex Danvers) immediately started showing up on my dash. Just as immediately, I dismissed the possibility of anything happening between them. The gifs of Sanvers' continued interaction did not convince me anything romantic was intentionally being set up between them because I had been heavily involved in the nature of queer lady fandom for some time, and I knew how easy it was to slow down or manipulate a gif and/or edit to make something appear gayer than it actually was on television. A brief glance can be slowed down to a lingering look; a slight rearranging of shot orders can make an innocuous exchange suddenly sensual. Without having watched a single episode of *Supergirl*, I was positive that I was just seeing more projecting fangirls desperate for mainstream representation.

Not that their hopes were entirely unfounded: about a month before *Supergirl*'s second season began, the CW's[15] executive producer of superhero shows, Andrew Kreisberg, announced at the 2016 Television Critics Association's press tour that "one of the characters on one of the [superhero] shows is going to be exploring their sexuality and coming out." The show, character, and even character's gender remained secret. Another executive producer, Greg Berlanti, explained, "The only reason we wouldn't [say who it is] is because we really want the audience to enjoy the character developments and not necessarily be ahead of the storyline."[16] This did little to quell my cynical belief that the "Surprise! Gay" would be someone totally disposable like a janitor Supergirl had spoken to once who would go on to be killed after adding nothing central to the plot. After all, as Reinhart said, content for women-loving-women belonged in work by fans, not mass media. Having been burned several times before, I was sure that Sanvers shippers were just getting their hopes up and that the CW producers were being coy about revealing the gay character as a means to ensure queer viewers tuned in to as many of the shows as much as possible.

Whatever the case, the ploy worked: Sanvers was all over my Tumblr dash and I was barraged with messages from fellow queer fans and friends asking me if I had seen the show and what I thought of the ship. What makes Tumblr live-blogging so much more intense than tweeting is the myriad of options one has to articulate one's fangirling. While the most popular (and quickest) response might be less than 160 characters of "keysmashing" (e.g., some variation of "AS;LDHFA;LSDJFKA," meant to indicate incoherent flailing), there are multitudes of reaction gifs and short treatises on various moments of the newest episode. While I would later be lucky enough to watch the reaction to Alex and Maggie's first kiss unfold live, I missed the Tumblr experience of watching people collectively lose their minds over Alex's coming out.

I do not think I will ever forget seeing a string of texts from a quiet and closeted friend the night of Alex's coming out episode.[17] I did not even believe my friend at first, assuming—as I had done all season—that she was just willing subtext into maintext. But she insisted that it was a plain and simple, cut-and-dried, no-bones-about-it coming out scene and urged me to check Tumblr. I doubted this was a reliable source and told her at the moment I had no

Wi-Fi available to visit the site, so she filmed the scene in question off her television and texted it to me.

I was stunned.

Later that night I was able to access a video on Tumblr, splicing together three key sequences in the episode, titled "Crossfire."[18] The first segment has Maggie in a sour mood, telling Alex that she's been dumped. "Who would do that?!" Alex asks incredulously. Okay—good supportive, hetero friend there. Just gals bein' pals. The second clip has them at a crime scene the next day, where Maggie just wants to focus on work but Alex persists in trying to help her get over being dumped. Her suggestions that they hang out one-on-one become increasingly earnest, at last cuing Maggie, with a look of happy surprise, to believe Alex is asking her out: "I think I read you wrong." When Alex asks what she means in a tone of innocent curiosity, Maggie elaborates, "I didn't know you were into girls." Alex is taken aback and after a heavy pause stammers, "I'm not." Looking disappointed but staying calm, Maggie apologizes for the mistake yet adds "you'd be surprised how many gay women have told me that [they weren't gay]." Alex awkwardly ends the conversation with as much grace as she can muster and walks away, looking clearly troubled.

It was not until this moment that I was prepared to concede my friend had not just been parsing for subtext; in fact, I was overwhelmed. Experience had taught me that outside of teen soaps, when a leading character was accused of being gay, their response would be disinterest if not disgust, or treated as a hilarious joke (see many sitcoms of the 1990s and 2000s, notably *Friends*). To have Alex react to Maggie's assumption with such quietness spoke very loudly to the show's intent.

Then came segment three, the big moment. Eyes are the window to the soul, and the soul is what we see as Alex's face lingers in a rare gradual close-up for her coming out. She stumbles through her thoughts, unable to bring herself to use certain buzzwords like "gay," "lesbian," or even "men," giving the scene a more authentic feeling than the manufactured way these moments often come about on television. She struggles to make eye contact with Maggie, but this does not make her conversation any less brave. Coming out is something that often happens in quiet moments in dark corners, and in this case, the bar where Maggie first told Alex she herself was gay. It is a reality rarely captured so poignantly on screen:

> ALEX: The one part of my life that I've never been able to make perfect was dating. I just never really liked it, and you know, I—I mean, I tried! I got asked out, I just … I never liked … being intimate. I just … I don't know, I thought maybe that's just not the way I was built. It's just not my thing. I never thought it was because of … the other. That… (laughs) Maybe, I—I mean, I don't know. Now I just can't stop thinking about…

MAGGIE: About what?
ALEX: That maybe ... there was some truth to what you said.
MAGGIE: About?
ALEX: About what you said. About me.[19]

The camera stays in close-up even for the one cutaway to Maggie, which happens the first time she prompts Alex to continue. Alex departs abruptly and Maggie stays behind, letting Alex leave to process.

I myself needed to process what I had just seen, and that naturally led me to Tumblr to see how others were doing it. Post after post—some already with thousands of "likes" and reblogs—related my fellow viewers' peerless elation at seeing our experience captured so well. "Alex's speech is so pure," gushed badlance.[20] "I'm so emotional about how Maggie is so comforting to Alex in this very vulnerable moment [...] She understands how hard it is for Alex and how she struggles with saying the words 'I'm gay,'" emoted hedaswarrior.[21] "I don't watch this show, but this gif feels beautiful," chimed in sonofabacchae.[22]

Unfiltered reactions like these are a moving contrast to what was intended to be an inspirational piece by *The Advocate*, listing LGBT characters who have helped redefine family television. Alex made the cut: "Supergirl's older sister Alex revealed she [also] had an identity she was keeping secret herself."[23] I suppose the urge to compare repressed sexuality to a superhero alter-ego was just too slick to ignore, but such a misinterpretation severely weakens Alex's arc. A significant part of what makes her story so unique in television and what made it resonate with so many millions of viewers is that unlike Kara Danvers purposefully hiding her identity as Supergirl, *Alex was not intentionally keeping her orientation a secret.* Viewers watched Alex's progression of her self-understanding unfold in the early episodes of season two as she got to know Maggie, picking up the codes planted to imply something not-heterosexual going on even while Alex remained quietly flustered about their meaning. There is a good chance that some straight viewers—not prone to parsing for subtext and not bothering to wonder if certain cues might point to more than friendship—were just as surprised as Alex when Maggie questioned Alex's orientation.

In the episode after Alex comes out, Maggie wants to follow up on the conversation and Alex begins doubting herself, citing her age: "I don't know what to do now, you know? I'm almost thirty and I feel like a kid again. [...] Maybe it's just a phase. Maybe it isn't real." Maggie's immediate response is, "No, it's real. You're real. And you deserve to have a real, full, happy life."[24] This sentimental, supportive dialogue might have sprung right off Tumblr, where mantras affirming queer kids are reblogged hundreds of thousands of times, reminding them that their existence—their orientation, their identity—is valid, pure, and valued. Another significant takeaway: as brought up by Stephen Tropiano, when television shows wanted to preach about tolerance in the past, they would often do so via an enlightened straight character telling a homophobic straight character why they needed to accept their gay friend—who, incidentally, would often just be making a one-episode appearance to teach a Very Special Lesson.[25] To have Maggie, an out and proud lesbian, be the one to comfort Alex and thus the viewer is a subtle but important detail: it is a reassurance to the queer spectator that we are able to affirm each other and ourselves and that affirmation takes priority over straight people's comfort.

Alex's coming out is not over and done within a single episode, which is another key change, showing that contextualizing your orientation is an ongoing affair, and does not always have to be painful. *Supergirl* swerves from standard queer storylines which put so much focus on the build-up to coming out, depicting the concept as a smoothly upward line until it plateaus with the one and only "I'm gay!" scene. Alex's coming out/self-acceptance arc subverts this approach in multiple ways. First, it spans several episodes rather than a one-and-done, wrapped-up-by-the-end-credits hour. Second, this storyline is seamlessly integrated with Alex's other professional and personal ties to the show's main plot, thus avoiding a common symptom Suzanna Walters identifies in television where "gayness is both everything and nothing as well"—meaning, gay storylines focus only on a character's sexual identity without bothering to consider how that intersects with other parts of their life.[26] Third and most crucially, *Supergirl* shows how the immediate coming out process is nonlinear: it can be freeing one moment, but angering and anxiety-inducing the next, then a relief, and back again. On that note, I think it is important to take a moment to unpack Alex's coming out to her canonically straight sister Kara (Melissa Benoist) because, again, the arc sidesteps the typical narrative, which focuses more on straight responses to gayness than the actual gay character in question.[27]

In the episode following Alex's coming out to herself and Maggie, with Maggie's admittedly pushy encouragement, Alex decides to come out to her sister.[28] Her first conversation with Kara is a striking contrast to the coming out she had with Maggie; in the latter scenario, Alex and Maggie are seated across from each other, and while Alex does get flustered and avert her gaze now and then, it is very much a face-to-face conversation. She is embarrassed as she processes her thoughts out loud, but feels safe in knowing that Maggie is someone who gets it and will not judge her. For Kara, Alex chooses a walk-and-talk, sparing her the psychological strain of having to watch Kara's reactions to her words. As it was with Maggie, Alex's speech is halted as she tries to navigate her way around definitive vocabulary ("I started to develop feelings … for [Maggie]. *Those* feelings"); unlike with Maggie, Alex is guarded and cagey.

To Kara's credit, as she questions her sister, she sounds like someone wanting to make sure she behaves as a good ally, not as someone who is doubtful or accusatory.

> KARA: So, [Maggie's] gay. And are you saying you are, too?
> ALEX: I don't know. I'm just trying to make sense of it all. It's so complicated.
> KARA: Alex, it kind of sounds like you're coming out to me. Have you felt like this before?
> ALEX: Not like this.
> KARA: Have you ever been with a girl?
> ALEX: No, never.
> KARA: Okay, what's different? I know you haven't been dating much lately…
> ALEX: (hotly) This isn't because I haven't found the right guy!
> KARA: I never said it was! I'm just trying to understand, okay?
> ALEX: I'm up all night just thinking about it. And if I'm being honest, you know, I realize that … maybe I've had thoughts like this before.[29]

Alex then relates the story behind why she and her best friend in high school had a falling out: Alex worried her affection for her friend was abnormally strong, and the fear of what that might imply caused her to lash out, leading to a fight and the end of the friendship: "I shoved that memory down so deep inside that it's like it never happened. I'm remembering stuff like that now."[30] When Kara asks if Maggie likes her back, Alex curtly walks off and says she does not want to talk about it anymore.

Sometime later, Alex comes to Kara's apartment and accuses of her being "weird" ever since Alex came out to her. Kara insists she only has not talked more about it because Alex had said she did not want to and what follows is an extremely rare case of an apology. Usually on television (and too much in real life), a person's coming out is joined with an apology for the straight listener's benefit: "I'm sorry I was keeping this from you/lying to you"; "I'm sorry I didn't come out to you first/sooner"; "I'm sorry if this throws off your plans for us to have a normal family life," and so on. From a storytelling perspective this not only serves to further illustrate a queer person's agony and self-loathing, but allows a straight character to show how gracious they are by dismissing the apology and voicing their surprise that the queer character was worried about them at all—thus kind of making the whole situation about themselves and what a great ally they are rather than validating the queer person's feelings.

Supergirl flips this approach by having Kara tell Alex she is sorry before Alex can even utter anything close to that:

> I think I owe you an apology [...] for not creating an environment where you felt like you could talk about this with me. All those years we spent together growing up, the endless nights of talking and sharing … now I realize that they were all about me and my secret [powers]. There's never been room for you, and that's my fault. And I'm so sorry.[31]

No doubt feeling bad for her testy attitude earlier, Alex tries to assure Kara that she did not do anything wrong but Kara will not let herself off the hook. She likens Alex's orientation to her secret identity as Supergirl, but unlike the *Advocate* article, she acknowledges that they are not the same at all: "but I do know how it feels to keep a part of yourself shut off, to keep it inside. And I know how lonely that can make you feel. Alex, you are not alone."[32]

What Kara does not have to apologize for is making homophobic comments, because in another huge break from televised tradition, distinguishable homophobic bullies are not the enemy here. Walters took major issue with the fact that in most coming-out episodes, tension is provided by a one-time appearance of a homophobic relative or even complete stranger who, if they have not come around by the end of the episode, at least will never be heard from again once it's over. This lessens the impact of their harmful attitudes and compartmentalizes it, brushing away the lasting effects homophobia can have. It also paints a very basic and restricting concept of what homophobia is; in Walters' words: "when homophobia is only evidenced as overt bashing, it is like depicting racism solely as cross-burning."[33] Instead of an archetypal homophobe, what Alex has had to come to terms with and overcome is the more nebulous opposition of heteronormativity, i.e., compulsory heterosexuality. As Ellen Page described it on her show *Gaycation*:

> We're all born into a homophobic society. We just are. [...] The moment you are a conscious being, every story you're told, every movie you see, almost every song you hear is heterosexual and typically also hetero-sexist. And infused in you is a feeling of shame. Sometimes I think you don't even know how much that's affecting you for a really, really long time.[34]

This concept is seldom explored in mainstream media. *Supergirl* destroys the idea that every girl knows her sexuality by age twelve and immediately recognizes her crushes for what they are. Alex's awakening was relatable for the thousands of women who did not figure out their orientation in high school, who did not figure it out after experimenting in college. Women who just went along, assuming they had not met the right man yet because they had been societally set up to expect less of men, to assume their own sex drive was less easily set off than men's. In these instances, all it can take is the right woman to open your eyes and go, "oh." There is no bully to tell off, no traumatic past to overcome—just the slow-burning realization that does not hatch until adulthood, telling you that maybe there is something alien about your experiences to the majority of society. Maybe you have some untangling of your past to do.

In a way, Alex's age and circumstances seem to indicate that we have come full circle in some aspects of depicting queer characters. Tropiano explains that until the mid–1980s, gay men and lesbian representation was limited to adult characters, who remained closeted until their late twenties or early thirties, so the networks could avoid the accusation that they were endorsing "the gay lifestyle" to kids.[35] By the twenty-first century, however, youth culture was making it clear that they were ready and angling for queer characters in media. As ABC Family's Vice President of Programming, Kate Juergens, put it in 2014: "With our millennial audience, it's what they expect to see. Don't Ask Don't Tell was such a vestige of an older generation."[36] Thus, while younger viewers in fandoms whose shows were aimed at "traditional" older women (i.e., TNT's buddy cop show *Rizzoli & Isles*—ask me about my bitterness) were pretty much stuck settling for subtext at best and derision at worst, shows for teens began paving the way for gay representation (*Glee, Faking It, Degrassi: The Next Generation, Skins, South of Nowhere, Pretty Little Liars*, to name a few). According to Dr. Caitlin Ryan, head of the Family Acceptance Project at San Francisco State University, decades of documented research on queer adolescents has shown that the average coming out age has dropped from early twenties in the 1970s to 13 in 2016—"and it's dropping down even more."[37] There is a chicken-and-egg effect in place here when we consider what media has had to do with this: is the representation of more gay youth intended as a reflection of American teenage culture today, to seem realistic, or is the increased representation what has helped teenagers come out? The answer is both.

With such a strong focus on the coming-out stories of teenagers, complex coming-out stories for adults have waned. These storylines are often mired in drawn-out angst, self-loathing, and an excruciating need to stay in the closet. While those situations are certainly authentic for many, the ubiquitous depiction of that angle seems unnecessary and often becomes an overwhelming aspect of the character's arc and/or personality. In a seemingly contradictory way, this fixation on the closet takes attention away from the queer characters themselves and focuses it on the reactions of others, stunting development for the queer character in question. This makes a case for depicting well-adjusted, happily out adults without coming-out commentary (e.g., *The Fosters, Grey's Anatomy, Orange Is the New Black, How to Get Away with Murder*, and so on), as it shares a comforting ideal for closeted viewers and is solid representation for those already out. In fact, *Supergirl* contributes to this canon of characters by introducing Maggie in season two as an already out woman with a girlfriend.

Partway through her first episode, Maggie brings Alex to a bar that caters to aliens, calling it a safe haven for them from humans. It is here where she casually comes out to Alex by mentioning that she used to date one of the waitresses, saying she finds it easier to relate to aliens than to most people: "Growing up a non-white, non-straight girl in Blue Springs, Nebraska? I might as well have been from Mars. I was an outcast and felt like it. Our alien neighbors [...] have to hide who they are in order to survive. I can sympathize."[38] The comparison here might be a tad on-the-nose, but at the same time, it is refreshing to have an allegory that is more than a symbolic gesture projected onto a canonically straight character.[39]

After coming out to Kara, Alex's shaky trajectory continues when she kisses Maggie and confesses her feelings. Maggie is wary of dating someone "fresh off the boat," telling Alex they are in two very different places when it comes to their orientation, which makes them romantically incompatible.[40] Embarrassed and heartbroken, Alex is brusque when Maggie expresses a keen interest in remaining good friends: "Initially, I was terrified, but ultimately I was proud to come out because it wasn't just some concept. It was about my feelings for this amazing woman. But now? I don't feel liberated, or like I'm on some great journey. All I feel is pain because you don't want me."[41]

That pain stings and does not go away until Maggie almost dies in the line of duty in the following episode—plausible in her line of work as a police officer, but the scene of Alex helping to bandage her up at the hospital definitely feels a bit "fan-fic-y" (the "hurt/comfort" trope is a common one in fan works, to the degree that it is listed as a genre on one of the best-known fansites, www.fanfiction.net). By this time, Maggie has apologized for causing Alex pain and reiterated her sincere desire for friendship. Faced with Maggie's near-death, Alex is finally ready to accept romantic rejection and embrace what is indeed her new "great journey":

> When you first suggested that I was gay, I denied it. Then I thought that it was just about you. I mean, how would I not like you? But, you know, deep down I think I wasn't comfortable that that was my new normal. But it *is* my new normal. And I'm happy that it is. Because um, I uh, I don't know; I finally get me. And now I realize that it wasn't about you, but it's about me living my life. So, thank you.[42]

Alex's honest ability to move past this romantic setback and even see it as a mark of personal progress provides the kind of heart-tugging emotion opposite of what queer viewers traditionally see: "not very empowering tears of romanticized self-pity."[43] Alex's heartache is not conflated with being gay, but is rather a result of personal rejection.

The real miracle occurs, however, when the episode ends with Maggie coming to Alex's apartment late at night. She confesses that she does in fact have feelings for Alex, but had panicked when Alex came onto her, anxious at the thought of Alex having come out for her. But her brush with death has reminded Maggie that life's too short to quibble about such things: "we should be who we are, and we should kiss the girls that we want to kiss. And I really just want to kiss you."[44] The night that episode aired, I saw that dialogue and the ensuing kisses reblogged on my Tumblr dash dozens of times, with each post adding their own ecstatic commentary.

The meteoric rise of social media has become an imperative way not only for fans to share each other's work and theories, but for bringing industry folks into unprecedented contact with their fans. Walters and others have posited that viewers feel a special connection to television characters as opposed to those on film because they are regularly scheduled visitors in our homes.[45] In that vein, I would suggest that some viewers have taken to considering actors and creators in much the same way: when your favorite celebrities' posts are interspersed with your friends' on Instagram, Facebook and Twitter with no notable format differences, a certain line becomes smudged. While I am sure there was power in inundating a person's mailbox with angry letters back in the day, an even more immediate message is sent on something like Twitter.

A striking illustration of this would be when *The 100* showrunner Jason Rothenberg lost thousands of followers in 2016 in the days immediately following the unexpected killing-off of beloved queer character Lexa.[46] Rothenberg and his team had spent months advertising their show's forward-thinking and queer-friendly cast of characters, garnering them a devoted fanbase of underrepresented queer women. The bait worked, but the showrunner was completely blindsided when his "twist"—where a lesbian is shot following a scene where she has just made love to her girlfriend for the first time—cost him almost a 50 percent decrease in 18- to 49-year-old viewers,[47] and garnered dozens of articles accusing him of homophobia. For older queer women, Lexa's brutal, post-coital murder was a throwback to Tara Maclay's on *Buffy the Vampire Slayer*—another show run by a cis straight white man who liked to boast about his progressiveness. Queer viewers of all ages felt used by Rothenberg and vowed never to tune in to *The 100* again. The outcry over this fictional death and its real-world implications led to Autostraddle's now famous ongoing list of lesbian and bisexual TV characters who have died. The list started with 65 characters but as of this writing is up to almost 200.[48] Queer women really needed a hero.

It was into this fractured fandom world that Alex and Maggie came to rise, with their creators promising viewers that the women will live and have happy endings—a needed reassurance when neither of those can be considered a given for queer female characters. Unlike creators such as Rothenberg or straight female actors who would use talk show appearances as an opportunity to deride the queer female fans clamoring for their characters to be gay, Chyler Leigh (Alex) has proven social media savvy when it comes to her queer fans: an Instagram picture shows her decked out in rainbow paraphernalia, with a shirt that says "Mama Bear," depicting a bear protectively clutching a rainbow-colored cub.[49] Another post from National Coming Out Day shows Leigh in a shirt that says "Support Positive LGBT Representation," and she goes on to address members of the LGBTQ+ community, acknowledging fans beyond the strictly gay and lesbian labels she might be expected to cater to.[50] Floriana Lima (Maggie) engages less frequently but has posted some Sanvers imagery on Instagram, such as Scrabble tiles laid out to connect Maggie and Alex's names.[51] These sorts of public affirmations establish a bond of trust between fans and actors, with fans often addressing their comments directly to the actor, thanking them for their work and support.

The Sanvers relationship has continued to progress on *Supergirl*, hitting its ups and downs as any heterosexual couple would without falling into the trap of normalizing queerness for the sake of tolerance. However, the fact that such a poignant same-sex couple has appeared on a family-friendly show does not mean that the days of fandom subtext parsing are over; in fact they are not even over for *Supergirl*. A significant portion of women not only ship Maggie and Alex but also Supergirl herself with her sometimes-nemesis Lena Luthor (Katie McGrath) under the ship name "Supercorp."[52] This would suggest, as Russo theorizes, that it is worth considering whether "the dichotomy [a] discussion posits between 'subtext' and 'maintext' is as transparent and unambiguous as it appears to be."[53] Many fans have been frustrated by cast members' dismissiveness of Supercorp, and even more so by Sanvers getting shunted aside to devote screen time to Kara's own blossoming romance with Mon-El, a character most Sanvers shippers find cruel and misogynistic. To them, the intense care that went into making Alex's romantic arc realistic and a departure from previous, harmful perpetuated stereotypes on television is missing for Kara. The show's propping up of the problematic "Kara-Mel" ship as a beacon of laudable heterosexuality and its intensive focus on Mon-El over characters such as James Olsen or Lena Luthor feels far less empowering than the show's early days.

And thus we return to Tumblr, where queer fans can delight in Sanvers gifs and isolated clips without having to sit through the show itself. In addition to saving them the time and effort of skipping through Karamel scenes, avoiding the show is also a purposeful political and economic move: many posts distribute links to illegal ways to view the show, so that viewers can access the content without giving the creators the benefit of counting their views and dollars. This can be an insidious practice, but there is intent driving it beyond a desire to save money; in fact by contrast, Tumblr posts often circulate urging viewers to use whatever legal means available to watch woman-friendly and queer-friendly shows to boost their ratings (e.g., *Agent Carter* and *Bomb Girls*, neither of which unfortunately made it past two seasons). The ethics and finances of that idea belong in another conversation. Regardless of how viewers feel about the progression of Kara's romantic life, *Supergirl* has already etched a place for itself in the hearts of queer women and the history of their depiction on television, and not at all without merit.

In her writing on lesbians and media, Clare Whatling criticized queer female viewers who complained about the "closetry" of storylines which teased but did not dare speak the name of the love shared by female characters.[54] She claims that "one of the chief delights of these films is that they allow free scope for, indeed even depend on, the viewer's imagination, teasing her to make the connections and fill in the silences," even as those same silences allow creators the comfort of knowing straight viewers can still comfortably impose heterosexuality on those moments. She continues: "There is a very particular pleasure in piecing together the lingering looks, smiles and moments of fingertips barely touching which form the covert lesbian subtext of such films."[55]

To that I would say Whatling entirely misses the only positive takeaway from subtext, which is that it can spark creative communities which hold value and pleasure distinct from the limits of money-grubbing mass media. To imply that queer female viewers ought to seek joy in being teased as opposed to anger at being suppressed is frankly insulting. The "particular pleasure" of piecing together subtextual moments is done out of a strong need to see ourselves organically represented, not out of a blind desire to impose ourselves on established characters. Any value in subtextual relationships, be they Xena and Gabrielle or Supergirl and Lena Luthor, is vested in the women who make them their own. They are not "overemotional and uncritical consumers"; they are appropriately emotional and often *the* most critical.[56] In fact, the propensity for criticism may be part of what makes the open reception of Sanvers so remarkable: for the weeks that Sanvers' relationship unfolded on *Supergirl* I immersed myself in the fandom on Tumblr, which is often a hyper-sensitive and hyper-critical place towards, especially, homophobia. Ian Bogost voiced concern that fans are not capable of true criticism because they are too easily satisfied, but all this tells me is that he has never met a queer girl scorned. If there is beauty to be found in femslash fandom culture, it is that it is filled with work and commentary by those who are not satisfied and demand to be seen.[57]

Consideration for *Supergirl* on the whole may be down on Tumblr but Sanvers continues to give its fans "all the feels," even when the couple was broken up in season three to free Floriana Lima for another show. Lima's departure did not end in Maggie's death, nor in Alex's orientation fading away. Gifs of their scenes continue to make the rounds on Tumblr and Tweets of gratitude to the actors continue to be posted with regularity; Sanvers continues to give a face and a voice to countless women trying to sort out their identities. Michael Renov asserted that "public declarations of private selves have come to be defining acts of contemporary life, often imbued with great urgency," and as the extent to which queerness may exist publicly continues to be debated, the ability to explore it privately (à la Tumblr) is crucial.[58] Television may not represent us accurately at all times, and *Supergirl* does not reflect every queer woman's experience—but it is not intended to. What it does aim to do is provide viewers with a platform with which they can discuss and think about what *is* true for their experiences. The representation validates those it speaks to, and reminds straight viewers that such stories are important. In that spirit, I hope Alex and Maggie's legacy continues to rise up, up, and never go away.

NOTES

1. Levi Grossman, "Foreword," *Fic: Why Fanfiction Is Taking Over the World* (Dallas: BenBella Books, 2013), xii.
2. Anthony Freitas, "Gay Programming, Gay Publics: Public and Private Tensions in Lesbian and Gay Cable Channels," *Cable Visions: Television Beyond Broadcasting* (New York: New York University Press, 2007), 217.
3. reigngooglesearches, Tumblr post, August 12, 2017: https://reigngooglesearches.tumblr.com/post/164086552100/someone-hey-do-you-know-whats-happening-on.
4. Stephen Tropiano, *The Prime Time Closet: A History of Gays and Lesbians on TV* (New York: Applause, 2002), 154.
5. Katherine Sender, "Dualcasting: Bravo's Gay Programming and the Quest for Women Audiences," *Cable Visions: Television Beyond Broadcasting* (New York: New York University Press, 2007), 307.
6. Emily Longeretta, "Riverdale Star Shoots Down Betty & Veronica Romance: It's Just Not Our Show," *Hollywood Life*, January 9, 2017: http://hollywoodlife.com/2017/01/09/riverdale-betty-veronica-romance-lesbian-relationship-lili-reinhart-interview/
7. The kiss occurs in the pilot during a cheerleading tryout. Veronica's spur-of-the-moment solution to spice up their routine is to kiss Betty, whispering, "don't freak out—just trust me." After a lengthy and romantically-lit kiss, Betty looks disgusted and the cheerleading captain looks bored: "Check your sell-by date, ladies. Faux lesbian kissing hasn't been taboo since 1994." It's still taboo enough to get exploited rather than represented in 2017, though.
8. Yvonne Tasker, *Working Girls: Gender and Sexuality in Popular Cinema* (London: Routledge, 1998), 152.
9. There are rare exceptions, such as when Twitter users bombarded *Glee* creator Ryan Murphy with messages insisting he follow-up on a line where Santana mentioned she and Brittany had sex. What was intended to be a throwaway joke resonated with a desperately under-represented community, and given the already gay-friendly nature of the show, the opportunity was taken to explore a canonical "Brittana" relationship.
10. Patricia White, *unInvited: Classical Hollywood Cinema and Lesbian Representability* (Bloomington: Indiana University Press, 1999), 1.
11. Tropiano, *Prime Time Closet*, 7.
12. Julie Levin Russo, "Textual Orientation: Queer Female Fandom Online," *The Routledge Companion to Media and Gender* (New York: Routledge, 2014), 453.
13. David Bordwell, "Cognition and Comprehension: Viewing and Forgetting in Mildred Pierce," *Film Theory & Criticism* (New York: Oxford University Press, 1974), 430.
14. *Supergirl*, "Welcome to Earth," season 2, episode 3, directed by Rachel Talalay, written by Jessica Queller and Derek Simon, aired October 24, 2016, on The CW.
15. After its first season, *Supergirl* was moved from CBS to the younger-skewing CW, a network co-owned by CBS.
16. Natalie Abrams, "Superhero Show Character to Come Out as Gay," *Entertainment Weekly*, October 2017: http://ew.com/article/2016/08/11/cw-superhero-gay-character.
17. The timing was unforgettable, too as this episode aired the day before the United States 2016 presidential election, which saw the election of Donald Trump. Trump had run a campaign that was hostile to members of the LGBTQ community and many within that community feared that rights previously granted under the Obama administration would be rolled back.

18. glenn-rhee, Tumblr post, November 7, 2016: http://glenn-rhee.tumblr.com/post/152882117782/sanvers-in-supergirl-205.

19. *Supergirl*, "Crossfire," season 2, episode 5, directed by Glen Winter, written by Gabriel Llanas and Anna Musky-Goldwyn, aired November 7, 2016, on The CW.

20. badlance, Tumblr post, November 8, 2016: http://underthegreensward.tumblr.com/post/152890683889.

21. hedaswarrior, Tumblr post, November 2016: http://sonofabacchae.tumblr.com/post/152885236710/hedaswarrior-im-so-emotional-about-how-maggie.

22. sonofabacchae, Tumblr post, November 2016: http://sonofabacchae.tumblr.com/post/152885236710/hedaswarrior-im-so-emotional-about-how-maggie.

23. Jacob Ogles, "35 Characters Who Redefined Family TV," *The Advocate*, February 2, 2017: https://www.advocate.com/arts-entertainment/2017/2/02/35-lgbt-characters-who-redefined-family-tv#slide-13.

24. *Supergirl*, "Changing," season 2, episode 6, directed by Larry Teng, story by Greg Berlanti, teleplay by Andrew Kreisberg and Caitlin Parrish, aired November 14, 2016, The CW.

25. Tropiano, *Prime Time Closet*, 192.

26. Suzanna Danuta Walters, *All the Rage: The Story of Gay Visibility in America* (Chicago: University of Chicago Press, 2003), 66.

27. Walters, *All the Rage*, 74.

28. *Supergirl*, "Changing," season 2, episode 6.

29. *Supergirl*, "Changing," season 2, episode 6.

30. *Supergirl*, "Changing," season 2, episode 6.

31. *Supergirl*, "Changing," season 2, episode 6.

32. *Supergirl*, "Changing," season 2, episode 6.

33. Suzanna Danuta Walters, *All the Rage*, 79.

34. Ellen Page (Producer), "Brazil," *Gaycation* (2016; Rio de Janeiro; Viceland).

35. Tropiano, *Prime Time Closet*, 154.

36. Jennifer Armstrong, "Gay Teens on TV," *Entertainment Weekly*, January 13, 2014: http://ew.com/article/2014/01/13/gay-teens-tv/

37. Shannon Keating, "Coming Out as Gay in Elementary School," *Buzzfeed*, April 27, 2015: https://www.buzzfeed.com/shannonkeating/coming-out-as-gay-in-elementary-school?utm_term=.cpjXrwQ9n#.ev4MrlX53.

38. *Supergirl*, "Welcome to Earth," season 2, episode 3.

39. A well-known example: on her site Pottermore, devoted to expanding information on the *Harry Potter* universe, J.K. Rowling explained that werewolf Remus Lupin's lycanthropy was a metaphor for stigmatized diseases like HIV and AIDS. Many fans were disappointed that a straight character was chosen to symbolize diseases with historical ties to homophobia.

40. *Supergirl*, "Changing," season 2, episode 6.

41. *Supergirl*, "The Darkest Place," season 2, episode 7, directed by Glen Winter, written by Robert Rovner and Paula Yoo, aired November 21, 2016, on The CW.

42. *Supergirl*, "Medusa," season 2, episode 8, directed by Stefan Pleszczynnski, written by Jessica Queller and Derek Simon, aired November 28, 2016, on The CW.

43. Alex Doty, *Making Things Perfectly Queer: Interpreting Mass Culture* (Minneapolis: University of Minnesota Press, 1993), 34.

44. *Supergirl*, "Medusa," season 2, episode 8.

45. Walters, *All the Rage*, 59.

46. Many viewers watched Rothenberg's follower count on Twitter drop in real time.

47. pineapple-pizza, Tumblr post, February 2017: http://inkybetterdays.tumblr.com/post/156877893367/pinnaple-pizza-saw-this-on-twitter-and-just-had.

48. Marie Lyn Bernard, "All 188 Dead Lesbian and Bisexual Characters on TV, and How They Died," *Autostraddle*, March 11, 2016: https://www.autostraddle.com/all-65-dead-lesbian-and-bisexual-characters-on-tv-and-how-they-died-312315.

49. Chyler Leigh, Instagram post, August 2017: https://www.instagram.com/p/BXoUUDLh7L-/?taken-by=chy_leigh.

50. Chyler Leigh, Instagram post, October 2017: https://www.instagram.com/p/BaHrKLThDn0/?taken-by=chy_leigh.
51. Floriana Lima, Instagram post, November 2016: https://www.instagram.com/p/BNGISFGjswv/?taken-by=florianalima.
52. On www.fanfiction.net, the most well-known hub for such works, as of this writing there are four times as many fan stories pairing Kara and Lena than Kara with Mon-El, the man the show is canonically setting her up with. Supercorp stories outnumber Sanvers stories as well (albeit by a much smaller margin), again indicating that the biggest source of fan works are couples whose potential is never actualized in canon.
53. Russo, "Textual Orientation," 451.
54. Whatling's analysis involves the 1991 screen adaptation of *Fried Green Tomatoes*, which erased the source material's romantic relationship in favor of a strong female friendship so as not to alienate straight women. Stripping down the maintext has left enough subtext for *Fried Green Tomatoes* to remain a frustrating benchmark film for queer women.
55. Clare Whatling, *Screen Dreams: Fantasising Lesbians in Film* (Manchester: Manchester University Press, 1997), 153.
56. Russo, "Textual Orientation," 456.
57. Ian Bogost, "Against Aca-Fandom," *Ian Bogost* (blog), July 29, 2010: http://bogost.com/writing/blog/against_aca-fandom.
58. Michael Renov, *The Subject of Documentary* (Minneapolis: University of Minnesota Press, 2004), xvii.

SELECTED BIBLIOGRAPHY

Abrams, Natalie. "Superhero Show Character to Come Out as Gay." *Entertainment Weekly.* October 2016. http://ew.com/article/2016/08/11/cw-superhero-gay-character
Armstrong, Jennifer. "Gay Teens on TV." *Entertainment Weekly.* January 13, 2014. http://ew.com/article/2014/01/13/gay-teens-tv/.
Bernard, Marie Lyn. "All 188 Dead Lesbian and Bisexual Characters on TV, and How They Died." Autostraddle. March 11, 2016. https://www.autostraddle.com/all-65-dead-lesbian-and-bisexual-characters-on-tv-and-how-they-died-312315.
Bogost, Ian. "Against Aca-Fandom." *Ian Bogost* (web log), July 29, 2010. http://bogost.com/writing/blog/against_aca-fandom/.
Bordwell, David. "Cognition and Comprehension: Viewing and Forgetting in Mildred Pierce." Edited by Marshall Cohen. In *Film Theory & Criticism*, edited by Leo Braudy, 427–49. 7th edition. New York: Oxford University Press, 1974.
Doty, Alex. *Making Things Perfectly Queer: Interpreting Mass Culture*. Minneapolis: University of Minnesota Press, 1993.
Freitas, Anthony. "Gay Programming, Gay Publics: Public and Private Tensions in Lesbian and Gay Cable Channels." In *Cable Visions: Television Beyond Broadcasting*, 215-33. New York: New York University Press, 2007.
Grossman, Levi. "Foreword." In *Fic: Why Fanfiction Is Taking Over the World*, by Anne Jamison, xi–xiv. Dallas: BenBella Books, 2013.
Keating, Shannon. "Coming Out in Elementary School." Buzzfeed. January 27, 2015. https://www.buzzfeed.com/shannonkeating/coming-out-as-gay-in-elementary-school?utm_term=.cpjXrwQ9n#.ev4MrlX3.
Leigh, Chyler. Instagram post. August 2017. https://www.instagram.com/p/BXoUUDLh7L-/?taken-by=chy_leigh.
———. Instagram post. October 2017. https://www.instagram.com/p/BaHrKLThDn0/?taken-by=chy_leigh.
Lima, Floriana. Instagram post. November 2016. https://www.instagram.com/p/BNGISFGjswv/?taken-by=florianalima.
Longeretta, Emily. "Riverdale Star Shoots Down Betty & Veronica Romance: It's Just Not Our Show." *Hollywood Life.* http://hollywoodlife.com/2017/01/09/riverdale-betty-veronica-romance-lesbian-relationship-lili-reinhart-interview/.
Ogles, Jacob. "35 Characters Who Redefined Family TV." *The Advocate.* February 2, 2017.

https://www.advocate.com/arts-entertainment/2017/2/02/35-lgbt-characters-who-redefined-family-tv#slide-13.
Page, Ellen, prod. "Brazil." In *Gaycation*. Viceland. March 9, 2016. pineapple-pizza. Tumblr post. February 2017. http://inkybetterdays.tumblr.com/post/156877893367/pinnaple-pizza-saw-this-on-twitter-and-just-had.
Renov, Michael. *The Subject of Documentary*. Minneapolis: University of Minnesota Press, 2004.
Russo, Julie Levin. "Textual Orientation: Queer Female Fandom Online." In *The Routledge Companion to Media and Gender*, 450–60. New York: Routledge, 2014.
Sender, Katherine. "Dualcasting: Bravo's Gay Programming and the Quest for Women Audiences." In *Cable Visions: Television Beyond Broadcasting*, 302–18. New York: New York University Press, 2007.
Tasker, Yvonne. *Working Girls: Gender and Sexuality in Popular Cinema*. London: Routledge, 1998.
Tropiano, Stephen. *The Prime Time Closet: A History of Gays and Lesbians on TV*. New York: Applause, 2002.
Walters, Suzanna Danuta. *All the Rage: The Story of Gay Visibility in America*. Chicago: University of Chicago Press, 2003.
Whatling, Clare. *Screen Dreams: Fantasising Lesbians in Film*. Manchester: Manchester University Press, 1997.
White, Patricia. *UnInvited: Classical Hollywood Cinema and Lesbian Representability*. Bloomington: Indiana University Press, 1999.

Supergirl's Sisterhoods: Feminism as a Family Affair

Sisterhood of Steel

The Powerful Bond That Is the Heart of The CW's Supergirl

Donna J. Cromeans

The story of Superman's female cousin, Supergirl, has been intriguing comic book readers since her first introduction in 1959.[1] There have been many incarnations of the character in the comics and in film and television since then, but perhaps none has captured the essence of the character more than the Ali Adler, Greg Berlanti, and Andrew Kreisberg creation and production of *Supergirl*, brought to life on CBS in 2015. Superhero shows at the time were seeing a resurgence, with the success of *Arrow* and *Flash* on The CW Network (a sister network owned in part by CBS). The decision to air not just a superhero show, but a female superhero show on the more mainstream CBS network was a risk, but the Berlanti/Adler/Kreisberg production premiered to mostly positive reviews and was the 2015 fall season's top-rated premiere with just over twelve million viewers.[2] In their retelling of the Supergirl story, they remained faithful to much of what was already DC canon, but they put a modern twist on the story that resonated with viewers. One of the most popular decisions they made in their version was to give Supergirl a sister, and not just any sister, but one that would become as great a hero to fans as she was to the title character. The special bond between Alex and Kara Danvers would become an aspect and theme of the show that attracted fans due to the touching and honest portrayal of a sibling relationship.

More times than not, siblings on television—particularly sisters—are portrayed as catty, back-biting, jealousy-driven characters to create drama and conflict on the show.[3] However, the Danvers sisters of *Supergirl* were just the opposite: Alex and Kara were not afraid or ashamed of expressing their familial love for one another and who would without hesitation fight or die for the other and defend their city and the world from alien aggressors. And outside of their superhero personas, they were just two normal sisters who binge-watch their favorite television shows together over pizza or ice cream, giggle like giddy school girls over their love lives, and squabble in one breath, but in the next, come to each other's defense when threatened by outside forces. The portrayal of the Danvers sisters since the pilot has been one of the most refreshing, honest, and healthy relationships on the show and critics have called it the show's heart and core.[4] At the 2016 CW upfronts, show lead Melissa Benoist even characterized the relationship as the most important relationship of the series.[5]

It is widely reported that Benoist, known for her roles on *Glee* and in the film *Whiplash*, was the first actor interviewed for the part of Kara Danvers/Supergirl and landed the part after a lengthy audition process.[6] Leigh, known primarily for her work on *Grey's Anatomy*, was reportedly the last actor seen for the part of Alex Danvers and according to Benoist, the "savior."[7] Both actors are quick to contend that the on-screen bond works so well due to the close bond they share off-screen. At a Paley Center panel on the show in 2016, Benoist declared that from day one, it was truly a sisterhood, while Leigh said meeting Benoist one of the most powerful—short of meeting her husband—relationships she had ever felt from an artistic standpoint, also calling her co-star one of the most genuine people she had ever met.[8] Their affection for one another has been evident from the earliest interviews through today.[9] It clearly comes across on screen, whether it be a shared look, a slight touch, or being able to present highly dramatic or emotional scenes, because of the trust they obviously have in one another. The genuine connection that Benoist and Leigh share in real life translates into their character's on-screen relationship. This chapter explores, whether planned or not, how the evolution of the Danvers sisters' bond has become the show's greatest superpower: a "Sisterhood of Steel."

Season One: The Sisterly Bond

Kara and Alex never refer to themselves as adopted siblings, but always as sisters. This aspect of their relationship has garnered both attention and praise.[10] Carrie Goldman, award-winning author and adoption advocate, took her three daughters to meet Melissa Benoist and Chyler Leigh at a rare dual fan appearance at the 2016 Chicago Comic Entertainment and Expo. Afterward, she penned "An Open Letter to *Supergirl* Stars Melissa Benoist and Leigh, From an Adoptive Mom" for her popular *Portrait of an Adoption* blog, praising both the show and the actors, calling them heroes her daughters had grown to love.[11] She writes:

During the scenes in *Supergirl* where Alex and Kara explore the painful aspects of their relationship as sisters through adoption, our whole family absorbs every word, every expression, because seeing this dynamic on mainstream television makes our family feel less alone. The fact that Alex and Kara are kickass, strong, smart, flawed, beautiful women who work hard, cry, laugh, yell, fight, and make mistakes has been an incredible model for our girls. [...] Watching *Supergirl* has normalized our experience where some parts of adoption are amazing and other parts are really difficult, but what never changes is that we are family, and we love each other. Thank you for that.[12]

Another key message that resonated with viewers was "El Mayarah," a philosophy that originated as part of Kara's heritage but quickly became something she built with her adoptive family, especially Alex. Throughout the first season, the show skillfully illustrated how it was a show about family, specifically about how Kara and Alex rely on one another for support and strength and are indeed "Stronger Together." Their reliance and love for one another often marked throughout the season by what came to be known as the Danvers sisters "couch" scenes: the two on the couch in Kara's apartment while sharing their day, their fears, their concerns and just time being normal sisters.

Moreover, without the strength of the Danvers sisters' bond, there might never have been a Supergirl in National City. It is not until midway through the pilot that Kara decides to use the powers she had kept hidden for years, and she only uses them and becomes Supergirl after learning Alex's life is in danger aboard an aircraft that is about to crash. Alex, in a typical protective older sister mode, is not thrilled that Kara shows herself to the world, yet later, after realizing that the world "needs her to fly," she is the one who convinces Kara to become Supergirl. This is a pivotal moment because Alex had grown into a big sister figure who wanted to shelter her baby sister even though Kara had powers. So, she had to step back and let Kara fly, a sign of acceptance that she would have to let Kara do dangerous things. Kara likely never knew Alex had threatened to quit working for the Department of Extranormal Operations (DEO) unless it welcomed her super sister, too.[13] She convinces Kara to become Supergirl by bringing her a holographic message from Kara's Kryptonian mother. As Kara starts watching the message, we see Alex trying to slip away, clearly feeling like an intruder. Then the simple gesture of Kara reaching out for Alex's hand and pulling her close as she watches. This moment of Kara making sure Alex is still connected to her ties back into the theme of "El Mayarah" and elevates the show from being a typical superhero series into something special.[14] That simple gesture establishes the Danvers sisters and their relationship as the heart and anchor of the show.

Since that moment, this core relationship has been tested, threatened, but more importantly, grown into an even stronger element that centers the show. Fans responded immediately to the Danvers sisters and the actors who portray them.[15] Finally, young female viewers had not one, but two female superhero role models. One of the key messages the show conveyed was that not all superheroes wear capes. Soon, fans admitted that they preferred watching the Danvers sisters and their relationship over superhero feats. Thousands of fan-made videos and fanfiction stories began appearing, celebrating and exploring the depth and strength of the relationship between Alex and Kara, demonstrating the power of the sibling relationship resonated with viewers.[16]

Protecting one's younger sibling is a heavy enough burden. Studies show that the oldest child does bear the brunt of parental strictness that often can turn that child into a perfectionist.[17] Prior to the "Livewire" episode,[18] Alex Danvers had proven herself to be fearless after being kidnapped by Kara's Aunt Astra[19] and taking down a Hellgrammite with her bare hands. Yet in this episode, we get a first glance at a rattled Alex Danvers, scared and nervous because her mother is coming to town to spend Thanksgiving with her girls.[20] Alex is afraid her mother will blame her for Kara coming out as Supergirl, for not protecting her sister, as her parents had asked her to do since she was fifteen. In Alex's case, the burden was made even more difficult because when their father went missing, she took on the responsibility of her alien sister at the expense of her own life. She gave up her dreams and ended up at the DEO, all for the purpose of protecting Kara. Her fears are not unfounded, as Eliza does blame Alex, despite Kara standing up for her sister and saying the decision to become Supergirl was hers. And Eliza, at first, is inexplicably even more upset that Alex has been hiding the fact she has been working at the DEO. In Alex's eyes, no matter what she does or how much she gives up for her sister, nothing has been good enough to win her mother's approval, which Alex clearly wants and needs. So, her mother's outburst and disapproval at this revelation was par for the course for Alex, a first insight into what drives her, adding more layers to an already compelling character.

If there is an episode in the first season that solidifies the strength of the Danvers sister's bond it is "For the Girl Who Had Everything." The episode is an homage to a classic Superman story involving a deadly plant known as the Black Mercy that traps a person in a dream-like fantasy world of their greatest desires as it slowly kills them. The victim, in this case, is Kara and is a showcase for Chyler Leigh as Alex. Alex's love for her sister is at the center of this episode, as she fights desperately to save Kara. She even agrees to collaborate with two of her enemies, Kara's Aunt Astra, whose blood ties to Kara threaten the foundation of her sisterhood, and arch-enemy Maxwell Lord, who has tried time and again to kill Kara. She must jump into Kara's dream world and convince her to return. Any doubts about Alex's devotion to Kara are put to rest when, just prior to jumping into her sister's subconscious, Alex tells James to stop Hank if he tries to pull her out before she reaches Kara: "I either come back with my sister, or I don't come back at all."[21]

The depth of her devotion proven by her willingness to sacrifice her own life to save her sister. Alex fights the entire episode, but never more fiercely than when she is placed on trial in Kara's dream world.

Leigh's passionate and heart-wrenching performance makes one feel every ounce of the desperation Alex feels, tearfully pleading with her sister to return, all the while handcuffed and struggling with the guards trying to hold her back. At their 2016 Chicago Comic Entertainment and Expo appearance, Leigh talked about filming that scene, saying there was a strange disconnect with Benoist.[22] She mentioned how the two had grown used to being there for one another and supporting one another during filming and how it felt strange, so she channeled that frustration into her performance. Benoist does admit that part of this disconnect was deliberate—further proof that the intensity of the scene between Alex and Kara would not have been as great had the connection between the actors not been as strong.

After rescuing Kara, Alex is forced to kill Astra to save J'onn during a battle, which is set up an interesting potential conflict since Kara's adopted Earth sister murders her only living blood relative. The twist to this was having J'onn lie to Kara and say that he was the one who killed Astra: "It's because you're Supergirl's hero and I don't want her seeing you as anything but that."[23] This is not an atypical notion; it just reaffirms a study conducted by Laurie Kramer, a professor of applied family studies at the University of Illinois at Urbana. Younger siblings start out adoring their older brothers or sisters, wanting to mimic their strengths and talents.[24] Other shows might have used this massive secret to drive a season-long mystery and wedge between siblings. *Supergirl*, however, took a more realistic approach, having a guilty Alex try to tell her sister the truth several times. In what became an iconic scene just two episodes later, Alex breaks. It has torn her apart watching Kara take out her anger about Astra's death on J'onn, even going so far as to walk away from the DEO. She loves her sister too much to keep the truth from her and the pain of being her protector is costing her a surrogate father. In another bravura moment from Leigh, Alex tearfully confesses to Kara that she was the one who killed Astra, fully aware her confession may destroy her relationship with her sister.

What turned that powerful moment into the iconic scene it became was that instead of having Kara lash out in anger and walk away from Alex, the show did the unexpected. Kara forgave Alex, embracing her sobbing sister and then reaching out for J'onn's hand as he tried to slip from the room to give them privacy. It was a powerful moment made even more so by the fact that it was done without dialogue. It takes a great deal of trust for an actor to make themselves as vulnerable as Leigh did in that scene, and it illustrated the trust she placed in Benoist to support her.

The audience sees this trust on display in "Falling," a showcase episode for Melissa Benoist. Under the influence of a synthetic Red Kryptonite, created by Maxwell Lord, Supergirl goes rogue, acting out all her repressed anger and feelings, and lashing out at those closest to her. Kara's most vicious attack was directed toward Alex. In a raw, powerful scene that both actors admit was difficult to film in part because of their off-screen closeness.[25] Kara cruelly reduces Alex to tears telling her they have never been sisters, that Alex would not have a life without her, that Alex never wanted her to acknowledge her powers because deep down she hated her, and that's why she killed Astra.[26] Alex is devastated and fears her sister is gone. Later, as Alex tries to administer an antidote for the Red Kryptonite, Kara physically attacks her, threatening to kill her. Once free of the Red Kryptonite, Kara is filled with remorse and tearfully begs Alex's forgiveness. Alex displays her unconditional love for her sister, telling her she loves her no matter what. While Kara's words have been harsh and hurtful, Alex recognizes that there was an underlying truth to them and admitted that there were things the two sisters needed to work on to strengthen their relationship.

Viewers are later given a glimpse further into their relationship and the sacrifices Alex had made up until this point. It had been obvious from the beginning of the series that Alex was very close to her father. His reported death had devastated her and placed even more of the burden of caring for Kara upon her young shoulders. But as a flashback shows, that responsibility grew to be too much for Alex, and she began drinking and partying, eventually ending up in a drunk tank. And that is when Hank Henshaw stepped into her life and offered her the opportunity to work for the DEO. Hungover and sullen when Hank first makes his offer, Alex blows him off until he mentions her alien sister. Alex goes on alert, sobering immediately, and ready to fight this man who at first seems to be a threat to Kara. So, no matter how resentful she was when the full responsibility of caring for Kara fell on her, she is ready to defend her sister, even behind bars. Hank finally convinces Alex that the best way to protect her sister is to come work for the DEO. This is the first glimpse of the pressures Alex had been under to protect her sister and what she had sacrificed to live up to her parents' wishes. There is a deleted scene from this episode included in the Season 1 DVD/Blu-Ray that shows a young Kara coming to see Alex at her apartment (which ironically is now Kara's apartment). Hungover, she tries to put on a façade that everything is fine as she hides the letter from her school saying she is about to be kicked out of the doctoral program. She must appear strong and in control in front of Kara. This cut scene shows the audience that Alex's pattern of burying her needs and feelings to take care of Kara began early on and remains today. This is obviously not healthy for Alex, but it is at the core of the person: always putting Kara first and in a roundabout way still doing it to seek approval from her parents.

Alex, however, is not the only Danvers capable of making a sacrifice. Kara makes a significant one herself in an episode where Alex and J'onn are arrested for treason and shipped off to the mysterious Cadmus, the equivalent of an alien concentration camp so heinous that it made Superman refuse to work for the government. Desperate to rescue her sister and surrogate father, Kara shows how much Alex means to her by revealing her secret identity to Lucy in exchange for her help. It is also in this episode that viewers learn that Jeremiah Danvers is alive and a prisoner of Cadmus. The sisters now have a common goal: finding their father. However, for the first time all season they must work apart, as Alex is now a fugitive from both the government and Cadmus. As they prepare to leave one another, Kara laments her life without Alex, showing, as Hank had pointed out, that Alex was her hero, and she relied upon her guidance. Alex tells her: "you don't need me, you never did."

At the end of the first season, the Kara and Alex Danvers that appear in "Myriad" and "Better Angels" are different women than those we met in the pilot. Throughout the season, Alex learned to share her little sister with the world and watched with pride as Kara grew into a hero. With the love and support of her sister, Kara embraced her new persona as Supergirl. Their bond grew as well, and the strength of it proved "El Mayarah": the Danvers sisters truly were stronger together. In the first of these two episodes, they were forced to stay apart because of the government search for Alex and J'onn. Kara's uncle, Non, has put humans in National City under a Kryptonian mind-control called Myriad, leaving Kara to face him virtually alone. To protect her sister Supergirl begged Alex to stay in Midvale with their mother, Eliza, where she and J'onn have taken refuge, but Alex is not about to let her sister face Non alone. She convinced J'onn to take her back to National City. But Non found the perfect weapon to fight Supergirl: her sister in a special suit laced with Kryptonite. Supergirl pleaded with Alex to fight the mind-control as she grew weaker from the suit's Kryptonite. The timely arrival of J'onn and Eliza prevented Alex from killing her sister and ultimately, Supergirl and her team are able to disarm Myriad.

The stakes are raised in "Better Angels," when it is discovered that although they had defeated the mind-control, Myriad contains a signal that will kill all life on Earth. The clock ticks as Kara realized she must face Non alone. She knew it would be a suicide mission and one-by-one she says goodbye to those closest to her except for one person: Alex. A wounded J'onn, who insisted on going with her, wondered why she did not tell her sister goodbye. Kara told him that if she has to say goodbye to her sister, she would never leave. That one, almost throwaway line of dialogue summed up just how important Alex was to Kara.

Another impactful moment came when Kara took the necklace her mother had given her before she left Krypton and gave it to Alex, asking her to take care of it for her; such a simple gesture, but so important. Just as her mother, who knew she was about to die, gave Kara the necklace as a remembrance of her love, Kara gave Alex the necklace for the same reason. Blood or not, they were bound as sisters by that necklace. Alex clung to the necklace as if it was her sister. In the episode's most emotional moment, Kara called Alex to tell her goodbye and Alex, clutching tightly to the necklace, tearfully refused to say goodbye.

Leigh and Benoist were not in the same room during the filming of that scene, yet one could feel their connection through the phone line. Both fought back tears, their voices trembling with emotion, Kara says: "[Jeremiah] needs to know everything good I did came from you being my sister!"[27] Alex, in a move just as heroic as her sister's sacrifice in space, took Kara's Kryptonian pod and rescued her. Alex returns the necklace, saying "You saved the world, and then I saved you, in your pod.... You're not the only bad-ass in the family."[28] These two scenes illustrated how these characters and actors, bound together by sisterly love, would and did sacrifice everything for one another.

Season 2: New Network, New City

Many significant changes were brought to the show during the second season of *Supergirl*.[29] For some time, there was doubt that the show would get a second season until, at the last minute, it was announced that the show was moving from the more conservative CBS to the more progressive The CW Network, which is also part-owned by CBS. It was a logical move, as The CW was already the home of several other successful DC superhero shows from executive producer, Greg Berlanti. While *Supergirl* was a better fit for the network, it differed from the other shows with its more optimistic, upbeat tone, and cinematic style. The change also meant that the cast and crew would need to move from Los Angeles to Vancouver, which resulted in the entire cast growing closer together, relying on one another on-screen and off as they worked long hours in an unfamiliar location.[30] It was a creatively positive move for the show. With it came a twenty-two-episode order that meant the show could take its time in developing deeper, richer storylines. This gave the show the opportunity to give each character the time to grow and no two characters had greater growth and development in the second season than the Danvers sisters.[31]

Their bond would become stronger not only on as sisters but also as women. The show's move to the more superhero-friendly and open network allowed the show to take on topics that would illustrate what remarkable women Kara and Alex Danvers were apart from each other, but most importantly, it re-emphasized the fact that they were still stronger together. Some lamented that they missed the couch scenes where the sisters would get together and discuss their day or what they were feeling. But while their actual screen time might have been less, the scenes they had together were of a richer, higher quality.

Alex and Kara went through many changes during the second season. Although she had not lost that joy and enthusiasm at being Supergirl, this season's Kara/Supergirl was a more self-assured and mature character. The near catastrophic events of the first season had left an impact, and she began taking her responsibilities as the Girl of Steel more seriously. She began thinking somewhat more of the consequences of her actions and became better at expressing her feelings to Alex. The two were sisters that deeply cared for one another, but who were not without issues between them to explore and conflicts between them to be resolved. In a Q&A hosted by The CW, Executive Producer Andrew Kreisberg spoke of his first-hand knowledge of this special bond: "Chyler and Melissa love each other so much that they're not worried about fights or people swinging guns or explosion. They get worried about the scenes where they have to fight with each other."[32] The second season was certainly replete with the type of material that the actors worried about the most.

The more complex nature of the Danvers sisters' relationship was explored in this second episode of the season. In the first episode "The Adventures of Supergirl," Kara was delighted when her cousin, Superman (Clark Kent) came to National City. Being her only living blood relative, he could give her insights into living on Earth as a Kryptonian. When Kara abruptly announced that she was considering moving to Metropolis to learn from Clark and no one in National City would have to deal with her anymore, Alex lashed out. In Kara's mind, she thought moving would be good for Alex; her sister would not have to take care of her anymore. But to Alex, this meant that everything she had done for Kara—giving up a medical career, joining the DEO, dedicating her life to protecting her—would have been for naught. In her mind, Kara was abandoning her, choosing her blood family over her adoptive family, even as she ironically reminded Kara that Clark abandoned her to them all those years ago. This was an important moment in the show for several reasons. It was the first time that Alex stood up for herself and also the first time we see her get genuinely angry at her sister. It also gave a hint of resentment at what she had had to give up for her sister. Later, in a sign of Kara's growth and maturity in the season, she sought Alex out to apologize, perhaps for the first time realized just how much Alex has sacrificed for her. She then rushed to rescue Alex who had been captured by Cadmus. The episode later revealed that the sisters were not only stronger together emotionally, but physically as well.

After watching Kara grow into the hero Supergirl had become, Alex began to realize that her little sister could take care of herself and maybe did not need her protection anymore. She began wondering who she was and what was out there for her. It was this journey of self-discovery and that gave *Supergirl* its most critically acclaimed storyline of the season. It was one of the best coming out stories told on television and featured (many believed) award-caliber work from Chyler Leigh,[33] with strong support from Melissa Benoist and Floriana Lima as Maggie Sawyer, Alex's new love interest. The introduction of Detective Maggie Sawyer earlier in the season[34] had a profound impact on Alex. Not only did she have a companion, but Maggie also helped Alex understand the feelings she had been having, ultimately questioning her own sexuality. In "Crossfire," Alex admits to Maggie there is "some truth" to Maggie's words about Alex being attracted to women. We gain insight into how difficult it has been for Alex to always be "perfect": the perfect daughter, the perfect sister, the perfect agent, and how she has hidden that part of herself that she thought was not "perfect."[35] It is an important step for the normally stoic and reserved agent, and one she does not quite fully take to, admitting Maggie was right without ever saying the word "gay."

If one could point to a single episode of the series in its first two seasons that is the definitive example of the power of the Danvers sisters' relationship, it would be "Changing." This was a critically acclaimed episode and contains one of Chyler Leigh's all-time favorite Danvers Sisters scenes: Alex coming out as gay to Kara.[36] This was a landmark episode for the series, which drew praise for its sensitive handling of a coming-out story.[37] Alex's experience was different in that she was a woman in her late twenties just discovering and embracing her sexuality. Reverting to type, she told Maggie that maybe it is just a phase, once again, letting her self-doubt take charge. Thankfully, Maggie told her otherwise, that she deserved a happy life. Maggie's role was to remind Alex that she had a life outside of the DEO, away from Supergirl. For all the bravura and self-confidence that Agent Danvers exudes, Alex Danvers was a mass of insecurities. She had always put others before her own needs, driven by a deep desire within her to always be perfect. This is especially true in watching as the normally confident, self-assured Alex stumbled nervously over her words as she tried to come out to her sister in the park. Leigh masterfully showed Alex's vulnerability and captured that Alex was struggling with her new reality. Again, the bond between the actors as well as the characters made this scene powerful and effective.

And when Kara did not immediately offer her acceptance, the confused and insecure Alex reappeared, threw her walls up and walked away. At first, it seemed that Kara was not accepting of her sister. However, later, in Kara's apartment, we saw a new level of maturity between the sisters. Alex came to her; fearful she had failed again and disappointed her sister. Yet in a moment that signaled a significant shift in the Danvers sisters' relationship, Kara told

Alex she was "so okay" with her being gay and then went on to apologize to her sister.[38] She saw now that since she came into the Danvers family, it had all been about her, even when they were growing up. She apologized for not creating an environment that would have allowed Alex to come talk to her about this.

The sister dynamic at this moment shifts and Alex's and Kara's roles are reversed. Kara became the fierce, mother-hen protector, telling Alex, "You go get the girl."[39] Unfortunately, for the moment, "the girl" did not want Alex, at least not in that way, which devastated Alex's delicate psyche. The result was a tour-de-force moment between two actors who many believe had become one of the strongest on-screen acting partnerships on television.[40] In portraying Alex's emotional breakdown after Maggie's rejection, Leigh gave a remarkably real, raw, and honest piece of acting. As she sat there gasping and sobbing on such a deep level, and Benoist's arms around her, one wonders at what point it went past Kara comforting Alex to Melissa comforting Chyler who had reached depths of despair in her performance rarely seen on television.[41] It was a prime example of Leigh's trust and faith in Benoist's support that she could take her performance to such levels. In lesser hands, the scene could have come across as trite or clichéd. Instead, it was real, honest, and heartbreaking emotion.

Following her first night spent with Maggie, a strange, unusual creature showed up for work at the DEO: a smiling, happy, almost giddy Agent Alex Danvers. And no one is happier for her than her little sister. But when Supergirl went missing, Alex reverted to her protective sister role and almost sabotaged her fragile new relationship with Maggie because she believed she was not allowed to be happy. That this was an example of what had been the norm in her life: anytime she had done something for herself it ended in disaster. After traveling across universes to rescue her sister, she returned to find she wanted to fight for a relationship with Maggie, a clear sign that Maggie was having a positive effect on Alex's self-worth. She learned that Maggie knew Kara was Supergirl and agreed with her that their relationship was worth fighting for, presenting an interesting twist to the Danvers sisters' bond. How was Kara going to feel having to share the big sister she had had all to herself all her life, with someone else?

Since she was adopted by the Danvers family, Kara was used to having much of Alex's attention. Alex was the one she first turned to in order to learn how to navigate her new life on Earth. Now, Alex had someone else, Maggie. While she was happy for her sister, she could not help but be disappointed when Alex asked to postpone her hastily planned "Earth birthday" celebration to attend a concert with Maggie. Kara had not realized what it would mean to her not to have Alex around all the time or that she was going to have to learn to share her now. Alex was learning too, not being used to having much of a life outside of the DEO and Kara, a life that now included time with Maggie.

When they searched for a White Martian together while trapped inside the DEO, the sisters got an opportunity for a heart-to-heart where Kara admitted her anxiety, her fear that Alex was going to abandon her now that she had Maggie.[42] It was an open and honest exchange which expressed a common fear among adoptees: abandonment. This exchange, in particular, and the episode itself again drew the praise of adoption advocate Carrie Goldman: "Adoptees need to talk again and again and again and again about their issues, not just once, and this show is modeling the best way for adoptees to work through their feelings over and over."[43] Some expressed an understandable disappointment that this touching scene was not really between Supergirl and Alex at all after it is revealed that the Alex in that scene was, in a plot twist, a second White Martian that had disguised itself as Alex.[44] The episode was redeemed in the final moments when Alex skipped the concert and goes to her sister bearing an "Earth birthday" cupcake to celebrate. She reassured Kara that due to a psychic bond with the Martian she remembered their conversation and that, even though she was with Maggie now, their sisterhood is still important.

This was especially necessary in the upcoming episodes, "Homecoming and Exodus," where their sisterly bond was tested more than anything before. In an emotional reunion with a rescued Jeremiah Danvers at the DEO, as Alex tearfully hugged her father, as Kara/Supergirl stood off to the side. She saw herself as the outsider, the adopted daughter, and wanted to give Alex, Jeremiah's blood daughter, the chance to welcome her father home, not wanting her presence to spoil this moment for her sister. After all, it had been her arrival that had resulted in Jeremiah's disappearance. As Alex and her father are embracing, she reached out for Kara and pulled her into the emotional hug. This was just one of many times viewers saw moments like this between the sisters, moves or gestures that seemed perfectly normal, but are so natural that viewers often do not know if they are scripted or improvised. Later, the two had a no-holds-barred fight with each other when Kara began having doubts about Jeremiah's loyalty. Both actors did not hold back and were not afraid to go for the jugular in an intense exchange where Alex told Kara, "Because you're either part of the family or you're not!"[45] A stunned Kara replied, "You don't mean that."[46] The story showed how deep the rift between the sisters was after it is discovered that Jeremiah had indeed betrayed his family and was now working for Cadmus, instead of turning to each other, Kara and Alex turned to their new significant others, Mon-El for Kara and Maggie for Alex, for comfort.

In "Exodus," even as their rift widened, Kara again asserted her new role as her big sister's protector. As difficult as was is for her, she backed J'onn suspending Alex from the search for Jeremiah when he escaped from the DEO. We soon learned, however, that their sisterly bond made them stronger than ever. Feeling betrayed by the two people she loved the most, J'onn and Kara, Alex went rogue and tracked her father to Cadmus, ultimately getting trapped on a spaceship full of aliens about to jump to lightspeed halfway across the universe.[47] Earlier, Kara had told Alex that her priorities were skewed, that she needed to be worried more about the aliens that Cadmus had abducted. Yet, at the end of Exodus, as that ship of aliens was about to fly away, Supergirl literally moved heaven and earth, expending all her energy to stop the ship. At that moment, it was not about the aliens on board, it was about saving the most important person in her life: her sister. Kara feared that she cannot do it until Alex, from inside the ship, ignored Kara's primal screams and the fearful look in her eyes, put her hand to the window, and smiled at her sister and told her she can do it.[48] She had unwavering faith in her sister. The end of "Exodus," however, was a missed Danvers Sisters moment because, after the intensity and emotion of that powerful scene, viewers were denied a physical Danvers Sisters reunion and hug that the scene clearly called for.

Following these events, there was a new aspect to the Danvers sister's relationship to consider: Maggie Sawyer. In "Alex," for the first time, the show devoted an episode to the effect of just how strongly the introduction of Maggie had impacted the dynamic between Alex and Kara. Kara and Maggie engage in a battle of wills, as they raced to rescue a kidnapped Alex. There was a line in the episode where the villain wonders aloud: "I wonder which one of you loves her more."[49] And in the end, the answer was that they loved her equally. Initially, Maggie and Kara had been at odds because of the detective's criticism of Supergirl's methods. However, Kara was willing to try with Maggie and responds to her criticism because she and Maggie both were trying to get along out of their love for Alex.

The second season ends with a two-part second season finale of *Supergirl* that does not contain many Danvers sisters' moments; however, the ones it does have are powerful and intense, none more so than the opening scenes of "Resist." The DEO was under attack from Daxamite forces, and Alex, in command since J'onn had been incapacitated by an earlier attack, orders the evacuation of the DEO.[50] Like a good leader, Alex had remained until all her team had escaped and calls Supergirl in for back-up. Supergirl raced to the rescue but knows that she would not arrive before the Daxamite squad overpowered the facility. She told Alex to meet her outside. And in a scene one reviewer calls "the most badass shot Alex has ever had on this show,"[51] Alex ran through the DEO, shooting attackers in her way and in one final dramatic move, turned and leaped off the balcony backward, continuing to fire as she began to fall. If ever there was a moment to illustrate Alex's faith in her sister that was it. She never doubts for a moment that her sister would be there to catch her. It was the ultimate act of blind faith.

It is also telling that Alex is there, splashing through the water of the fountain to support Supergirl following her battle with Superman in the season finale, having had to stand by helplessly and watch her little sister fight toe-to-toe with the Man of Steel. And finally, after the Daxamites are defeated, Alex tried to console her heartbroken sister on the balcony of the DEO, telling her how proud of her she was, echoing her sister's support when she came out. This time, it was Kara that offered the small but more mature act of telling her sister basically to live her life and never let Maggie go. It was clear that the Sisterhood of Steel had grown stronger and further anchored itself as the heart of the Supergirl series in the second season.

In early interviews discussing the show's third season, Kreisberg acknowledged the importance of Kara and Alex's relationship. Showrunners had clearly recognized the strength of the sister's relationship and the positive audience reaction to episodes featuring the two. They took steps to further solidify Supergirl's greatest superpower: the Danvers sisters' relationship when they announced that the show was returning to its roots and planned to make Season 3 more Danvers sisters-centric.[52] *Supergirl*, the series, is fortunate to have two actors that share such a strong and heartwarming personal bond in Melissa Benoist and Chyler Leigh as well as faith in the characters they have created. That bond shows in the strength of the performances in the scenes they share. There is no doubt that Supergirl's greatest superpower is the Sisterhood of Steel.

NOTES

1. Supergirl first appeared in DC *Action Comic* Vol. 1 #252, May 1959: http://dc.wikia.com/wiki/Action_Comics_Vol_1_252.
2. Rick Kissell, "CBS' 'Supergirl' Premiere Ratings Strong: Top New Show of the Fall," http://variety.com/2015/tv/news/supergirl-premiere-ratings-1201626577.
3. See "Sibling Rivalry," http://tvtropes.org/pmwiki/pmwiki.php/Main/SiblingRivalry and Sally
4. For examples, see Jen Stayrook, "'Supergirl': Rainbow Hearts for Everyone in 'Changing,'" November 16, 2016: https://www.theworkprint.com/supergirl-review-changing/123, and Megan Logan, "Why Our Superhero-Hungry World Needs a 'Supergirl' Season 2," May 9, 2016: https://www.inverse.com/article/15389-why-our-superhero-hungry-world-needs-a-supergirl-season-2; "Performers of the Month—October Winner: Outstanding Actress—Chyler Leigh," https://www.spoilertv.com/2016/11/performers-of-month-october-winner.html.
5. CW Upfront Interview with Melissa Benoist, YouTube, June 4, 2016: https://www.YouTube.com/watch?v=1X8GkRiD-Ic; and Leanne Aguilera, "'Supergirl' Melissa Benoist Talks Superman's 'Dream' Debut and How the Danvers Sisters Will Grow," *ET*, October 10, 2016: http://www.etonline.com/tv/199989_exclusive_supergirl_melissa_benoise_season_2_superman_crossover_danvers_sisters.
6. James Hibberd, "'Supergirl': How Melissa Benoist Convinced CBS She Would Fly," *Entertainment Weekly*: http://ew.com/article/2015/09/14/supergirl-3.

Sisterhood of Steel (Cromeans) 175

7. 2016 Chicago Comic & Entertainment Expo 2016, Voice of E, YouTube, March 23, 2016: https://www.YouTube.com/watch?v=wOdrC8i_3aI, 3:20–3:45.

8. 2016 Paley Center Honors Supergirl Panel, Tori Love, YouTube, Jan 3, 2017: https://www.YouTube.com/watch?v=jm5OuXiVp8o&t=517, 8:45.

9. Christian Saclao, "'Supergirl': Chyler Leigh Reveals Why She's Thankful for Melissa Benoist," Yahoo! Sports, November 24, 2016: https://sports.yahoo.com/news/supergirl-chyler-leigh-reveals-why-073642009.html; Alyse Whitney, "Supergirl Melissa Benoist Opens Up About the Pressures of Playing a Female Superhero, from Sexuality to Comic Fans," *Teen Vogue*, October 22, 2015: https://www.teenvogue.com/story/melissa-benoist-supergirl-interview.

10. Ong, "'Supergirl' TV Series: Actress Who Portrays Kara's Sister Says People Should Watch the Show Because of Its Message of Empowerment," *Christianity Daily*, http://www.christianitydaily.com/articles/6970/20151125/supergirl-tv-series-actress-who-portrays-karas-sister-says-people-should-watch-the-show-because-of-its-message-of-empowerment.htm.

11. Carrie Goldman, "An Open Letter to Supergirl Stars Melissa Benoist and Chyler Leigh, from an Adoptive Mom," *Chicago Now*, March 22, 2016: http://www.chicagonow.com/portrait-of-an-adoption/2016/03/an-open-letter-to-supergirl-stars-melissa-benoist-and-chyler-leigh-from-an-adoptive-mom.

12. Goldman, "An Open Letter to Supergirl."

13. *Supergirl*, "Pilot," season 1, episode 1, directed by Glen Winter, story by Greg Berlanti, Ali Adler, and Andrew Kreisberg, teleplay by Ali Adler, aired October 26, 2015, on CBS.

14. *Supergirl*, "Pilot," season 1, episode 1.

15. Chyler Leigh talks about a Chicago fan experience in Meredith Woerner, "'Supergirl' Cast Explains How the Series Affects the Lives of Its Audience, Especially Young Girls," *Los Angeles Times*, October 10, 2016: http://www.latimes.com/entertainment/herocomplex/la-et-hc-supergirl-20161010-snap-story.html.

16. See "Kara and Alex | Danvers Sisters" has 917,000 views as of January 17, 2017: https://www.YouTube.com/watch?v=Hg5vdNcqmvI; and "Kara & Alex | Heartbeats" has 179,000 views as of July 11, 2016 https://www.YouTube.com/watch?v=2o6aik0tUzo.

17. Melissa Dahl, "The Plight of the Older Sibling," *NBC News*, May 5, 2008: http://www.nbcnews.com/id/24397323/ns/health-childrens_health/t/plight-older-sibling/#.WeOx2VtSyUk.

18. This episode aired out of order due to the November 12, 2015, terrorist attack in Paris, see Michael Ausiello, "CBS Replaces Monday's Terrorism-Themed Supergirl, NCIS: Los Angeles Episodes in Wake of Paris Attacks," *TV Line*, November 15, 2015: http://tvline.com/2015/11/15/supergirl-paris-attacks-cbs-schedule.

19. Astra was revealed as Kara's aunt and only surviving member of her immediate family.

20. *Supergirl*, "Livewire," season 1, episode 5, directed by Kevin Tancharoen, story by Roberto Aguirre-Sacasa and Caitlin Parrish, aired March 28, 2016, on CBS.

21. *Supergirl*, "For the Girl Who Has Everything," season 1, episode 13, directed by Dermott Downs, written by Ted Sullivan, Derek Simon, and Andrew Kreisberg, aired February 8, 2016, on CBS.

22. 2016 Chicago Comic & Entertainment Expo 2016.

23. *Supergirl*, "For the Girl Who Has Everything," season 1, episode 13.

24. Francine Russo, "The Science of Siblings," *Parade*, June 22, 2013: https://parade.com/23970/francinerusso/the-science-of-siblings.

25. Nora Dominick, "SDCC 2016: 'Supergirl' Star Chyler Leigh Talks Daddy Danvers, Sisterly Bond with Melissa Benoist & Project Cadmus," *Entertainment Monthly*, July 27, 2016: http://emertainmentmonthly.com/index.php/sdcc-2016-supergirl-star-chyler-leigh.

26. *Supergirl*, "Falling," season 1, episode 16, directed by Larry Teng, written by Robert Rovner and Jessica Queller, aired March 14, 2016, on CBS.

27. *Supergirl*, "Better Angels," season 1, episode 20, directed by Larry Teng, written by Andrew Kreisberg and Ali Adler, teleplay by Robert Rovner and Jessica Queller, aired April 18, 2016, on CBS.

28. *Supergirl*, "Better Angels," season 1, episode 20.

29. Katharine Trendacosta, "It" Official: Season Two of Supergirl Will Be on the CW," Io9, May 12, 2016: https://io9.gizmodo.com/its-official-season-two-of-supergirl-will-be-on-the-cw-1776348480.

30. Christina Radish, "'Supergirl' Season 2: Melissa Benoist Says Superman's Arrival Is a 'Natural Progression,'" *Collider*, October 10, 2016: http://collider.com/supergirl-season-2-melissa-benoist-interview; see also Jeremy Jordan's comment in Meredith Woerner, "'Supergirl' Cast Explains How the Series Affects the Lives of Its Audience."

31. DJ Riter, "Supergirl Growing Stronger on the CW," *Spoiler TV*, March 14, 2017: http://www.spoilertv.com/2017/03/supergirl-growing-stronger-on-cw_13.html

32. Craig Byrne, "'Supergirl': Chyler Leigh and EP Andrew Kreisberg Tease 'Homecoming,' Family Fallout," Collider, February 27, 2017: http://collider.com/supergirl-chyler-leigh-andrew-kreisberg-interview.

33. See Mike Cecchini, "Supergirl Season 2 Episode 6: Changing Review," *Den of Geek*, November 15, 2016: http://www.denofgeek.com/us/tv/supergirl/260048/supergirl-season-2-episode-6-changing-review; Amy West, "Supergirl: Why Alex Danvers' Authentic Coming Out Journey Means So Much to LGBT+ Viewers," *International Business Times*, November 16, 2016: http://www.ibtimes.co.uk/supergirl-why-alex-danvers-authentic-coming-out-journey-means-so-much-lgbt-viewers-1591645; Brian Grubb, "Our Writers Offer Picks for the Best Performances of 2016," *Uproxx*, December 14, 2016: http://uproxx.com/tv/best-tv-performances-2016-uproxx; and Aimee Hicks, "2016 Performer of the Year—Chyler Leigh *Includes Special Message from Chyler*," Spoiler TV, March 11, 2017: https://www.spoilertv.com/2017/03/2016-performer-of-year-chyler-leigh.html.

34. Detective Maggie Sawyer first appears in "Welcome to Earth," season 2, episode 3, directed by Rachel Talalay, written by Jessica Queller and Derek Simon, aired October 24, 2016, on The CW.

35. *Supergirl*, "Crossfire," season 2, episode 5, directed by Glen Winter, written by Gabriel Llanas and Anna Musky-Goldwyn, aired November 7, 2016, on The CW.

36. Damian Holbrook, "Here's Why the Women of 'Supergirl' Hold All the Power," *TV Insider*, September 11, 2017: https://www.tvinsider.com/274373/heres-why-the-women-of-supergirl-hold-all-the-power/

37. Carly Lane, "The Importance of Not Underestimating the CW," *Syfy Wire*, November 28, 2017: http://www.syfy.com/syfywire/importance-not-underestimating-cw and Amy West, "Supergirl: Why Alex Danvers' Authentic Coming Out Journey Means So Much," and Ashley Victoria Robinson, "Alex Danvers Is the Real Supergirl on DCTV," Crave, February 28th, 2017: http://www.craveonline.com/entertainment/1222049-alex-danvers-real-supergirl-dctv.

38. *Supergirl*, "Changing," season 2, episode 6, directed by Larry Teng, story by Greg Berlanti, teleplay by Andrew Kreisberg and Caitlin Parrish, aired November 14, 2016, The CW.

39. *Supergirl*, "Changing," season 2, episode 6.

40. Aimee Hicks, "Performers of the Month—November Winner, Outstanding Actress—Chyler Leigh," Spoiler TV, December 31, 2016: https://www.spoilertv.com/2016/12/performers-of-month-november-winner.html; Carly Lane, "Supergirl Is Best When It Sticks to the Heart of the Show: The Women," *Syfy Wire*, November 28, 2017: http://www.syfy.com/syfywire/supergirl-is-best-when-it-sticks-to-the-heart-of-the-show-the-women; Christian Saclao, "'Supergirl': Chyler Leigh Reveals Why She's Thankful for Melissa Benoist," Kevin Smith comment. Vicki Hyman, "Kevin Smith on Directing 'Supergirl' and Why It Makes Him Regret Being a Man," *NJ*, January 23, 2017: www.nj.com/entertainment/tv/index.ssf/2017/01/kevin_smith_directing_supergirl_lives.html; and Allison Shoemaker, "Supergirl" Recap: Kara Says Goodbye to Season One (And Everyone Else)," *Comic Book Resources*, April 19, 2016: https://www.cbr.com/supergirl-recap-kara-says-goodbye-to-season-one-and-everyone-else.

41. Hicks, "Performers of the Month" and "2016 Performer of the Year."

42. *Supergirl*, "The Martian Chronicles," season 2, episode 11, directed by David McWhirter, written by Gabriel Llanas and Anna Musky-Goldwyn, aired February 6, 2017, on The CW.

43. Carrie Goldman. "Supergirl Deftly Explores Adoptee Abandonment," *Chicago Now*, February 8, 2017: http://www.chicagonow.com/portrait-of-an-adoption/2017/02/supergirl-deftly-explores-adoptee-abandonment.
44. Mike Cecchini, "Supergirl Season 2 Episode 11 Review: The Martian Chronicles," *Den of Geek*, February 8, 2017: http://www.denofgeek.com/uk/tv/supergirl/47135/supergirl-season-2-episode-11-review-the-martian-chronicles.
45. *Supergirl*, "Homecoming," season 2, episode 14, directed by Larry Teng, written by Jerry Siegel, aired February 27, 2017, on The CW.
46. *Supergirl*, "Homecoming," season 2, episode 14.
47. *Supergirl*, "Exodus," season 2, episode 15, directed by Michael Allowitz, written by Paula Yoo and Eric Carrasco, aired March 6, 2017, on The CW.
48. *Supergirl*, "Exodus," season 2, episode 15.
49. *Supergirl*, "Alex," season 2, episode 19, directed by Rob Greenlea, written by Eric Carrasco and Greg Baldwin, aired May 1, 2017, on The CW.
50. *Supergirl*, "Resist," season 2, episode 21, directed by Millicent Shelton, story by Jessica Queller and Derek Simon, aired May 15, 2017, on The CW.
51. Teresa Jusino, "Supergirl Recap: Cat Grant Returns to Remind National City to "Resist," *The Mary Sue*, May 16, 2017: https://www.themarysue.com/supergirl-recap-s2-ep21.
52. Natalie Abrams, "Spoiler Room: Scoop on Supergirl, Arrow, the Good Place and More," *Entertainment Weekly*, September 7, 2017: http://ew.com/tv/2017/09/07/spoiler-room-supergirl-arrow-good-place.

Selected Bibliography

Abrams, Natalie. "Spoiler Room: Scoop on Supergirl, Arrow, the Good Place and More." *Entertainment Weekly* (online), September 7, 2017. http://ew.com/tv/2017/09/07/spoiler-room-supergirl-arrow-good-place.
Aguilera, Leanne. "Exclusive: Supergirl, Melissa Benoist Talks About Superman's 'Dream' Debut and How the Danvers Sisters Will Grow Stronger." *ETOnline*. October 10, 2016. http://www.etonline.com/tv/199989_exclusive_supergirl_melissa_benoise_season_2_superman_crossover_danvers_sisters.
Ausiello, Michael. "CBS Replaces Monday's Terrorism-Themed Supergirl, NCIS: LA Episodes in Wake of Paris Attacks." TVLine.com, November 15, 2015. http://tvline.com/2015/11/15/supergirl-paris-attacks-cbs-schedule.
Burt, Kayti. "Supergirl Season 2 Episode 21 Review: Resist." *Den of Geek*, May 16, 2017. http://www.denofgeek.com/us/tv/supergirl/264817/supergirl-season-2-episode-21-review-resist.
Byrne, Craig. "Supergirl: Chyler Leigh and EP Andrew Kreisberg Tease 'Homecoming,' Family Fallout." *Collider* (online), February 27, 2017. http://collider.com/supergirl-chyler-leigh-andrew-kreisberg-interview/#images.
Cecchini, Mike. "Supergirl Season 2 Episode 6: Changing Review." *Den of Geek*, November 15, 2016. http://www.denofgeek.com/us/tv/supergirl/260048/supergirl-season-2-episode-6-changing-review.
_____. "Supergirl Season 2 Episode 11 Review: The Martian Chronicles." *Den of Geek*, February 8, 2017. http://www.denofgeek.com/uk/tv/supergirl/47135/supergirl-season-2-episode-11-review-the-martian-chronicles.
Cromeans, Donna J. "Supergirl Growing Stronger on the CW." *SpoilerTV*, March 14. 2017. http://www.spoilertv.com/2017/03/supergirl-growing-stronger- on-CW_13.html.
Dahl, Melissa. "The Plight of the Older Sibling." *NBCNews* (Children's Health), Today.com (with video), May 5, 2008. http://www.nbcnews.com/id/24397323/ns/health-childrens_health/t/plight-older-sibling/#.WeOx2VtSyUk.
Dominick, Nora. "Supergirl Star Chyler Leigh Talks Daddy Danvers, Sisterly Bond with Melissa Benoist and Project Cadmus." San Diego Comic Con, *Entertainment Monthly* (online). July 27, 2016. http://emertainmentmonthly.com/index.php/sdcc-2016-super girl-star-chyler-leigh/.

Goldman, Carrie. "An Open Letter to Supergirl Stars Melissa Benoist and Chyler Leigh from an Adoptive Mom." BLOG-Portrait of an Adoption. *ChicagoNow*. March 22, 2016. http://www.chicagonow.com/portrait-of-an-adoption/2016/03/an-open-letter-to-supergirl-stars-melissa-benoist-and-chyler-leigh-from-an-adoptive-mom/.

_____. "Supergirl Deftly Explores Adoptee Abandonment." BLOG-Portrait of an Adoption. *ChicagoNow*. February 8, 2017. http://www.chicagonow/portrait-of-an-adoption/2017/02/supergirl-deftly-explores-adoptee-abandonment.

Grubb, Brian. "Our Writers Offer Picks for the Best Performances of 2016." *Uproxx*. December 14, 2016. http://uproxx.com/tv/best-tv-performances-2016-uproxx.

Hibberd, James. "How Melissa Benoist Convinced CBS She Could Fly." *Entertainment Weekly* (online). September 14, 2015. http://ew.com/article/2015/09/14/supergirl-3.

Hicks, Aimee. "Performers of the Month—October Winner: Outstanding Actress—Chyler Leigh." *SpoilerTV*. November 16, 2016. http://www.spoilertv.com/2016/11/performers-of-month-october-winner.html.

_____. "Performers of the Month—November Winner: Outstanding Actress—Chyler Leigh." *SpoilerTV*, December 31, 2016. http://www.spoilertv.com/2016/12/performers-of-month-november-winner.html.

_____. "2016 Performer of the Year—-Chyler Leigh—*Includes Special Message from Chyler." *SpoilerTV*, March 11, 2017. http://www.spoilertv.com/2017/03/2016-performer-of-year-chyler-leigh.html.

Holbrook, Damian. "Here's Why the Women of Supergirl Hold All the Power." *TVInsider*. September 11, 2017. https://www.tvinsider.com/274373/heres-why-the-women-of-supergirl-hold-all-the-power.

Hyman, Vicki. "NJ.com Kevin Smith on Directing Supergirl and Why It Makes Him Regret Being a Man." *NJ Advance Media*. January 23, 2017. http://nj.com/entertainment/tv/index.ssf/2017/01/kevin_smith_directing_supergirl_lives.html.

Jusino, Teresa. "Supergirl Recap: Cat Grant Returns to Remind National City to 'Resist.'" *The Mary Sue*. May 16, 2017. https://themarysue.com/supergirl-recap-s2-ep21.

Kissell, Rick. "CBS' Supergirl Premiere Ratings Strong: Top New Show of the Fall." *Variety* (online). October 27, 2015. http://variety.com/2015/tv/news/supergirl-premiere-ratings-1201626577.

Lane, Carly. "The Importance of Not Underestimating the CW." *Syfywire*. November 28, 2018. http://www.syfy.com/syfywire/importance-not-underestimating-cw.

_____. "Supergirl Is Best When It Sticks to the Heart of the Show." *Syfywire*. November 27, 2018. http://www.syfy.com/syfywire/supergirl-is-best-when-it-sticks-to-the-heart-of-the-show-the-women.

Logan, Megan. "Why Our Superhero-Hungry World Needs a Supergirl Season 2." *Inverse Entertainment*. May 9, 2016. https://www.inverse.com/article/15389-why-our-superhero-hungry-world-needs-a-supergirl-season-2.

Ong, Sally. "Supergirl TV Series Actress Who Portrays Kara's Sister Says People Should Watch the Show Because of Its Message of Empowerment," *Christianity Daily* (online), November 25, 2015. http://www.christianitydaily.com/articles/6970/20151125/supergirl-tv-series-actress-who-portrays-karas-sister-says-people-should-watch-the-show-because-of-its-message-of-empowerment.htm.

Radish, Christina. "Supergirl Season 2: Melissa Benoist Says Superman's Arrival Is a Natural Progression." *Collider* (online), October 10, 2016. http://collider.com/supergirl-season-2-melissa-benoist-interview.

Robinson, Ashley Victoria. "Alex Danvers Is the Real Supergirl on DCTV," *Crave* (online), February 28, 2017. http://www.craveonline.com/entertainment/1222049-alex-danvers-real-supergirl-dctv.

Russo, Francine. "The Science of Siblings." *Parade Magazine* (online), June 22, 2013. https://parade.com/23970/francinerusso/the-science-of-siblings.

Saclao, Christian. "'Supergirl': Chyler Leigh Reveals Why She's Thankful for Melissa Benoist," *Yahoo Sport-International Business Times*, November 24, 2016. https://sports.yahoo.com/news/supergirl-chyler-leigh-reveals-why-073642009.html.

Shoemaker, Allison. "Supergirl Recap: Kara Says Goodbye to Season One (and Everyone

Else)." *Comic Book Resources*. April 19, 2016. http://www.cbr.com/supergirl-recap-kara-says-goodbye-to-season-one-and-everyone-else/.

Siegel, Katherine. "Supergirl Review: 'Pilot' (Episode 1.01)." *Paste Magazine*. October 27, 2015. https://www.pastemagazine.com/articles/2015/10/supergirl-review-pilot.html

Stayrook, Jen. "Supergirl: Rainbow Hearts for Everyone in 'Changing.'" *The Workprint*. November 16, 2016. https://www.theworkprint.com/supergirl-review-changing/123

Trendacosta, Katherine. "It's Official: Season Two of Supergirl Will Be on the CW." *io9*. May 12, 2016. https://io9.gizmodo.com/its-official-season-two-of-supergirl-will-be-on-the-cw-1776348480.

West, Amy. "Supergirl: Why Alex Danvers' Authentic Coming Out Journey Means So Much to LGBT+ Viewers." *International Business Times*. November 2016. http://www.ibtimes.co.uk/supergirl-why-alex-danvers-authentic-coming-out-journey-means-so-much-lgbt-viewers-1591645.

Whitney, Alyse. "Supergirl Melissa Benoist Opens Up About the Pressures of Playing a Female Superhero, from Sexuality to Comic Fans." *Teen Vogue* (online). October 12, 2015. https://www.teenvogue.com/story/melissa-benoist-supergirl-interview.

Woerner, Meredith. "Supergirl Cast Explains How the Series Affects the Lives of Its Audience, Especially Young Girls." *Los Angeles Times* (online with video). October 10, 2016. http://www.latimes.com/entertainment/herocomplex/la-et-hc-supergirl-20161010-snap-story.html.

"Women of power and the mothers who molded them"
Matriarchal Mentorship and Symbols of Sisterhood in Supergirl

Courtney Lee Weida

As an educator and researcher, I observe the prevalence of comic books and related representations of women throughout recent graphica-inspired television with rapt interest. Comic book researcher Mike Madrid notes enduring conditions among female superheroes' depictions in popular culture, in which most are called "girls" rather than acknowledged as women, and many are associated with lesser power and prestige than male counterparts. Yet, Madrid maintains that these female heroes are also idealized and goddess-like, for their efforts are remarkably more concerned with the complexities of improving humanity rather than merely besting foes.[1] Perhaps Supergirl, lesser-known cousin of Superman, is a primary example of these predicaments and possibilities. In a recent show airing first on CBS (2015–2016) and then The CW (2016–present), the *Supergirl* series presents viewers with an array of compelling mythic female characters beyond its iconic lead. Like other recent superhero shows focused on women such as *Agent Carter* (2015–2016) or *Jessica Jones* (2015–2019), and even contemporary series centered on male protagonists, *Supergirl* handily passes the Bechdel test for meaningful dialogue by female characters.[2]

Just as Supergirl/Kara and her friends frame Supergirl's story as the untold counterpart to Superman's legacy, their experiences also highlight the message that there are many female leaders: multiple women who qualify as heroic in their various roles and responsibilities. Catherine "Cat" Grant, Kara's boss and mentor, repeatedly asserts herself as "the hero" of the world of news and even claims to be the "Queen of all media." Cat also dubs Kara "Supergirl,"[3] claims control of Supergirl's narrative within CatCo media, and later even expresses her desire to adopt Supergirl. In turn, Kara reflects that Cat is an integral part of Supergirl: acknowledging the consistent wisdom, mentoring, and support Grant provides both Kara and Supergirl results in a sort of collaboration. In a very real sense, the influence of myriad news media at CatCo inspires Kara's heroism, from immediate heroic responses to danger viewed in news reports, to deeper rumination on the roles of heroes gleaned from editorials and analyses from Cat and other colleagues.

Kara's budding brand of heroism offers a particular sense of collaboration and community throughout the series so far, perhaps stemming from a yearning to belong since her girlhood separation from Krypton and biological family. She notes a contrast between her own approach and that of Superman, observing how she does not wish to be a solitary hero like Superman, but rather to openly collaborate with her friends, family, and colleagues. Supergirl's beginnings as Kara Zor-El (sent to Earth with Superman) also reveal an interesting twist on the superhero origin story. Unlike her cousin, Kara is sent to Earth as a thirteen-year-old, a teen whose development becomes arrested by prolonged suspended animation while her infant cousin is adopted, matures, and becomes a famed superhero on Earth. Oddly enough, while Clark's rare appearances on the show include archaic sayings hearkening to the past, adult Kara is more immersed in Earth's contemporary popular culture in terms of language, music, and food preferences, including affinities for fast food like pizza, popular television such as *Homeland*, and women in contemporary American politics. Though both Clark and Kara work in media, perhaps because adolescent Kara was also a girl trapped in time and between lives, she grows into an alien refugee who is well-versed in Kryptonian culture as well as Earth customs. Kara's evolving identities as both Danvers and Supergirl strongly reflect her relationships and the shifting roles and definitions of women and heroism in National City. This essay will outline these iconic female characters and analyze their relationships within the first two seasons of *Supergirl*.

My analysis will center on the inner circle of Kara's female family members and mentors who are privy to her three identities as Danvers, Supergirl, and Zor-El. The trinity of her identities is reflected in her work as a sort of first, second, and third shift within the show. Specifically, Kara works not only as an aspiring human journalist, but also moonlights as a superhero, and thirdly serves as an informal consultant with the DEO (Department of Extranormal Operations), a *Men in Black*–like government organization where her sister is an agent and sometimes interim/acting director. Within this essay, I contextualize *Supergirl* as a collection of valuable narratives and symbolism centered on women's identities, ethics of leadership, and practices of care, offering comparisons to related feminist superhero stories and ancient mythology. From my perspective, it is valuable to locate Supergirl in this way: not only as a subversive gender representation among superheroes, but also as part of a legacy of lesser known narratives and images of female strength.

Establishing the Female Superhero as Mythic Muse and Goddess

So far, Supergirl has been steeped in subtle and overt references to ancient mythology. Markers of horns and wings are juxtaposed early on in the show as a binary classification of National City's aliens, posing the flying figures as either devils or as angels. For example, Kara appears in angelic white within flashbacks to Krypton, whereas her aunt Astra is clad in black as she plots against humans. So too, Lena Luthor often wears either bright white or black in contrast with her surroundings as a sort of juxtaposition that mirrors her outsider nature and her moral quandaries. Further, Kara's first heroic, public act of flight and strength as Supergirl occurs before her friend Winn crafts her Superman-like costume. She appears in dark clothing, first dampened by rain and then illuminated by flame, looking like more of an elemental force than a superhero or villain (neither angel nor devil, but perhaps goddess). Supergirl is also classified as a sort of guardian angel, and repeatedly noted as inspiration to humanity to heed its "better angels."[4] Similarly, the heavens and stars also feature as a frequent theme, with Supergirl as someone who might "touch the stars."[5] Young Kara had also studied the stars under her aunt Astra's teachings on Krypton, and she still loves space as an adult. Later, in season 2, Kara's friend Winn, a colleague at both CatCo and the DEO, dates an alien named Lyra (whose name references both the brightest star in a constellation as well as Greek mythology).

Other mythic references from Greco-Roman traditions abound in *Supergirl*. Cadmus, a shadowy research organization led by Lex Luthor's mother, Lillian Luthor, creates villainous man-and-machine cyborgs, enhanced with artificial alien elements, such as synthetic kryptonite. The name Cadmus intentionally hearkens back to the Greek king who fought monsters and even opposed the god, Zeus. Cadmus himself, like the cyborg creations of the organization bearing his name, was a sort of hybrid of god and mortal ancestry. Meanwhile, Medusa is a more well-known female figure from mythology. Her name is invoked in *Supergirl* as a virus created by Kara's father as an emergency measure in times of invasion or war to eradicate alien life on Krypton. In Cadmus' hands, the files on the virus are used to actually create a virus against all aliens on Earth. Realizing the deadly nature of the virus and the implications of engineering it, Kara awakened to the monstrousness of her own father, making the myth a foreboding and appropriate name for the project.

Other mythical references are more positive than associations with Cadmus and Medusa. Kara's boss and mentor Cat Grant's offices at CatCo feature massive colorful panther statues that evoke both her name and the mythical creatures Dionysus rode. Cat's frequent references to actual actors and actors from Hollywood and real politicians also lend her a sense of knowledge and broken fourth wall otherworldliness between the universe of National City and our world as viewers. Her mentions of Hollywood often involve comparisons between Supergirl characters and *The X Files*' Agent Mulder or James Bond, or refer to real or fictional relationships with popular actors such as Jennifer Lawrence. Cat also reveals her entrée into journalism involved her keen perception about and failure to reveal a famed actor was an abusive (and later murderous) spouse. It is Cat's perceptive observation into the world of Supergirl that enables her to guess Kara's identity as Supergirl without being told. Further, besides calling herself the "queen" of her media empire and beyond, Cat claims to be a more goddess-like "muse to the world," perhaps a sort of human Calliope or Clio. Notably, the original Greco-Roman muses were goddesses and the sources of humanity's literature. Nearly all of the heroes of National City prize forms of writing as an ultimate vocation, enshrining creativity itself. Writing histories and record-keeping through journalism and photojournalism are the shared practices and noble occupations of Kara, Cat, James Olsen, Snapper Clark, and Clark Kent. Cat's estranged mother is a novelist as well. Further, additional literary references include villainous characters such as Maxwell Lord's quoting of *Prometheus Unbound* and Lillian Luthor's references to Nietzsche.

While both Superman and Supergirl share overlapping double identities in journalism and in heroics, Supergirl initially suffers under the watchful eye of a particularly critical audience within the news media, public commentary, and government personnel. Frequently anxious about public perceptions and feeling "defined by my victories and my losses."[6] Kara is initially consumed by a particularly self-conscious sense of herself, related to her fears of how others will see her. This phenomenon is described by Berger as a difficult condition of women plagued by a sort of double surveillance of watching themselves being observed by men.[7] Kara's consciousness of the watchful eye of others is amplified by her daytime job in media and frequent exposure to footage about herself as Supergirl. Further, the show also suggests that Supergirl is being treated differently on the basis of her gender or that she fears she may be: from DEO trainings, to government requests, to news media criticisms ranging from her tights and sexuality to any imperfections in her tactical approaches in saving human lives. Notably, Kara's favorite image of herself (in the midst of media saturated with her likeness) is where she has temporarily lost her superpowers and successfully appeals to the humanity of criminals who could actually kill her due to her weakened state, while Cat is concurrently broadcasting an appeal to her viewers to be heroic.[8] This moment represents her synchrony and collaboration with Cat, as well as a merging of her superhero self and her powerless human persona. Toward the end of season one, Supergirl also draws on her voice over her might, inspired by Cat to employ a powerful broadcast to speak directly to National City's people and break the hold of Myriad's mind control. These moments represent shifts in her concepts of identity and heroism, allowing her to frame her own narrative.

Additionally, the show's focus on writings and media, of creators and creations could also be seen as part of a greater legacy for us as readers and viewers, given the growing longevity of superheroes. With Superman originally imagined and written with DC Comics in the 1930s,[9] yet still represented as youthful in contemporary mythologies, superheroes take on immortal qualities of gods and goddesses. Just as humans preserve superheroes across generations by reading, writing, and creating television shows about them, superheroes offer us a sort of parallel longevity and love by serving as enduring symbols of protection for our very humanity. Further, Kara's status as a best friend to Lena Luthor is sealed with the similar promise to "always" be her friend and protector. J'onn J'onzz makes a nearly identical protective promise to Jeremiah with regards to the care-taking of Kara and Alex. He also promises to always protect M'Gann. Even Cat pledges to Kara that she will always have a job with her and admits Kara has become the "best assistant" she's ever had, which is the closest to a proclamation of eternal love and commitment that may be possible from Cat. These parental promises and practices of eternal protection are linked with memory and written record: Supergirl's legacy as a hero is initiated and maintained by her public acts of saving and protecting human beings who will in turn record and remember her.

Heart of a Hero: United by Blood, United by Love

Kara contributes to literature as a journalist, and she acts as a researcher both within her writing roles and her work as Supergirl, perusing Kryptonian documents via a hologram interface of her mother's records. As part of a maternal trinity of influences, Kara's biological mother, Alura, appears in memories and through historical record via artificial intelligence, while her adoptive human mother, Eliza, serves as a human protector, and her aunt,

Alura's identical twin Astra, once acted as a surrogate mother to Kara. As a trinity of maternal figures, each of these characters represents and inhabits different spaces that have served as home to Kara: Krypton, her hometown on Earth, and National City. Along these lines, her multiple mother figures could be realized in a triple goddess matriarchal configuration of the *maiden* aunt (Astra), biological *mother* (Alura), and wise *crone* (Eliza). With her background as a powerful Kryptonian judge, Alura might be associated with the Greek goddess, *Themis*, a goddess of divine law, righteousness, and justice. Further, mirroring Alura and Kara, Themis had a daughter who also personified justice but with a focus on human matters. Themis' sister, *Phoebe*, is like Alura's sister Astra in that Phoebe possesses oracular powers, just as Astra accurately foretold the fall of Krypton, and just as Cat is a sort of mother/mentor to Supergirl and muse. Eliza, as a gifted scientist and caring mother, could be seen as akin to *Urania*: a muse of science who is also associated with love.

Supergirl's family members and family records stand in stark contrast with Superman's substantially smaller support system and his isolated fortress of solitude, a family memorial and resource space in a remote location where he seeks knowledge of Krypton and beyond. Supergirl's headquarters are arguably the DEO where a hologram of her mother is housed, to a lesser extent in storage closets at CatCo, and most frequently in her own warm apartment where pizza, potstickers, and conversations with her family and friends accompany her superhero strategy sessions. Her apartment is fittingly airy with several floor to ceiling windows and curtains blowing in the wind, often illuminated by fairy-lights and glowing jars that evoke flight. Supergirl's aura of warmth and light carries into the cold space of the fortress of solitude, a space Kara typically accesses in the presence of various companions, which markedly alters the solitary name and impenetrable/undisturbed quality of the fortress.

Kara's relational approach to life and work is so exhaustive that she shares nearly every aspect of her life with others. While her biological mother is the identical twin of Astra, Kara is also symbolically a sort of double to her own adoptive sister, who she spends a great deal of time with at the DEO and during leisure time. Her sister "from another planet," Alex Danvers, is her confidant, protector, and colleague. They often appear as equals and mirror reflections of one another, particularly through juxtaposed simultaneous fighting sequences, and Alex is called a hero almost as frequently as Supergirl. Alex first characterizes Kara's identification as Supergirl as "coming out," which indirectly mirrors both Alex's subsequent coming out to her mother about her work as a DEO agent and her coming out later as gay. Kara's friends from CatCo, James and Winn, attempt to come out as the team behind new hero Guardian to Kara on the same night that Alex wishes to tell her mother she is gay. Closets frequently figure as secret and often sexual spaces between work and home in *Supergirl*. Both Winn and Mon-El engage in trysts with women in a CatCo supply closet on two separate occasions and interrupted by Kara, and Supergirl slipped away to meet Winn and James in a different CatCo storage space to strategize plans. In some ways, since many of Kara's friends and family are already aware of her superhero identity, the closet is less of a secret space for Kara's own coming out and more a symbol of her awakening/awareness of sexuality in herself and others. In fact, her blurred transformations on screen suggest much of her changing from Kara to Supergirl takes place publicly in super-fast motion, rather than within a closet or other hiding space. These closet spaces act instead as liminal, transitional spaces on the threshold of various relationships and identities, and they expand on Superman's iconic phone booth as changing space with a more makeshift and communal quality.

Transition is a common theme for both Kara and Alex. As heroes, both sisters are often torn between work and family spaces and alliances, with different family and cultural loyalties leading to both Alex's suspension from the DEO and Kara's dismissal as a journalist at CatCo. However, as Kara is an alien adoptee and Alex is a human daughter, there was originally some discord and competition between the two within their Earth family. As Alex bemoans to their mother, Eliza, Kara risks her life to protect others and is "a hero," but when she does the same, she is "in trouble." However, the sisters' destinies become more clearly intertwined, as Eliza suggests, "Take care of your sister; take care of yourself," a saying that would seem to evoke a catchphrase from NBC's 2006–2010 *Heroes*: "Save the cheerleader, save the world."[10] Rather than depicting one sister as a savior and the other as a victim, *Supergirl* highlights the sisters' mutual protection of one another and their deepened friendship as adults: a sisterhood that reflects growth and maturity.

Additionally, DEO Director J'onn J'onzz serves as a surrogate father and protector to both Alex and Kara, for her allegedly deceased father asked J'onzz to fulfill this role as his dying wish. J'onzz becomes close to both Alex and Kara, sharing his superhero/alien identity with them, and noting that while he tragically lost his biological daughters and fathering others can never be quite the same, "any man would be glad to call you his daughters."[11] In this way, Alex and Kara are the core of two different symbolic family units in which their sisterhood is a constant. When Alex eventually meets Astra, they grapple with their own connections and alliances pertaining to Kara, while Astra poses a sort of syllogism: "If she is your sister, and I am her aunt, what does that make us?"[12] These kinds of questions of surrogacy and symbolism reverberate with other biological, blended, and adopted family relationships throughout the series, causing Kara to alter her Kryptonian proverb of "blood bonds us all" to become "love bonds us all."[13]

The sisters' sense of deep bond echoes the ethics of heroism and care from other female superhero stories, such as *Buffy the Vampire Slayer* (1997–2003) and Buffy's adopted sister, Dawn. The sisterhood bond is held above all other considerations in both series. Further, linguistic similarities to BTVS's creator Joss Whedon's world pop up throughout the *Supergirl* series thus far seemingly as a sort of homage, with invented superhero adjectives like "killy,"[14] and an episode where Supergirl mocks her foes by taunting: "blah, blah" in a very Buffy-esque manner. References to epically failed Thanksgiving dinners tainted by supernatural disturbances are mentioned in both BTVS[15] and *Supergirl*[16] demonstrating the attempts and extreme challenges of work life balance for female superheroes. Finally, the growing urban underworld of National City throughout the second season mirrors the demon haunts of Whedon's 1999–2004 BTVS spin-off, *Angel*. Against this seedy backdrop, actor Dichen Lachman (recognizable to fans from two of Whedon's series: *Dollhouse* 2009–2010 and *Agents of Shield* 2013–present) also appears as an intriguing recurring villain, Veronica Sinclair (Roulette), on *Supergirl*.

Also like BTVS, the thematic constant of a special bond between sisters Kara and Alex is developed through heroism and superpowers. Within an iconic flashback to their childhood, Kara first uses her super ability to fly from Earth through the night sky with Alex, providing viewers a rare and powerful tribute to girlhood bonding and childhood fantasy come true. This soaring imagery is a unique representation of two young women wielding magic and power with delight and as a shared bond. Compared with familiar boy-dominated imagery of flight from *Harry Potter* to *E.T.* or even Superman's often-recreated flying scenes with Lois Lane, this imagery is striking for young women viewers as the blending of sisterly love and magic. Further, this flight is a symbol of forged family, a symbolic sisterhood across cultures. It is also notable as the first shared flight scene in the series, with a training sequence of J'onn J'onzz as the second, and a brief collaboration with Superman as the third. Kara shares her gift of flight as an act of family love and collaboration.

Superhero Powers: Personal, Political and Patriotic

Beyond Kara and Alex's remarkable lives as strong female characters, additional women figure as powerful heroic symbols and historic references for *Supergirl's* storytelling, such as 2016 presidential candidate Hillary Clinton. Clinton's campaign message: "stronger together" echoes in the series as a guiding message in the script.[17] Cat Grant also compares her sparring with a female subordinate employee to earlier disputes about Clinton's first presidential run: "you and I got through your not supporting Hillary in 2008; we can get through this."[18] Later, Cat's emails are hacked and publicly released, resulting in a near collapse of her career that might be reminiscent of Clinton's email server controversy as well. Other episode titles like "Nevertheless she persisted"[19] reference Massachusetts Senator Elizabeth Warren's refusal to be silenced on the senate floor. The world of *Supergirl* even features a female U.S. president whose voice, gestures, and pantsuit-like clothing are all somewhat reminiscent of Hillary Clinton. For viewers, these cameos from the 1970s *Wonder Woman*, Lynda Carter, and Teri Hatcher (who played Lois Lane in *Lois & Clark: The New Adventures of Superman*), also evoke a legacy of female strength and community that permeates the show.

The fictional female President Marsdin is also revealed to be an alien refugee, who has lived on earth for many years and exhibits a goddess-like quality of strength and perseverance when she survives a plane crash. Eternal life or extended life takes on provocative potential in politics, where a politician might benefit from years of historical and political study before becoming a candidate. Politically, the president makes a monumental gesture toward granting intergalactic aliens U.S. citizen rights within an executive order.[20]

Relating back to literature, Marsdin is a talented orator, and Supergirl is often in awe of her speeches and sayings. Like Marsdin, Kara identifies strongly with the U.S., though both are aliens. Kara characterizes her superhero identity as particularly and unabashedly American, noting she is the "personification of the American way."[21] Kara also worries about a central concern of many Western women, of balancing work and life. Her mentor, Cat, dismisses this issue to be "the most annoying question of the century," yet she continues to offer Kara anecdotes and advice about the difficulties of juggling a calling, a career, and the possibility of romantic relationships and motherhood.[22] Cat also observes that too many women burn out when trying to do too much, a concern Kara struggles with as well. Supergirl later recommends the show *Call the Midwife* to Maxwell Lord, a 2012–2018 PBS series based on a midwife's memoirs during the 1950–1960s that often celebrates the strength of ordinary women and mothers in childbirth, which also might suggest Kara's potential interest in motherhood. Yet, Supergirl rejects simplistic assumptions about gender and family publicly, observing to Cat during a news interview (appearing as Supergirl) that no one ever asks her cousin about plans to start a family. Kara similarly notes that her own biological mother sent her to earth not to acquire "love, children … or a white picket fence" but rather for the protection of Kal El, and now Earth.[23]

Another convention of women's experiences in television shows encompasses the make-over trope.[24] Instead of more traditional dressing room shots, Kara's first date outfit with James is preceded by a montage of flashes of super quick changes. She also dons a Vera Wang wedding dress within an imp-induced hallucination, performing the possibility of becoming a bride.[25] Kara's refusal to marry the magical imp, Mr. Mxyzptlk and her prowess in tricking him into leaving Earth results in his childish retort that she is a "nasty woman." This particular insult would seem to reference Hillary Clinton again within the final presidential debate in which the same insult was leveled, as well as a longer tradition of "nasty woman" as feminist rallying cry.[26] This epithet also juxtaposes a desirable woman with one who refuses a relationship. The "nasty woman" comment is later used toward media personality-turned-villain, Livewire.[27] In the same episode, Livewire points out her observation of sexism among not only male villains but also male vigilantes, sardonically noting, "I love little boys who think they can do a better job than the woman who's an actual superhero." Supergirl's world reveals sexism as one of the greatest threats to humans and aliens, superheroes and villains alike across the galaxy.

Missing Mothers: Mentored/Mothered in Krypton and Beyond

In addition to presenting sexism, *Supergirl* often offers viewers complex models of motherhood and matriarchy. Nearly all of Supergirl's heroic actions are collaborative leadership efforts with other women and select male allies, as she notes, "I save the world better when I save it with people."[28] Notably, Cadmus plans its major attack for when Superman has chosen to leave Supergirl, as they believe that the two will be weaker apart. Kara and Supergirl rely most heavily on the advice and support of boss and mentor, Cat Grant. To my ears, Cat's frequent mispronunciation of Kara's name as "Ker-Rah" has a striking auditory similarity with "She-Ra," a 1980s warrior princess cartoon. This notion might be supported by the title of an article Kara proposes to Lena Luthor: "Women of Power and the Mothers Who Molded Them," which evokes She Ra's epithet: Princess of Power.

Just as Kara's biological mother offers her the advice to "Find your way back to the brave girl you always were,"[29] Cat recalls that she too has always seen the potential in Kara. Cat proves this fact by producing Kara's original resume on which she had scrawled the word "reporter" during their first meeting. The theme that mentors and mothers alike truly see us carries on from season 1 into season 2, in which Cat acknowledges she actually knows Supergirl is Kara.[30] Cat consistently mentors Supergirl as well as Kara, offering criticism of her for having little to say as a new superhero, and yet subtly praising her earnestness, and offering Kara a brief hug and reminding her she is "smart, talented, and astonishing."[31] Cat insists that her employees refrain from critiquing Supergirl on the basis of her body or sexuality, suggesting a particular journalistic integrity, as well as protective tendency toward Supergirl. Cat even forbids her own mother from criticizing Kara as her assistant, which is the only time she actually stands up to her mother.[32] Cat even helps to encourage and redeem Supergirl when she is under the influence of Red Kryptonite and the public loses faith in her as well.[33]

This point of reckoning in the show is somewhat jarring, as Kara increasingly acts out angrily in all spheres of her life with lowered inhibitions and no restraint. She has been unknowingly corrupted by Red Kryptonite developed by Maxwell Lord. Under the increasing influence of this kryptonite, Kara appears as Supergirl to Cat. Cat is understandably worried about Supergirl's behavior and offers support and a referral for psychiatric medication. Threatened by this perceptive comment, Supergirl throws Cat off the side of a building and catches her a few feet from the pavement, barely saving her from death. Cat is visibly pained and later issues a warning to the public to be careful of Supergirl, describing Supergirl's actions as a type of "fall," in fact interpreting her own literal fall at Supergirl's hands as a moral fall from grace. Then Cat comforts Supergirl once she is restored to health and suggests that Supergirl can work to regain the trust of others.

It should be noted that many of Kara's extreme actions while affected by Red Kryptonite are less menacing than her interaction with Cat, as she pursues James more openly and aggressively, is ruder to her rival Siobhan, harshly calls her sister jealous, and is rather careless with the capture of minor villains. Supergirl's extreme violence against Cat is difficult to reconcile without considering that Cat stands as a sort of mentor and mother to Kara in a world where she has lost her biological mother and her aunt. If we consider Supergirl's tossing Cat off the roof as a symbolic testing of Cat's love, the moment might make more sense. Cat responds rather appropriately as a symbolic parent, setting boundaries for human safety and yet remaining emotionally available to Supergirl. This episode is mirrored when Cat returns to National City to help save the Earth from Rhea and falls from Air Force One.[34] Supergirl again rescues Cat from a fall, this time prioritizing Cat's life over the life of the U.S. president, who luckily is an alien and able to withstand the crash.

Importantly, Cat consistently exemplifies not only sustained mentorship, but also heroic hard work and morality. She rarely rests, pursues her goals with unfettered passion, and emphasizes how hard she had to work to rise to her current leadership role. Both Kara and Lucy Lane characterize Cat as a "badass," noting that Cat's nine companies (an interesting number that also evokes the rumored nine lives of cats) are all led by women.[35] Calista Flockheart as Cat Grant evokes a toughened, wizened version of her 1997–2002 Ally McBeal role; and the combined effect of her name, cat-related nicknames, and appearance subtly evokes Michelle Pfeiffer's 1992 Catwoman (from Tim Burton's *Batman Returns*). Cat exercises extensively, eats remarkably healthy food and is keenly perceptive and observant. Her excellence in career endeavors is represented with humor within the show, but also with evidence of genuine effort. Meanwhile, Supergirl has the extraordinary gastronomical power to overindulge in massive quantities of sticky buns, pizza, and alcohol without ill effects due to her superior alien DNA. Yet as a writer and a warrior, we observe her very human effort, practice, and growth. Kara admits that she expected being a writer would be very hard, and yet, the work is even harder than she thought, similarly to her superhero work. During several meetings on Cat's balcony after hours as both Supergirl and as Kara, the appearance of having drinks or debriefing sessions after lengthy work days can be readily perceived, cementing Cat as a mentor for both careers goals.

Another connection point between Cat and Kara is that Cat's eldest son, Adam, is nearly Kara's age and has also grown up somewhat motherless. Like Adam, Kara has longed for her mother since their separation. Cat struggles as an estranged biological parent, but Kara observes Cat's willingness to sacrifice her prized career for Adam's sake. Initially, Kara and Cat are potentially placeholders for one another to imagine what the missing family member might have felt. Cat struggles to connect with her adult son upon meeting him, and Kara acts as a sort of facilitator or translator between Cat and her Adam, explaining what each feels to the other.[36] Cat also notes what she most missed about being a parent, summarizing and affirming her concept of parenthood in a similar light to her prized vocations: hanging her son's drawings on the fridge (art), telling him stories (literature), and teaching him not to be afraid of the world (mentorship and/or heroism).

Beyond this fraught reconciliation, missing mothers is a resonant theme throughout this show. Kara's friend Lena Luthor, like Kara, desperately seeks female mentorship to fill the void of motherhood she hoped to receive from her stepmother, Lillian. She appears in lush garments and rich makeup amidst pristine white L-Corp offices, perhaps reflecting the juxtaposition of her warmth and creative genius with cold, scientific atmosphere of her family. Interestingly, her adopted mother Lillian Luthor discloses that Lena is not adopted but rather the lovechild of Lionel Luthor through an extramarital affair. Lillian also claims that she and Lena have always been at odds in the past because of Lex and Lionel, suggesting that now there are "no men to divide us."[37] While her analysis does not ring entirely true, it does allude to the complexities of stepparents, extramarital affairs, toxic masculinity, and patriarchy.

Queen Rhea, Mon-El's mother, acts as a supportive mentor and pseudo mother figure to Lena when she cannot reconnect with her own son. Her words to Lena echo J'onzz's fatherly words to both Kara and Alex: "Any mother should be proud to call you daughter."[38] Ultimately, Rhea even attempts to position Lena as her daughter-in-law by trying to arrange a marriage with her son Mon-El. Thus far in the series, Lena's morality is sustained by her deep friendship with Kara. Lena resists the lure of her stepmother's love and her stepmother's criminal alliances on several occasions, and she resists Rhea's alliances as well. This rejection is parallel to Kara's rejection of her Aunt Astra's alliance. Kara praises Lena's goodness and intelligence, urging her to become her "own hero" like Supergirl.[39] Alex similarly reminds Kara in her own weak moment that "pain ... makes you a hero."[40] These complexities of pain and female friendship are threads of the show, suggesting that we can move beyond the sins of our families of origin and forge new families and lives.

If mothers and mentors are a major theme of the women of *Supergirl*, frail and/or failed father figures might be their counterpart among male characters. Kara's father was a Kryptonian scientist who developed Medusa, a genocidal virus that in the hands of Cadmus murders scores of aliens and nearly claims Mon-El's life. Though Kara frequently converses with her mother's hologram as if she were living, she does not pursue additional conversation with her father, but rather seeks comfort from J'onn. Kara literally carries the burden of her people's problems to Earth, especially because the Fort Rozz prison had accompanied her pod when it landed. But her human peers struggle with toxic fathers and the sins of their fathers as well. Adoptive father Jeremiah Danvers is assumed dead, but later found to be compromised by Cadmus, morally corrupted in a similar way to her biological father. Kara's best friend Lena Luthor is fatherless, but finds the deceased Lionel Luthor did not adopt her, but rather fathered her through an extramarital affair. General Lane is estranged from her daughter Lois and struggles with his relationship with Lucy Lane. Winn's father is a genius toy maker turned terrorist who tries to force Winn to commit murder, while Maggie Sawyer's father refuses to accept her sexuality, and James' father is tragically deceased. Mon-El's father, who graciously honors his son's decision to remain on Earth and with Kara, is swiftly overpowered and disposed of by Queen Rhea, literally stabbed in the back.[41]

J'onn J'onzz is the only stable, strong, and surviving father figure in the show's first two seasons, demonstrating extraordinary strength, wisdom, power, and care. His identity is perhaps the most complex of any *Supergirl* character: he is a Green Martian and father of two, later assumes the form of an African American man after seeking refuge on Earth, takes on Henshaw's role as the director of the DEO, becomes known as the Martian Manhunter, transforms into a White Martian briefly, and even occasionally assumes the forms and identities of Kara and Supergirl to aid her. He is generally sensitive to the complexities of other family figures in his friends' lives, assuring Kara that despite her doubts about her parents' morality, her heroism is their legacy. However, his care is tempered by his professional role as Kara's boss and head of the DEO, and his fatherly heroism is countered by the fact that the human whose form he has adopted, Hank Henshaw, has become a terminator-like cyborg of Cadmus and appears in National City as J'onzz' terrifying double. J'onzz ultimately occupies a fatherly mentor position not unlike Buffy Summers's watcher, Giles in *Buffy the Vampire Slayer*. Despite her struggles with multiple male family members, Kara remains fairly grounded in her relationship with J'onn and fiercely loyal to family and the very concept of family. For example, she urges former nemesis Maxwell Lord to collaborate with her to save the Earth by compelling him to "honor your parents and mine."[42] Kara's responsibility to family, which transfers to protection of her adopted family and adopted home planet, trumps all other considerations.

Beyond Accessories: Symbolism in Supergirl's Attire and Kara's Support System

Through all her relationships, Kara strives to "figure out what Supergirl means."[43] Part of her identity and appearance relates to her family and builds on her cousin's legacy. Kara's costume, clearly influenced by Clark's, lacks the protective element of his cape. Kal's mother wrapped him in a red baby blanket in his pod, and this bright red cloth became his superhero cape. Kara's only tangible relic from her mother is a necklace that once belonged to Alura. In the season two finale, Kara ultimately gives this necklace away to Mon-El as a parting gift.[44] Her gift mirrors the moment when Kara's mother gave her the necklace and sent her to Earth but also leaves her empty handed of both a partner and the tangible memento of her mother. Kara's enduring strength in such moments is subtle, but constant.

Her identity is also forged by trappings and trainings from her friends and relatives. Kara's eyeglasses, like her cousin's, reflect a desire to assume a dual identity with a mask-like accessory within a non-superhero persona. While it may seem laughable that the slight shift of glasses, hair, and costume would obscure Kara's identity as Supergirl, we might read this situation as a parable for many women unnoticed as heroes in everyday life. Society would not expect Cat Grant's assistant to be a Superhero, so the only person who recognizes her in this role is Cat herself. Additionally, Kara's glasses take on an additional dimension as they are chiefly a piece of technology fitted to her by her adoptive father, Jeremiah Danvers, to suppress her super sight. This added feature makes her glasses a strange inversion of assistive technology and a marker of very real weakness (the muting of her powers). Further, this adaptation represents a dulling of the senses and perception that is leveled on Kara but not on Clark. Kara often hesitates to use not only her x-ray vision, but also her super hearing. Given the pressures placed on many women to conform and not flaunt their talents, the restriction of her glasses is notable. Some critics have observed that as Kara increasingly casts off these glasses, she gains confidence in her superhero identity.[45] Kara's black glasses also look stylistically similar to those of Cat, which links the two women visually. Additionally, both women perhaps reveal their truest self without their glasses: for Kara becomes Supergirl *sans* glasses, and Cat often removes her glasses to make a personal comment or connection with Kara.

Kara not only tosses her glasses in her transformation, but also releases her ponytail or bun, allowing her wavy hair to be free and flowing. Finally, Kara rips apart her blouses, revealing her iconic "S" symbol on her blue costume. Notably, when Kara is experiencing difficulty both at CatCo and as Supergirl, she convalesces in her apartment wearing an awkward combination of her wrinkled work blouse and obscured superhero tunic as if caught between the two identities and purposes.[46] While Superman's hair remains rather similar to Clark's, Supergirl's shirt-ripping and hair release takes on a different quality than Superman, perhaps highlighting her female body and physicality in a way not unlike other female superheroes. Specifically, fellow superhero Power Girl (sometimes written as Kara Zor-El in a parallel universe)[47] has a costume lacking the typical defining letter or symbol emblazoned across the chest. Rather than a blank space, however, Power Girl has a hole in her costume. Because she is female, her uniform's hole reveals (and even highlights) her ample chest.[48] In this way, the corporal sexuality of her costume is linked to its symbolic ambiguity and openness. As viewers, Supergirl's transformation also reminds us to grapple with her body, her gender, and obscured versus imagined aspects of her identity all at once, because of our own potentially objectifying and sexualizing gaze. Supergirl's blouse-ripping move also reminds us that she's not really undressing, but rather that she is transforming from one profession to another: journalism to heroics. Further, with Supergirl's glasses tossed aside, perhaps she also can gaze back at us, subverting the male gaze.

Concluding Collaborations: "This isn't his story"

Also in contrast with the Man of Steel, Supergirl's most frequent show of power, aside from flight, is often her "freeze" vision. While other superheroes employ aggression and might, Supergirl seems instead to use multifaceted perception and to stop foes in their tracks with her gaze. Supergirl's x-ray vision is an extra perception, whereas her heat vision rivals a laser, and her freeze vision can execute protective walls of ice. Interestingly, we do not see her powers of vision patrolled as closely in the DEO as her fight and flight is monitored and muted by friends and foes. Her vision as a hero and as a writer is important, and it functions in many different ways. When Kara cannot save the world as a superhero or a journalist, she attempts community blogging to spread her views.[49] In parallel fashion, *Supergirl* is not just the untold story of Superman's cousin, but also the "sister-centric storytelling"[50] of Supergirl's adopted sister, of Lois Lane's younger sister, of Lex Luthor's lesser-known half-sister (Lena Luthor), and others. Kara is the keeper of most of Krypton's memories by virtue of her childhood experiences there, and Superman even asks her to tell him stories of their ancestral home. Kara consistently claims her own messages and meanings as Supergirl, too. For example, there is an interesting sort of layering of syllogisms by herself and Hank Henshaw who observes of J'onn J'onzz, "you may be an alien, but I'm Cyborg Superman" to which Supergirl amends and concludes: "you may be a cyborg, but you are no Superman."[51]

Not only does Supergirl best Superman in contest, but her show even replaces him to a certain extent within moments such as the above dialogue, and with extended collaborations with other males such as the Flash or with Daxamite prince, Mon-El. Aside from assisting Supergirl as a new hero, Mon-El also works as a CatCo intern, then a bartender, and finally devotes much of his time to cook at home for Kara. These valid but somewhat less traditionally ambitious career choices stand in contrast with Superman and with some prevailing expectations about males, careers, and relationship roles.

Supergirl's peers also reconfigure expectations of identity, family, and self through the addition of unexpected characters. Many characters in the show initially believe themselves to be the sole surviving daughter or son of a lost culture and later find an unexpected larger family, including Kara, Clark, M'Gann, and J'onn. First, Superman is joined by Supergirl. The title character—the last daughter of Krypton—Kara finds that Astra is actually still living. The last son of Mars, J'onn, discovers not only M'Gann, a fellow Martian, but also other survivors on Mars who come to his aid on Earth. Kara herself draws strength from the complicated but loving relationships of Kryptonian mother figures Alura and Astra, as well as Earth mother figures Eliza and Cat. Supergirl's interdependence in her personal life as Kara carries great weight in a web of comprehensive professional collaborations with individuals throughout media, business, science/technology, police, government, and the DEO. Rather than centering on a special, solitary figure, *Supergirl* explores sharing heroism and expanding the definitions and spheres of family into a fascinating web of inter-relationships. The growing group of female characters and their male allies represent an elegant symmetry in their mentoring, mothering, and heroic roles with one another, and they are the ones crafting their own stories and forming meaningful family relationships and professional partnerships.

Notes

1. Mike Madrid, *The Supergirls: Fashion, Feminism, Fantasy, and the History of Comic Book Heroines* (Minneapolis: Exterminating Angel Press, 2009).
2. Hannah Lodge, "Five Superhero Shoes Put to the Bechdel Test: Only One Fails," *The Beat: The News Blog of Comic Culture*, http://www.comicsbeat.com/five-superhero-shows-put-to-the-bechdel-test-only-one-fails.
3. *Supergirl*, "Resist," season 2, episode 21, directed by Millicent Shelton, story by Jessica Queller and Derek Simon, aired May 15, 2017, on The CW.
4. *Supergirl*, "Human for a Day," season 1, episode 7, directed by Larry Teng, written by Yahlin Chang and Ted Sullivan, aired December 7, 2015, on CBS.
5. *Supergirl*, "Pilot," season 1, episode 1, directed by Glen Winter, story by Greg Berlanti, Ali Adler, and Andrew Kreisberg, teleplay by Ali Adler, aired October 26, 2015, on CBS.
6. *Supergirl*, "Fight or Flight," season 1, episode 3, directed by Dermott Downs, written by Michael Grassi and Rachel Shukert, aired November 9, 2015, on CBS.
7. John Berger. *Ways of Seeing* (New York: Penguin Press, 1990).
8. *Supergirl*, "Human for a Day," season 1, episode 7, directed by Larry Teng, written by Yahlin Chang and Ted Sullivan, aired December 7, 2015, on CBS.
9. "Superman," *DC Comics*, http://www.dccomics.com/characters/superman.
10. *Heroes*, "Hiros," season 1, episode 1, directed by Paul Shapiro, written by Michael Green, aired October 23, 2006, on NBC.
11. *Supergirl*, "Strange Visitor from Another Planet," season 1, episode 11, directed by Glen Winter, written by Michael Grassi and Caitlin Parrish, aired January 25, 2016, on CBS.
12. *Supergirl*, "For the Girl Who Has Everything," season 1, episode 13, directed by Dermott Downs, written by Ted Sullivan, Derek Simon, and Andrew Kreisberg, aired February 8, 2016, on CBS.
13. *Supergirl*, "The Adventures of Supergirl," season 2, episode 1, directed by Glen Winter, story by Greg Berlanti and Andrew Kreisberg, teleplay by Andrew Kreisberg and Jessica Queller, aired October 10, 2016, on The CW.
14. *Buffy the Vampire Slayer*, "Blood Ties," season 5, episode 13, directed by Michael Gershman, written by Steven S. DeKnight, aired February 6, 2001, on WB.
15. *Buffy the Vampire Slayer*, "Pangs," season 4, episode 8, directed by Michael Lange, written by Jane Espenson, aired November 23, 1999, on WB.
16. *Supergirl*, "Medusa," season 2, episode 8, directed by Stefan Pleszczynnski, written by Jessica Queller and Derek Simon, aired November 28, 2016, on The CW.
17. *Supergirl*, "Stronger Together," season 1, episode 2, directed by Glen Winter, story by Greg Berlanti and Andrew Kreisberg, teleplay by Andrew Kreisberg and Ali Adler, aired November 2, 2015, on CBS.
18. *Supergirl*, "Livewire," season 1, episode 5, directed by Kevin Tancharoen, story by Roberto Aguirre-Sacasa and Caitlin Parrish, aired March 28, 2016, on CBS.
19. *Supergirl*, "Nevertheless, She Persisted," season 2, episode 22, directed by Glen Winter, story by Andrew Kreisberg and Jessica Queller, teleplay by Robert Rovner and Caitlin Parrish, aired May 22, 2017, on The CW.
20. This action takes on stark contrast with our recent political situation, in which the U.S. president has signed three executive orders against immigrants with Muslim backgrounds.
21. *Supergirl*, "Luthors," season 2, episode 12, directed by Tawnia McKiernan, written by Robert Rovner and Cindy Lichtman, aired February 13, 2017, on The CW.
22. *Supergirl*, "How Does She Do It?," season 1, episode 4, directed by Thor Freudenthal, written by Yahlin Chang and Ted Sullivan, aired November 23, 2015, on CBS.
23. *Supergirl*, "Better Angels," season 1, episode 20, directed by Larry Teng, written by Andrew Kreisberg and Ali Adler, teleplay by Robert Rovner and Jessica Queller, aired April 18, 2016, on CBS.

24. Katherine Silva, 'Why the 'Nerd Girl Makeover' Needs to Die," *The Odyssey Online*, https://www.theodysseyonline.com/beautiful-all-along.
25. *Supergirl*, "Mr. & Mrs. Mxyzptlk," season 2, episode 13, directed by Stefan Pleszczynski, written by Jessica Queller and Sterling Gates, aired February 20, 2017, on The CW.
26. Megan Garber, "'Nasty': A Feminist History," *The Atlantic*, https://www.theatlantic.com/entertainment/archive/2016/10/nasty-a-feminist-history/504815/
27. *Supergirl*, "We Can Be Heroes," season 2, episode 10, directed by Rebecca Johnson, written by Caitlin Parrish and Katie Rose Rogers, aired January 30, 2017, on The CW.
28. *Supergirl*, "Exodus," season 2, episode 15, directed by Michael Allowitz, written by Paula Yoo and Eric Carrasco, aired March 6, 2017, on The CW.
29. *Supergirl*, "Pilot," season 1, episode 1.
30. *Supergirl*, "Nevertheless, She Persisted," season 2, episode 22.
31. *Supergirl*, "Stronger Together," season 1, episode 2.
32. *Supergirl*, "Red Faced," season 1, episode 6, directed by Jesse Warn, written by Michael Grassi and Rachel Shukert, aired November 30, 2015, on CBS.
33. *Supergirl*, "Falling," season 1, episode 16, directed by Larry Teng, written by Robert Rovner and Jessica Queller, aired March 14, 2016, on CBS.
34. *Supergirl*, "Nevertheless, She Persisted," season 2, episode 22.
35. *Supergirl*, "Childish Things," season 1, episode 10, directed by Jamie Babbit, written by Yahlin Chang, teleplay by Anna Musky-Goldwyn and James Dewille, aired January 18, 2016, on CBS.
36. *Supergirl*, "Strange Visitor from Another Planet," season 1, episode 11.
37. *Supergirl*, "Luthors," season 2, episode 12.
38. *Supergirl*, "Nevertheless, She Persisted," season 2, episode 22.
39. *Supergirl*, "Medusa," season 2, episode 8.
40. *Supergirl*, "For the Girl Who Has Everything," season 1, episode 13.
41. *Supergirl*, "Distant Sun," season 2, episode 17, directed by Kevin Smith, written by Gabriel Llanas and Anna Musky-Goldwyn, aired March 27, 2017, on The CW.
42. *Supergirl*, "Myriad," season 1, episode 19, directed by Adam Kane, written by Yahlin Chang and Caitlin Parrish, aired April 11, 2016, on CBS.
43. *Supergirl*, "Fight or Flight," season 1, episode 3.
44. *Supergirl*, "Nevertheless, She Persisted," season 2, episode 22.
45. Hanh Nguyen, "Supergirl: Why the Hell Does Supergirl Wear Sunglasses" *TV GUIDE*, http://www.tvguide.com/news/supergirl-kara-glasses/
46. *Supergirl*, "Manhunter," season 1, episode 17, directed by Chris Fisher, story by Derek Simon, teleplay by Cindy Lichtman and Rachel Shukert, aired March 21, 2016, on CBS.
47. Alan Kistler, "Supergirl, Superwoman & Power Girl Historical Timeline Part 1: 1938–1986," *The Mary Sue*, https://www.themarysue.com/supergirl-superwoman-historical-timeline-part-1-1938-1986.
48. Courtney Weida, "Wondering Women: Investigating Gender Politics and Art Education Within Graphica," *Journal of Visual Culture and Gender* 6, no. 1 (2011): http://vcg.emitto.net/6vol/Weida.pdf.
49. *Supergirl*, "Ace Reporter," season 2, episode 18, directed by Armen V. Kevorkian, written by Paula Yoo and Caitlin Parrish, aired April 24, 2017, on The CW.
50. Caroline Siede, "Supergirl Fights for Immigrant Rights in an Episode That Doesn't Pull Its Punches," *AV Club*, http://www.avclub.com/tvclub/supergirl-fights-immigrant-rights-episode-doesnt-p-251617.
51. *Supergirl*, "Medusa," season 2, episode 8.

Selected Bibliography

Berger, John. *Ways of Seeing*. New York: Penguin Press, 1990.
Garber, Megan. "'Nasty': A Feminist History." *The Atlantic*. October 20, 2016. https://www.theatlantic.com/entertainment/archive/2016/10/nasty-a-feminist-history/504815.
Kistler, Alan. "Supergirl, Superwoman & Power Girl Historical Timeline Part 1: 1938–1986."

The Mary Sue. June 25, 2015. https://www.themarysue.com/supergirl-superwoman-historical-timeline-part-1-1938-1986.

Lodge, Hannah. "Five Superhero Shoes Put to the Bechdel Test: Only One Fails." *The Beat: The News Blog of Comic Culture*. February 12, 2016. http://www.comicsbeat.com/five-superhero-shows-put-to-the-bechdel-test-only-one-fails.

Madrid, Mike. *The Supergirls: Fashion, Feminism, Fantasy, and the History of Comic Book Heroines*. Minneapolis: Exterminating Angel Press, 2009.

Nguyen, Hahn. "Supergirl: Why the Hell Does Supergirl Wear Sunglasses." *TV Guide*. October 26, 2015. http://www.tvguide.com/news/supergirl-kara-glasses.

Siede, Caroline. "Supergirl Fights for Immigrant Rights in an Episode That Doesn't Pull Its Punches" *AV Club*. March 6, 2017: http://www.avclub.com/tvclub/supergirl-fights-immigrant-rights-episode-doesnt-p-251617.

Silva, Katherine. "'Why the 'Nerd Girl Makeover' Needs to Die" *The Odyssey Online*. February 8, 2017. https://www.theodysseyonline.com/beautiful-all-along.

"Superman." *DC Comics*. http://www.dccomics.com/characters/superman.

Weida, Courtney. "Wondering Women: Investigating Gender Politics and Art Education Within Graphica." *Journal of Visual Culture and Gender* 6, no. 1 (2011). http://vcg.emitto.net/6vol/Weida.pdf.

El Mayarah

The Danvers Sisters as Chosen Family

Sarah J. Palm

When CBS first debuted *Supergirl* in the fall of 2015, it was clear that family would be the thematic bedrock of the show. The family grounding this show, however, was anything but a traditional one. Centering on the titular super-powered alien hero as she teams up with her human adoptive sister and the DEO to defend the Earth against alien threats, the show deals extensively with themes of family, both chosen and biological. Though the concept is explored through many characters on the show, it is embodied most clearly in the characters of, and relationship between, Kara and Alex Danvers. At some point in their shared history, the two women came to identify as "sisters," dropping the qualifier of "adoptive" entirely, and forgoing any number of other potential labels that could describe their relationship. In doing so, the heroines of *Supergirl* enact "sisterhood"—and by extension, "family"—as a choice. This portrayal of chosen family is continuously reiterated throughout the series, through specific and indicative use of language, action, and creative choices.

Portrayals of adoptive families are still rare in the television landscape. Adoption itself, while modeled on biological networks, has traditionally been thought of in Western society as more of a social connection.[1] However, in recent years, fictive kinship—kinship not based on biological or marital ties—such as adoption and chosen family, has been the focus of renewed interest and study.[2] Carsten suggests that "instability and divorce in heterosexual marriage, the advent of same-sex marriage, gender equality, gay rights, falling fertility rates, and increasing numbers of people living on their own all suggest some profoundly new practices and experiences of Western kinship."[3] Such evolving real-life experiences of family and kinship inevitably seep into contemporary media and popular culture, which reflect such lived experiences while also acting as wish-fulfillment for what remains to be desired. Television scholar Jillian Sandell writes:

> Recent decades have witnessed major reconfigurations of what counts as "family": from the Moynihan report of the 1960s to the rising divorce rate, from feminism and abortion rights to reproductive technologies and surrogate motherhood, from blended families and adoption to teenage single mothers, and from the increased reporting of child abuse to other dysfunctional familial patterns. The question of which relationships receive social legitimacy, and are represented in the media, remains a highly political one.[4]

She further observes that working-class families, many ethnic and racial groups, and those in the LGBTQ community often create kinship patterns that bear little resemblance to the "mythical American family,"[5] or what author and historian Stephanie Coontz termed "the way we never were."[6] While this myth of white, heterosexual, upper middle-class, biological family continues to dominate the media, "from watching TV you would never know that in the United States, the majority of the population does *not* live in a nuclear family."[7]

With its pop culture references and sly political jabs, *Supergirl* is very much a product of our times. As such, it is also a reflection of current anxieties and a reactant fantasy to combat perceived injustices and societal deficits. It challenges the status quo through the themes it explores—immigration politics, tolerance of "others," and LGBTQ experiences, to name a few. But family is the thematic through-line. By questioning what constitutes "real" family, the series reflects a need for an expanded, more inclusive and thoughtful concept of "family."

Despite the rarity of representations of adoptive families in television at large, Supergirl is not the only current superhero show to have a similar protagonist duo: *Marvel's Jessica Jones* and DC's *The Flash* both focus on a pair of adoptive siblings brought together after a family tragedy. In the former, the two identify as best friends and in the latter, romantic partners. *Supergirl*'s decision to immediately establish Kara and Alex as sisters then, foregoing any number of alternate labels and embracing them fully as family, makes it unique. In doing this, while also presenting their relationship as primary in the narrative, the show asserts that shared genes are not a necessary component of family.

This notion is at the heart of "chosen family"—the idea that true family is not simply ready-made at birth, but rather a support network carefully curated throughout our lives, comprised of individuals who "accept you for who you are, not for who they want you to be."[8] Feminist author Courtney E. Martin writes that choosing one's family "is the nature of growing up and growing away, of being someone who sheds some legacies while embracing others, of turning a critical, albeit compassionate, eye on our origins."[9] Echoing those sentiments, Executive Producer Sarah Schechter acknowledges chosen family as one of *Supergirl*'s most important aspects, noting that "this show in particular is about the family that you choose and the family that, as an adult, you build."[10]

Chosen or alternative families have become much more commonly accepted in recent years, particularly among young and queer people. Creating such a family then makes sense for the mostly young and diverse characters of *Supergirl*, as well as for the demographically similar audience wanting to see their own experiences represented in the media they consume. Kara and Alex both have families they were born into, as well as families they choose—namely one another. Their relationship has been singled out by viewers and creators alike—including the actors themselves—as the most important relationship in the show. Bookending the first season with two major Danvers sisters' moments, the series places their relationship front and center in the narrative. And by surrounding them with relationships that serve as direct counterpoints to their own, the show further emphasizes the women's singular bond.

"Here's to the Danvers sisters": Choice Through Language

The choice of "chosen family" begins with words—that is, the language one uses to address and refer to others. The labels Kara and Alex choose, for example, immediately indicate how they view themselves and their relationship, and how we, the audience, are to perceive them. From the moment in the first episode when Kara opens her door to an exasperated Alex with, "Because you're my sister and you love me,"[11] we understand their relationship as genuinely familial. This initial introduction of our heroines sets the linguistic standard for their relationship for the rest of the series, with "sister" used exclusively. And apart from the episode recaps, which utilize the same opening voice-over from Kara, in which she explains (for new viewers) how she works with her "adoptive sister" at the DEO, the qualifier of "adoptive" is dropped entirely from the show's vocabulary. The accuracy of the chosen label "sister" is never questioned or clarified by any other character, but rather, readily accepted as simply the most accurate descriptor of the two women, and as mere fact. The legitimacy of their relationship is only called into question once when Kara is affected by Red Kryptonite. Under its personality-altering effects, she cruelly snaps at a confused and tearful Alex, "Cut the big sister act, Alex! We have never been sisters. We don't share blood."[12] Upon being released from the substance's influence, Kara is overcome with guilt and remorse for her words and actions over which she had no control. Alex wipes her tears and tells her, "Kara, you're my sister. And I love you no matter what. Okay?"[13] It is both an act of forgiveness and a reaffirmation of their familial bond, effectively putting the issue to rest permanently.

The choice of language used by both Alex and Kara is significant because its simplicity and directness stand in sharp contrast to Kara's other relationships, particularly with the rest of her adoptive family members. While Alex is simply "sister," Eliza and Jeremiah are always "Eliza" and "Jeremiah," or "Alex's [parents]." When Winn once refers to Eliza as "your mom," Kara immediately corrects him: "Foster mom."[14] Though she credits both Eliza and Alex for giving her "a great life, a life I never thought I'd be able to find outside of Krypton,"[15] she also refers to them as "my sister and my foster mom,"[16] tellingly using a qualifier for Eliza but not for Alex.

It makes sense that young Kara was hesitant to embrace new parents, when her birth parents were still fresh in her memory and in her heart when she landed on Earth. Her decision to continue enforcing the distinction, keeping them at a certain distance through language, allowing them to supplement but never replace (even symbolically) her parents, is understandable. Fully accepting Alex as her sister, however, threatens no memory of a previous family, as Kara was an only child on Krypton. The bond between her and Alex, therefore, is allowed to be the most unassailable, not only in the show generally, but also in the Danvers family.

A similar contrast appears when considering the mercurial dynamics between Kara and the various other characters. Over the course of just two seasons, James Olsen vacillates between friend and romantic interest; Winn goes from friend to rejected love interest, back to friend; Mon-El is introduced as an antagonist, before becoming Kara's protégé and later love interest; and J'onn goes from colleague to father-figure. Amidst the ever-changing dynamics and labels in Kara's life, Alex—"sister"—is the one constant.

Adopting the title of "sisters" is one way of pronouncing an intentional familial bond, but the word "family" itself is also used nearly as often, for instance, when Kara tells J'onn early on, "I know to you she's just an agent, but to me, she's my *family*."[17] Kara, in particular, makes the linguistic distinction between her blood family and her chosen family, while making it clear which one she prioritizes. When Astra is revealed to be alive, for example, Alex empathizes with Kara, saying, "I can't even imagine what you must be feeling right now—finding out you still have family..."[18] to which Kara immediately replies, "*You're* my family.... We have to stop my aunt."[19] Likewise, when Astra appeals to Kara's familial loyalties, Kara spits back, "You're not my family."[20]

The labels Kara and Alex choose for themselves and their relationship inform, and in turn, are informed by, their dynamic in the series—one that remains constant amidst shifting loyalties, alliances, and relationships. As the series progresses, Kara surrounds herself with a select few others whom she eventually comes to call "family" (i.e., Winn, James, J'onn), but it is constantly reaffirmed that when she thinks of family, it is Alex she thinks of first and foremost, and vice versa.

Earth Family vs. Birth Family: Choice Through Action

The act of choosing one's family, of course, is also an embodied one. Repeatedly, Alex and Kara make clear, tangible choices to be and remain close to one another, both physically and emotionally. Upon our first introduction to the Danvers sisters, several of these choices are already established: Alex has given up a promising medical career to join the DEO and watch over Kara, the two have remained in National City together, and by the end of episode one, Kara has revealed herself to the world as Supergirl, in order to save Alex's life. Though the choice to reveal her powers is ultimately the first step in her larger journey of self-discovery, the fact that Alex's life being threatened was the triggering moment of choice for Kara to expose her deepest secret to the world—a secret she has kept hidden for thirteen years—is expressive. This act also allows Alex to reveal to Kara that she has been working with the DEO for many years to watch over her. With both secrets out, Kara then doubles down on her commitment to remain near to her sister, first forgiving her for the years of lying, and then seizing the opportunity to form an even closer relationship, by joining her at the DEO. But even before learning of the existence of the DEO, Kara made the choice to remain in National City, to live and work close to Alex, when she could have just as easily found a similar assistant job at *The Daily Planet* in Metropolis, nearer her Kryptonian cousin. When Kara does briefly consider moving to Metropolis with Clark early in season two, her sister is understandably hurt. She reminds Kara, with no regret or resentment, of the sacrifices she has made to keep her safe over the years: her career, her childhood, and her father. She reminds her of their promise to look out for each other. Kara protests, "this is not about one family over the other. This is about me not feeling alone anymore. When I'm with Clark, I feel like I'm connected to somebody who actually understands what it's like to be me." Alex counters, "So does he understand that he abandoned you with us? Do *you*?"[21] After all, Clark was not there for his cousin growing up; he did not stick around to teach her Earth customs, or how to blend in to life as a human, or calm her down when her powers or anxiety threatened to overwhelm her. As Alex once tells the hologram of Kara's mother, Alura, "I'm sure you had hoped that she would find people that would take care of her, who would love her like she was their own? *I* did."[22]

Whether or not Kara wants to pit birth family against chosen family, their respective track records are clear: her mother and father sent her away; the Danvers gave her a home. Clark is the one who left; Alex is the one who stayed. Time and choice, the show seems to say, surpass biology. Thrust together at such formative ages, after a trauma, no less, for fourteen years spent guarding the same secret and protecting one another from the world— all that outweighs whatever house loyalty or blood ties Kara has to her cousin, who may share her abilities, but whom she hardly knows. Inevitably realizing this, Kara later apologizes to Alex, telling her, "I'm sorry if I have ever made you feel like you are less to me than Clark. You are the *only* reason I have *ever* felt at home on this planet."[23] By blood, Clark may be the closest thing Kara has ever had to a sibling. But it is her sibling of choice, Alex, who is "the person that is most important to me."[24] Ultimately, both women realize that they are simply "better when we're together."[25]

This is not the first time Kara makes a deliberate choice regarding her family members either. Upon learning that Alex has killed Astra in order to save J'onn's life, Kara is angry at first, but only until she sees how distraught Alex is at the thought that she has done something to drive Kara away. In the next moment, Kara wordlessly wraps her sister in a hug, choosing to forgive her and to salvage their relationship, rather than harbor resentment over the loss of a blood relative, even one whom she did once love like a second mother.

Perhaps the most literal example of Kara choosing her Earth family over her Kryptonian one, however, is the result of the Black Mercy.[26] With Kara trapped inside a fantasy of her home world, her friends at the DEO realize that the only way to save her is to convince her to reject the fantasy on her own. They know if anyone can bring her back, it is Alex. Inside the dreamscape, Alex is beaten and restrained by Kryptonian guards as she struggles to reach Kara, pleading with her to remember her friends and family in reality: "Kara, I can't choose this for you," she sobs, "You have to choose it yourself. Please come back to us, Kara. Please."[27] Alex had already made her choice before she entered the Black Mercy, when she told James, "Either I come back with my sister, or I don't come back at all."[28] Kara's choice is laid out before her inside the Black Mercy, with her Earth sister and her birth mother standing before her. She turns to the vision of Alura, decision in her eyes. "Krypton will be in my heart forever," she tells her. "But Alex is right. My *sister* is right. I have to go."[29] As the fantasy world crumbles around them, Alex and Kara reach for each other, surfacing back in reality moments later. "I chose to come back because I realized that I belong here with you," she later tells her friends, looking at Alex when she says, "My family."[30]

"Harnessing Anger" and Creative Choice

While dialogue and narrative action are hugely important in establishing relationships, the beauty of television is that writing is only one of the many devices used to convey information, emotion, and complexities to an audience. Editing, music, and performances further develop and emphasize relationships between characters, adding layers, contextualities, and emotional depth to a scene. In this realm, *Supergirl* makes a number of creative choices to express the singularity of the bond between the Danvers sisters.

Early on in the series, the use of certain editing techniques is significant in establishing some non-verbalized aspects of Alex and Kara's relationship. For instance, after Kara loses her powers for the first time, she is understandably shaken. The Alura hologram's voice-over tells her, "Do not be afraid ... and lean on those you trust,"[31] as the camera first shows us a vulnerable-looking Kara in a med-bay chair, then slowly pans from her hand clasped in both of Alex's, up to her sister's concerned face as she watches the monitors. So much is communicated in these ten seconds: Kara's fear, matched by Alex's worry for her, signifies a deep empathic connection; Alex in the role of protector gives us a sense of their dynamic; and through the combination of voice-over and visual, we understand that when Kara is at her most vulnerable, there is no one she trusts more than her sister. And in the very first episode, the hologram of Alura tells Kara, "though you were sent to Earth to protect young Kal-El, your destiny is not tied to his."[32] As she speaks, Alex moves to give Kara and her mother some privacy, but Kara catches her hand, and the camera cuts to a close-up of their intertwined fingers. With just this simple yet powerful editing choice, we recognize that Kara's destiny is now linked with Alex's. Her mandate has evolved, by her own choice, from blood kin to chosen kin.

Editing and camera choices such as these speak volumes to the viewer, on a conscious and subconscious level. One strategic cut or close-up can sometimes say more than an entire scene of vocalized exposition. Music, likewise, is a powerful communication tool, and composer Blake Neely's score does much to enhance our heroines' bond. The sheer number of musical pieces composed specifically for Danvers sisters scenes—"Alex Brings Kara Back,"[33] "Afraid of Losing You,"[34] "I Am So Proud of You,"[35] "Almost Losing Alex,"[36] "Saving Her Sister and the Ark"[37]—speaks to the care he and the creative team take with portraying this relationship, above all others. Some of these pieces are repeated as motif, but none more noticeably or memorably as "Harnessing Anger." This score is first used in episode six of season one, during Kara's battle with Red Tornado. The scene is intercut with flashbacks of the destruction of Krypton, of Kara losing her family and her world. Only by channeling the rage conjured by those most painful memories is she able to defeat the machine.

The score here is "not your typical action music," as Neely himself describes it. "It's more of an adagio and it's more emotional than sometimes you see in these fight sequences.... In this case, it was a slower, bigger arc, [an] emotional thing that ties into her thoughts of her home and her mother."[38] Here, the editing—specifically the use of flashbacks—informs the score's meaning and function, infusing it with overtones of family and loss. "It was one of those pieces I just really wanted to get in [Kara's] head," Neely says. "Because it was not just about beating [Red Tornado]. [People] call it the 'Red Tornado Track'... It's not the 'Red Tornado Track', it's about her inner struggle and her loneliness, actually."[39]

Apart from the main *Supergirl* theme, "Harnessing Anger" is easily the most recognizable and iconic piece of music used in the show. When it appears in the second season then, as Kara races to stop Lillian Luthor from launching the Ark, it lends even greater weight and emotion to a scene that is already one of the most memorable of the series. Struggling to stop the speeding mammoth of a spaceship carrying her sister and dozens of innocent people, as it hurtles toward the other side of the galaxy, the stakes are clear: if Kara fails, she will never see Alex again. This time, no flashbacks are necessary to cue the audience in to what our hero is thinking or feeling. The moment Alex puts her hand to the glass that separates them, in a gesture of unwavering faith, Neely's adagio swells once more, and we are reminded, as is Kara, of her family on Krypton and how much she has already lost. This time, her anger is not over that painful childhood memory, but the thought of history repeating itself. She presses her hand to Alex's, her face changing from panic to determination, and once again harnesses that anger, now on behalf of her chosen sister. Through sheer force of will and brute strength, while looking into the eyes of her family, she does the impossible, bringing the Ark to a halt just in time.

The two scenes are strikingly similar, both visually and aurally: in both, Neely's adagio takes over the soundscape entirely, all other sounds fading away, with the exception of Kara's muted screams of rage and exertion. Both scenes utilize the same editing and filming style, cutting between Kara and the object of her emotion (i.e., Red Tornado and Alex, respectively), with heavy use of close-ups on Kara's face conveying the intensity of her emotions (and the powerful performance from Melissa Benoist). And both follow the same sequence of action—Kara's initial fear and doubt in herself, then hardening resolve and a channeling of rage into the obstacle in front of her, followed by cathartic success and a collapse in exhaustion, her powers spent.

The use of repeated score, working in tandem with themes enhanced through editing, blurs the distinctions between Kara's two families, with the latter family perhaps coming to eclipse the former. Her greatest source of pain and anger when we first met her was the loss of her parents and her home world. Now, her greatest pain stems from the possibility of losing Alex, and her greatest anger is directed at herself for not being strong enough to save her sister. Anger, in both scenes, is the key that enables her to save herself and her family, where she was powerless to do so as a child, hence, the track title. The second scene hits harder emotionally, however, because it is about an anger borne from love, rather than from pain. Building on the first scene, it demonstrates an evolution in the way Kara has come to think of family.

Breaking Ties and Coming Out

Much research over the past few decades has recognized the social, emotional, spiritual, and psychological importance friends and chosen family can have. Often "families are not the truly loving and supportive havens they are meant to be," writes psychologist Gerald Schoenewolf.[40] He notes the importance of choosing one's own family when it becomes necessary to break ties with unsupportive or toxic birth families, particularly parents. "Letting go of ties that bind [one] to unhealthy values and attitudes," he writes, is instrumental in actualizing one's fullest potential.[41]

We see this idea borne out clearly in Kara, as she breaks away from her destructive ties with Astra and Non, surrounding herself instead with people who share her values and make her a better hero. But we also see a number of other characters strive to do the same: Winn sends his "homicidal maniac" father back to prison,[42] Lena distances herself from the Luthor name[43] and from her step-mother and brother's anti-alien vendetta,[44] and Mon-El helps Supergirl thwart his mother's plan for world domination.[45] Even M'gann came to Earth in order to break away from her genocidal race of White Martians,[46] and as a result finds a family in J'onn.[47]

To a less homicidal, but no less painful extent, many of the remaining bio-familial relationships in the show are unsupportive at best (e.g., Cat and her mother) and non-existent at worst (e.g., Maggie and her parents). And as much as they loved their daughters, both Alex and Kara's birth mothers ended up letting them down, forcing them to learn the hard way that parents can be extremely hurtful, even while proclaiming to have their children's best interests at heart. For Kara, this realization comes after discovering that her mother's willful blindness lead to Krypton's destruction and the deaths of everyone she knew and loved, and was further reiterated upon learning that her father created the Medusa virus. For Alex, it was a lifetime of never feeling like "enough" for her mother, who placed the unfair responsibility of Kara's safety on her shoulders when she was just fourteen years old. In Kara's eyes, though, Alex is not only enough, she is "Supergirl's hero."[48] And as for Alex, she always had faith in her sister, "way before you put on that 'S.'"[49]

The death of family members is equally instrumental in the formation of a new family unit, with Winn and James each having lost at least one parent, and J'onn having lost his entire family. Abandonment by one's blood kin, whether by death, emotional distance, or an irreconcilable and even lethal difference of ideals, is a consistent theme for every major character in *Supergirl*. As such, it is also the driving force behind each of their desires to create for themselves a new, reliable, and loving family based on shared values and unconditional support.[50]

Such rebuilding of support networks may be increasingly accepted as a necessary part of growing up in modern society, but it has its roots in a much more specific experience: LGBTQ culture. "Chosen family" has been a pillar of the queer community throughout history, though only in recent decades has it gained merited study and appreciation. American anthropologists such as Kath Weston and Ellen Lewin found that queer individuals tended to consider

> biological kinship as temporary and uncertain because biological kin had been known to disrupt or sever kin ties upon learning of a relative's homosexuality. Meanwhile ... friendships were invested with certainty, depth, and permanence and were discussed in an idiom of kinship by those whose experience of biological kin had been thoroughly disrupted.[51]

Anna Muraco concurs that "through discourse ... and practice, friends are often defined as family, [but] for many gay men and lesbians, friendship and family are combined into chosen family networks" often borne out of necessity.[52] Biological, legal, and financial limitations have historically made the formation of a "traditional" family inaccessible to those in the LGBTQ community,[53] forcing many such individuals to form alternative support networks.

Kara's secret identity has doubled as a metaphor for sexual identity since the pilot, with many characters, including Kara herself, often referring to the incident in which she reveals herself to the world as her "coming out." In this metaphor, her chosen family are the people she trusts with her secret, and who support her for it—namely Alex, Winn, James, and J'onn. The show goes beyond allegory, though, when Alex comes out as a lesbian in the second season, and the term "chosen family" takes on even greater meaning for the Danvers sisters.

Alex's total absence of a social life in season one left much room for character exploration. Over the course of the following season, as she meets and falls in love with Detective Maggie Sawyer, it becomes clear that her all-consuming work at the DEO was a cover of sorts. In subsequent interviews, the show's creative team noted that Alex threw herself into her work, protecting Kara and her secret, in large part because she had her own secret she was struggling with.[54] After Alex's own revelation, her initial panicked reaction to Kara "coming out ... as Supergirl"[55] and her anxiety about telling Eliza is, in hindsight, quite understandable.

Alex's coming-out narrative has rightly been praised for its exceptional honesty and relatability, conveying the emotional roller coaster of the coming-out experience as it swings between liberating and terrifying. One of the smartest things the show does is demonstrate how coming out is not simply a one-and-done event, but rather a series of small coming-outs, beginning with oneself. Alex essentially does this in her conversation with Maggie,[56] who serves as an audience surrogate for us, as well as a sounding board and a safe-space for Alex. Maggie says almost nothing in this scene, instead letting Alex process and say the words herself, for the first time accepting that this may be who she really is. The second person she comes out to, at Maggie's urging, is Kara. Though the conversation causes an initial disconnect between the two, after a Danvers sisters heart-to-heart, Kara admits it was because she felt ashamed for not creating a space where Alex felt comfortable talking about her own secret with her. Deeply apologetic, Kara tells her, "I know that this is not the same at all, but I do know how it feels to keep a part of yourself shut off, to keep it inside. And I know how lonely that can make you feel. But Alex, you are not alone."[57]

Courtney E. Martin writes that sometimes the most important thing chosen families can do for us is to "give us what we need, whether that's praise or space or just the simplest of utterances: *I'm proud of you, I see you, I love you*."[58] All Alex, like anyone on a journey of self-discovery, wants to hear from the person she loves most in the world are these three things, which Kara freely gives her, reassuring her that she could "never be disappointed" in her, that she is "so okay with it," and telling her to "go get the girl."[59] While said girl, Maggie, accepts Alex's sexuality, she does not initially reciprocate Alex's feelings for her, which Alex takes as overall rejection. This sends her into a spiral of panic, regretting her decision to come out and doubting the validity of her feelings. But even when Alex struggles with accepting herself, Kara accepts and loves her unconditionally, and for those in the queer community, that is the essence of "chosen family." It is Kara's support that gives Alex the confidence to, in turn, come out to her friends, co-workers, and parents. It was Kara who first accepted her in the way that she needed, and who, in one of her darkest and most painful moments, wrapped her arms around Alex and said, "I'm proud of you."[60]

Kara continues to be her sister's greatest champion, encouraging her to spend time with Maggie and expressing excitement at each of their relationship milestones. When facing death, Kara tells Mon-El to tell her sister "to keep living life on her own terms,"[61] making sure Alex knows she loved and supported her to the end. We see a similar steadfast support on Alex's part for her sister's identity as Supergirl. While there is no doubt that Kara's adoptive parents loved her, much of their concern and energy went into helping Kara hide her powers, her true self, in order to blend in with humans. The glasses Jeremiah makes for Kara to block her X-ray vision and Eliza's ban on displays of superhuman abilities were well-intentioned but ultimately misguided attempts to keep Kara from becoming the person she was meant to be, and roadblocks to achieving her fullest potential. Alex, on the other hand, defends Kara's coming out to Eliza (who would rather Kara continue to hide her abilities) and goes beyond her job at the DEO to protect and aid Supergirl in her mission. Alex was Kara's true-self champion (and flying companion) before anyone else, just as Kara is there for Alex, when it is her turn to come out.

From "Blood Bonds" to "Love Bonds": The Evolution of "El Mayarah"

The ways families have been depicted on television over the decades have been subject to a series of shifts that simultaneously mirror and rework larger societal trends.[62] Family is not so much an institution but rather an ever-changing socio-cultural construct,[63] and as our lived experiences of family increasingly diverge from normative definitions, we begin to question the "pervasive cultural belief that biolegal family connections are the most salient and durable bonds between individuals."[64] If television "speaks to our collective worries and to our yearning to improve, redeem, or repair our individual or collective lives, to complete what is incomplete,"[65] then perhaps what feels incomplete to us currently is the notion of family. And perhaps the real power of television—and *Supergirl*—is its ability to offer us "new models of family, new ideas about who counts as kin."[66]

The "traditional" American family may be more myth than reality; nevertheless, it continues to be perpetuated in the media.[67] *Supergirl* refutes this heteronormative, biological definition of family, however. By portraying a family instead comprised of adoptees, refugees, friends, queer kin, and parental-figures, it pushes for a broader understanding of what really constitutes a family. The show uses every creative tool at its disposal—writing, editing, music—to offer a more evolved, culturally relevant definition. It provides numerous counter-points to the central relationship between the Danvers sisters, thereby drawing our attention to it and asking us to consider it more deeply: Why is this relationship so unique, both on the show, and in the larger television landscape? How, and at what point, did the two become so close? The answer to these questions ultimately comes down to choice, embodied in the characters' words and deeds.

"Abandoned" by her birth parents, Kara ends up with the Danvers through a combination of tragedy, chance, and her cousin's inability or unwillingness to take care of her.[68] But because of her alien family's shortcomings, not simply in spite of them, Kara finds a new family on Earth, with Alex. Though the two may not have initially chosen to be placed together, somewhere in between the bathroom-sharing and secret-guarding they made a conscious decision to truly claim one another as family. Alex, in reflecting on their years growing up, expresses remorse over the way she treated Kara when she first landed on Earth. "All Kara wanted was a family," she tells Alura's hologram. "And that's what she is to me. She is my *sister*."[69] The before-and-after attitudes that Alex expresses toward Kara indicate a turning point of choice, and the bond initially forced on them now finds itself actively and mutually reinforced. Even though Alex admits, "You don't need me. You never have," Kara responds, "Yeah, but you still took care of me anyway."[70] In a commitment that goes beyond mere responsibility or need, Alex made the choice, and continues to make the choice, to say, "I'm here. Always."[71]

This conscious decision made by the Danvers sisters stands in stark contrast to the Kryptonian adage of "blood bonds us all," an "ancient proverb [that] comes from a time when Krypton was little more than a wasteland of warring tribes."[72] For as many times as the words are invoked, they are refuted: blood did not keep Alura from sentencing her own sister to Fort Rozz; it did not prevent the destruction of Krypton, nor move Kal-El to take care of his orphaned cousin; and it does not stop Astra and Non from repeatedly trying to kill their niece. The words imply a bond of duty rather than love. But duty—a feeling of compelled responsibility over which one has little control—only goes so far, and often breeds resentment. The lack of choice inherent in the biological connections presented in the show makes them tenuous, easily broken, or forgotten at any perceived slight or betrayal. Love, on the other hand, borne from choice and free from duty, *Supergirl* says, is the one truly unbreakable bond. The Danvers sisters' mutual realization of "better together" is a deliberate amendment to the words of the House of El ("El Mayarah": "stronger together"). It is the show's assertion that chosen family has the ability to transcend whatever loyalty shared names and lineage inspire, to be not merely stronger together, but wholly better. Because if there is one clear constant in the series, it is that Kara and Alex make each other better every day: better people, better heroes, and better sisters.

In the end, "blood bonds us all" is nothing more than the dying gasp of a dead planet. And like its Earthly equivalent—"blood is thicker than water"[73]—its relevance has passed into the realm of antiquity, replaced by a new, necessary ideal of family, one of greater inclusion and acceptance, but most of all, choice. In the final scene of the first season, Kara Zor-El, the last daughter of Krypton, surrounded by the family she has chosen, gives a toast: "To family," she says, looking at Alex. "*Love* bonds us all."[74]

212 Supergirl's Sisterhoods: Feminism as a Family Affair

NOTES

1. Janet Carsten, "Kinship," *Encyclopædia Britannica*, 2012, https://www.britannica.com/topic/kinship/Kinship-terminology.
2. Carsten, "Kinship."
3. Carsten, "Kinship."
4. Jillian Sandell, "I'll Be There for You: 'Friends' and the Fantasy of Alternative Families," *American Studies* 39, 2 (1998): 148, https://journals.ku.edu/amerstud/article/view/2714/2673.
5. Sandell, "I'll Be There for You," 148.
6. Sandell, "I'll Be There for You," 144.
7. Sandell, "I'll Be There for You," 148.
8. Gerald Schoenewolf, "Friends Are Your Chosen Family," *Psych Central* (blog), October 18, 2015: https://blogs.psychcentral.com/psychoanalysis-now/2015/10/friends-are-your-chosen-family.
9. Courtney Martin, "In Praise of Chosen Family," *On Being, with Krista Tippett*, last modified December 26, 2014: https://onbeing.org/blog/in-praise-of-chosen-family/.
10. Meredith Woerner, "Supergirl Cast Explains How the Series Affects the Lives of Its Audience, Especially Young Girls," *Los Angeles Times*, October 10, 2016: http://www.latimes.com/entertainment/herocomplex/la-et-hc-supergirl-20161010-snap-story.html.
11. *Supergirl*, "Pilot," season 1, episode 1, directed by Glen Winter, story by Greg Berlanti, Ali Adler, and Andrew Kreisberg, teleplay by Ali Adler, aired October 26, 2015, on CBS.
12. *Supergirl*, "Falling," season 1, episode 16, directed by Larry Teng, written by Robert Rovner and Jessica Queller, aired March 14, 2016, on CBS.
13. *Supergirl*, "Falling," season 1, episode 16.
14. *Supergirl*, "How Does She Do It?," season 1, episode 4, directed by Thor Freudenthal, written by Yahlin Chang and Ted Sullivan, aired November 23, 2015, on CBS.
15. *Supergirl*, "Better Angels," season 1, episode 20, directed by Larry Teng, written by Andrew Kreisberg and Ali Adler, teleplay by Robert Rovner and Jessica Queller, aired April 18, 2016, on CBS.
16. *Supergirl*, "How Does She Do It?," season 1, episode 4.
17. *Supergirl*, "Stronger Together," season 1, episode 2, directed by Glen Winter, story by Greg Berlanti and Andrew Kreisberg, teleplay by Andrew Kreisberg and Ali Adler, aired November 2, 2015, on CBS.
18. *Supergirl*, "Stronger Together," season 1, episode 2.
19. As for her uncle Non, Kara never even bothers to call him such—he is "Astra's husband," nothing more.
20. *Supergirl*, "Hostile Takeover," season 1, episode 8, directed by Karen Gaviola, written by Roberto Aguirre-Sacasa and Caitlin Parrish, aired December 14, 2015, on CBS.
21. *Supergirl*, "The Last Children of Krypton," season 2, episode 2, directed by Glen Winter, written by Robert Rovner and Caitlin Parrish, aired October 17, 2016, on The CW.
22. *Supergirl*, "For the Girl Who Has Everything," season 1, episode 13, directed by Dermott Downs, written by Ted Sullivan, Derek Simon, and Andrew Kreisberg, aired February 8, 2016, on CBS.
23. *Supergirl*, "The Last Children of Krypton," season 2, episode 2.
24. *Supergirl*, "Alex," season 2, episode 19, directed by Rob Greenlea, written by Eric Carrasco and Greg Baldwin, aired May 1, 2017, on The CW.
25. *Supergirl*, "The Last Children of Krypton," season 2, episode 2.
26. *Supergirl*, "For the Girl Who Has Everything," season 1, episode 13.
27. *Supergirl*, "For the Girl Who Has Everything," season 1, episode 13.
28. *Supergirl*, "For the Girl Who Has Everything," season 1, episode 13.
29. *Supergirl*, "For the Girl Who Has Everything," season 1, episode 13.
30. *Supergirl*, "For the Girl Who Has Everything," season 1, episode 13.
31. *Supergirl*, "Human for a Day," season 1, episode 7, directed by Larry Teng, written by Yahlin Chang and Ted Sullivan, aired December 7, 2015, on CBS.
32. *Supergirl*, "Pilot," season 1, episode 1.

33. *Supergirl*, "For the Girl Who Has Everything," season 1, episode 13.
34. *Supergirl*, "Solitude," season 1, episode 15, directed by Dermott Downs, written by Rachel Shukert, Anna Musky-Goldwyn, and James DeWille, aired February 29, 2016, on CBS.
35. *Supergirl*, "Nevertheless, She Persisted," season 2, episode 22, directed by Glen Winter, story by Andrew Kreisberg and Jessica Queller, teleplay by Robert Rovner and Caitlin Parrish, aired May 22, 2017, on The CW.
36. *Supergirl*, "Alex," season 2, episode 19.
37. *Supergirl*, "Exodus," season 2, episode 15, directed by Michael Allowitz, written by Paula Yoo and Eric Carrasco, aired March 6, 2017, on The CW.
38. Blake Neely, "'The X-Files' Star William B. Davis & 'Supergirl' & 'Arrow' Composer Blake Neely," *Pop Culture Tonight with Patrick Phillips*, Podcast audio, January 14, 2016: http://popculturetonight.com/william-b-davis-blake-neely/.
39. Blake Neely, Interview with Eric Johnston, *SDCC 2017 Discussion with Blake Neely*, Supergirl.TV, July 21, 2017.
40. Schoenewolf, "Friends Are Your Chosen Family."
41. Schoenewolf, "Friends Are Your Chosen Family."
42. *Supergirl*, "Childish Things," season 1, episode 10, directed by Jamie Babbit, written by Yahlin Chang, teleplay by Anna Musky-Goldwyn and James Dewille, aired January 18, 2016, on CBS.
43. *Supergirl*, "The Adventures of Supergirl," season 2, episode 1, directed by Glen Winter, story by Greg Berlanti and Andrew Kreisberg, teleplay by Andrew Kreisberg and Jessica Queller, aired October 10, 2016, on The CW.
44. *Supergirl*, "Luthors," season 2, episode 12, directed by Tawnia McKiernan, written by Robert Rovner and Cindy Lichtman, aired February 13, 2017, on The CW.
45. *Supergirl*, "Nevertheless, She Persisted," season 2, episode 22.
46. *Supergirl*, "The Darkest Place," season 2, episode 7, directed by Glen Winter, written by Robert Rovner and Paula Yoo, aired November 21, 2016, on The CW.
47. *Supergirl*, "The Martian Chronicles," season 2, episode 11, directed by David McWhirter, written by Gabriel Llanas and Anna Musky-Goldwyn, aired February 6, 2017, on The CW.
48. *Supergirl*, "For the Girl Who Has Everything," season 1, episode 13.
49. *Supergirl*, "Stronger Together," season 1, episode 2.
50. While the word "family" is invoked liberally throughout the series, it is not used carelessly, and, thus far, has not extended to romantic partners. Lucy Lane, Maggie Sawyer, Lyra, and Mon-El are all romantic interests of varying importance and duration in the main characters' lives, none of whom have earned the title of "family."
51. Carsten, "Kinship," 3.
52. Anna Muraco, "Intentional Families: Fictive Kin Ties Between Cross-Gender, Different Sexual Orientation Friends," *Journal of Marriage and Family* 68, 5 (2006): 1313.
53. "Chosen Family," *Queer Queries: Connecting and Complicating Queer Theory, Stories, and Understandings* (blog), https://complicatingqueertheory.wordpress.com/queer-families/chosen-family/.
54. Sydney Bucksbaum, "'Supergirl' Boss on 'Thoughtful' Coming Out Story and 'Bury Your Gays' Fears," *The Hollywood Reporter*, November 7, 2016, http://www.hollywoodreporter.com/live-feed/supergirl-gay-character-storyline-944838.
55. *Supergirl*, "Survivors," season 2, episode 4, directed by James Marshall and James Bamford, written by Paula Yoo and Eric Carrasco, aired October 31, 2016, on The CW.
56. *Supergirl*, "Crossfire," season 2, episode 5, directed by Glen Winter, written by Gabriel Llanas and Anna Musky-Goldwyn, aired November 7, 2016, on The CW.
57. *Supergirl*, "Changing," season 2, episode 6, directed by Larry Teng, story by Greg Berlanti, teleplay by Andrew Kreisberg and Caitlin Parrish, aired November 14, 2016, The CW.
58. Martin, "In Praise of Chosen Family."
59. *Supergirl*, "Changing," season 2, episode 6.
60. *Supergirl*, "Changing," season 2, episode 6.
61. *Supergirl*, "The Darkest Place," season 2, episode 7.

62. Ella Taylor, *Prime-Time Families: Television Culture in Postwar America* (Berkeley, CA: University of California Press, 1989), 3.
63. Jillian Sandell, "The Cultural Necessity of Queer Families," *Bad Subjects: Political Education for Everyday Life*, 12 (1994): 1, https://bad.eserver.org/issues/1994/12/sandell.
64. Muraco, "Intentional Families," 1313.
65. Taylor, *Prime-Time Families*, 3.
66. Sandell, "I'll Be There for You," 154.
67. Stephanie Coontz, *The Way We Never Were: American Families and the Nostalgia Trap* (New York: Basic Books, 1992).
68. In "Pilot," Kara tells us that her cousin wanted her to have "the same, safe, human-type childhood he did." However, the way the show presents this history, with Clark flying off so abruptly after leaving her with the Danvers, and his continued absence over the next fifteen years, makes one inclined to agree with Alex in her assessment of his actions as "abandonment."
69. *Supergirl*, "For the Girl Who Has Everything," season 1, episode 13.
70. *Supergirl*, "Manhunter," season 1, episode 17, directed by Chris Fisher, story by Derek Simon, teleplay by Cindy Lichtman and Rachel Shukert, aired March 21, 2016, on CBS.
71. *Supergirl*, "The Last Children of Krypton," season 2, episode 2.
72. *Supergirl*, "Blood Bonds," season 1, episode 9, directed by Steve Shill, written by Ted Sullivan and Derek Simon, aired January 4, 2016, on CBS.
73. Recent claims arising in the last few decades have asserted that the phrase was originally "The blood of the covenant is thicker than the waters of the womb," indicating an original meaning quite the opposite of the current understanding. However, there is no evidence to support this claim, and no substantiated references to such "original" phrase. In fact, all historical sources cite the twelfth-century German proverb *Blut ist dicker als Wasser* as the first known iteration of the phrase, aligning with its modern usage.
74. *Supergirl*, "Better Angels," season 1, episode 20.

Selected Bibliography

Bucksbaum, Sydney. "'Supergirl' Boss on 'Thoughtful' Coming Out Story and 'Bury Your Gays' Fears." *The Hollywood Reporter.* http://www.hollywoodreporter.com/live-feed/supergirl-gay-character-storyline-94488.
Carsten, Janet. Encyclopædia Britannica, s.v. "Kinship," *Encyclopædia Britannica*, Inc., 2012. https://www.britannica.com/topic/kinship/Kinship-terminology.
"Chosen Family." *Queer Queries: Connecting and Complicating Queer Theory, Stories, and Understandings* (blog). https://complicatingqueertheory.wordpress.com/queer-families/chosen-family/.
Coontz, Stephanie. *The Way We Never Were: American Families and the Nostalgia Trap*. New York: Basic Books, 1992.
Martin, Courtney. "In Praise of Chosen Family." *On Being, with Krista Tippett*. Last modified December 26, 2014. https://onbeing.org/blog/in-praise-of-chosen-family/.
Muraco, Anna. "Intentional Families: Fictive Kin Ties Between Cross-Gender, Different Sexual Orientation Friends." *Journal of Marriage and Family* 68 no. 5 (2006): 1313–1325. doi: 10.1111/j.1741-3737.2006.00330.x.
Neely, Blake. Interview with Eric Johnston. *SDCC 2017 Discussion with Blake Neely.* Supergirl.TV, July 21, 2017.
———. "'The X-Files' Star William B. Davis & 'Supergirl' & 'Arrow' Composer Blake Neely." *Pop Culture Tonight, with Patrick Phillips*. Podcast audio, January 14, 2016. http://popculturetonight.com/william-b-davis-blake-neely/.
Sandell, Jillian. "The Cultural Necessity of Queer Families." *Bad Subjects: Political Education for Everyday Life* 12 (1994). https://bad.eserver.org/issues/1994/12/sandell.
———. "I'll Be There for You: 'Friends' and the Fantasy of Alternative Families." *American Studies* 39, no. 2 (1998): 141–155. https://journals.ku.edu/amerstud/article/view/2714/2673.
Schoenewolf, Gerald. "Friends Are Your Chosen Family." *Psych Central* (blog). Last modified

October 18, 2015. https://blogs.psychcentral.com/psychoanalysis-now/2015/10/friends-are-your-chosen-family/.
Taylor, Ella. *Prime-Time Families: Television Culture in Postwar America.* Berkeley: University of California Press, 1989.
Woerner, Meredith. "Supergirl Cast Explains How the Series Affects the Lives of Its Audience, Especially Young Girls." *Los Angeles Times.* October 10, 2016. http://www.latimes.com/entertainment/herocomplex/la-et-hc-supergirl-20161010-snap-story.html.

About the Contributors

Johanna **Church**, Ph.D., serves as an associate professor of humanities at Johnson and Wales University and has a doctorate in literature from Drew University.

Donna J. **Cromeans** is a public relations specialist with experience in newspaper, radio, and television promotions and is the owner of Cromeans Consulting Associates, LLC. She is also a writer, playwright, and screenwriter and is a part of *Star Trek* history, having sold a story idea to *Star Trek: The Next Generation* for the episode "The Next Phase" with a writing partner.

Chelsea M. **Gibbs** is a film historian working as an educator and archivist. She has an MA in cinema studies from the University of Southern California with specializations in classic Hollywood and fan studies. Her publications include an essay on Greta Garbo for *Hollywood Heroines*.

Nicholas William **Moll**, Ph.D., is a freelance academic, educator and researcher. He is chiefly engaged by FGM Consultants, where he works with young adults. His research has focused on the franchising of the Western genre and popular culture as a whole. As a practicing educator, he is intensely interested in the gamification of the classroom as a means to interlink students' popular interests and their educational needs.

Sarah J. **Palm** is a Seattle-based writer and pop culture critic. Her previous publications include "'What Will We Leave Behind?': Claire Underwood's American Dream" for Blackwell's *House of Cards and Philosophy* anthology. She is writing about identity and morality in *Orphan Black* for a collection on ethics in science fiction.

Tim **Rayborn**, Ph.D. (University of Leeds, UK), has written three books for McFarland (*The Violent Pilgrimage*, 2013; *Against the Friars*, 2014; *A New English Music*, 2016), as well as three popular arts histories for Skyhorse Publishing (*Beethoven's Skull*, 2016; *Shakespeare's Ear*, 2017; *Weird Dance*, 2018). A musician, he has appeared on dozens of recordings and toured North America, Europe, and Australia. He has written articles for journals and magazines, in both the U.S. and UK.

Marcie Panutsos **Rovan**, Ph.D., serves as an assistant professor of English and director of first-year writing at Central Penn College. She has a Ph.D. in literature from

Duquesne University with a specialization in children's literature. Her publications include "The 'Broken Mirror,'" in *Impressions*, and "Dumbledore's Army" in *Lessons from Hogwarts*, a forthcoming collection on pedagogy and praxis in the *Harry Potter* series, for which she is coeditor.

Melissa **Wehler**, Ph.D., a professor of interdisciplinary studies, has published essays in a variety of edited collections where she discusses topics including the gothic, feminism, performance, and popular culture. She has published on Neil Gaiman's *Coraline*, PBS's *Downton Abbey*, Netflix's *Jessica Jones*, and Disney's *Maleficent*. She is the coeditor for the forthcoming *Lessons from Hogwarts*, about the representations of teaching in the *Harry Potter* series.

Courtney Lee **Weida** is an associate professor of art education in the College of Education & Health Sciences at Adelphi University in New York. As a practicing artist, her work includes both university teaching and community-based arts education. Her research emphasizes gender issues through intersecting topics of education, craft, and media literacy.

Jaime Chris **Weida**, Ph.D., is an assistant professor of English at BMCC-CUNY and earned her Ph.D. in literature from the CUNY Graduate Center. Her areas of interest include popular culture, modernism, pedagogy, gender and Queer theory, and the intersections between literature and science.

Justin **Wigard** is a Ph.D. candidate at Michigan State University, where he was awarded a University Distinguished Fellowship and develops pedagogical video games. He co-authored, with Ted Troxell at Central Michigan University, a chapter on the visual and cultural semiotics embedded in *Street Fighter II*. You can find more of his writing, work, and projects at wigardju.msu.domains.

Index

Adler, Ali 1, 14, 37, 66, 161
adoption 67–68, 73–74, 107–108, 122–123, 162–163, 169, 172, 184–186, 191–193, 199–202, 210
Agent Carter (series) 153, 180
Arias, Samantha *see* Reign
Arrow 21, 133; series 1, 96, 118, 128, 161

Batman 103–104, 108, 119–121, 132–134
Bechdel Test 6, 119, 136n6, 180
Benoist, Melissa 128, 133, 147, 162, 165–166, 168, 170–171, 174
Berlanti, Greg 1, 16, 19, 36, 105, 144, 161, 168
Black Mercy 108, 164, 204
Buffy the Vampire Slayer (series) 119, 152, 187, 193

Cadmus 48, 76, 97, 112, 167, 169, 172–173, 182–183, 189, 192–193
Carr, Snapper 95–98, 183
Carter, Lynda *see* Marsdin, Olivia
CatCo Worldwide Media 28–29, 31–32, 34–36, 39–40, 41n22, 46, 71, 78, 85, 89, 91–93, 95–98, 123, 134, 181–183, 185–186, 194–195
Clinton, Hillary 3, 187–189
costume 16, 49, 93–94, 122–123, 132–133, 182, 193–194, 210
Cyborg Superman 182, 193, 195, 110, 112–114; *see also* Henshaw, Hank

Danvers, Alex 1–2, 21, 45–46, 48–51, 59–60, 107, 135, 152–153; coming out 7, 58, 122–125, 128–131, 143–151; sister 68, 70–71, 94–95, 98, 161–174, 184–187, 191–192, 199–211
Danvers, Eliza 46, 123, 130–131, 164, 167, 184–186, 195, 207
Danvers, Jeremiah 12, 104, 108, 114, 122–123, 124, 164, 166–168, 172–173, 184, 186, 192–193, 202–203, 210
Daxam 46–48, 52, 57, 173–174, 195
DC Universe 1, 6, 37, 103–104, 112, 126
Department of Extranormal Operations (DEO) 1, 5, 15, 19, 46, 49, 51–52, 59, 70–71, 78, 85, 89, 90, 94–96, 104, 106–110, 123–124, 163–166, 169–174, 181–183, 185–186, 192–193, 195, 199, 201, 203–204, 208, 210
discrimination 6, 12, 48, 125–126

faux feminism 13–15, 17–18, 23
The Flash 1, 15, 21, 195; series 1, 48, 96, 105, 118, 200

GLAAD 2, 60n6, 135
Grant, Catherine "Cat" 1, 3, 5, 7, 11–17, 21–22, 27–40, 45, 67, 69, 71–72, 78, 85, 89, 91–98, 110–111, 123–124, 129, 134–135, 180–181, 183–185, 187–191, 193–195, 207
Grant, Katherine 36–37, 190
Green Lanterns 104, 107, 114; *see also* Red Lanterns
Guardian 53, 134, 184; *see also* Olsen, James "Jimmy"

Henshaw, Hank 51, 85, 90, 107, 111, 113, 124, 164, 166–167, 193, 195; *see also* Cyborg Superman; J'onzz, J'onn; Martian Manhunter
homophobia 134, 147, 149, 152, 154

In-Ze, Astra 1, 3, 21, 164–166, 182, 185–186, 192, 202, 204, 207, 211
Indigo 1, 134

Jessica Jones (series) 3, 118, 180, 200
J'onzz, J'onn 46–47, 51–52, 58–60, 85, 89–92, 94–96, 111, 124–129, 133, 165, 167, 172–173, 184, 186- 187, 192–193, 195, 202–204, 207–208; *see also* Henshaw, Hank; Martian Manhunter

Kal-El *see* Superman
Kant, Immanuel 55
Kent, Clark *see* Superman
Kreisberg, Andrew 1, 36–37, 144, 161, 169, 174

Index

Krypton 7, 11, 47–48, 53, 68, 76, 89, 95–96, 102–106, 108–110, 113–114
kryptonite 16, 106, 109, 167, 182; see also Red Kryptonite

L-Corp 65, 67, 73–74, 77, 191
Lane, Lois 73, 120, 134, 187–188, 192, 195
Lane, Lucy 1, 2, 15, 32, 45, 167, 190, 192
Leigh, Chyler 61n30, 143, 152, 162, 164, 169–171, 174
Lima, Floriana 61n30, 62n39, 143, 153–154, 170
Livewire 1, 21, 29, 32, 41n34, 42n38, 134, 189
Lord, Maxwell 31–34, 45, 112, 123, 164, 166, 183, 188, 190, 193
Lorde, Audre 86–87, 90–92, 94, 96
Luthor, Lena 1–2, 5, 7, 21, 45, 47, 65–69, 72–78, 79n35, 98, 107, 113, 153–154, 182, 184, 189, 191–192, 195, 207
Luthor, Lex 65, 67, 73–75, 103, 182, 191
Luthor, Lillian 21, 45, 47, 73, 75, 77, 182–183, 191, 206
Luthor, Lionel 73, 191–192
Luthor Corp see L-Corp

Marsden, Olivia 3, 49, 111, 134–135, 188, 190
Martian Manhunter 95, 102–104, 107, 109, 111, 114, 124, 126, 192; see also Henshaw, Hank; J'onnz, J'onn
Martians 46, 51–52, 58, 85, 95, 107, 112, 124–127, 172, 192, 195, 207
millennial 2, 11, 37–39, 43n67, 43n72, 67, 70–71, 150
Mon-El 21, 45–48, 57–58, 60n4, 61n18, 61n22, 76–77, 129, 153, 172, 186, 191–193, 195, 202, 207, 209
M'orzz, M'gann 1, 45, 46, 51–52, 125, 127, 129, 207
Myriad 35, 167, 184

Non 108, 133–134, 167, 207, 211

Olsen, James "Jimmy" 15, 21, 29, 46, 53, 59, 71, 89, 95–96, 98, 103, 108, 111, 129, 134, 153, 164, 183, 185, 188, 190, 192, 202–204, 208; see also Guardian

Queen Rhea 48, 77, 190–192

race 125–127, 207
Red Kryptonite 34, 37, 40n5, 41n23, 68, 93, 107, 112, 166, 190, 201; see also kryptonite
Red Lanterns 104, 107–111; see also Green Lanterns
refugee 47, 51, 181, 188
Reign 1, 3, 106
Riverdale (series) 142, 155n7
Roulette 68, 187

Sawyer, Maggie 1, 6–7, 21, 45–52, 58, 60n4, 110, 128–131, 135, 143–148, 150–155, 170–174, 173, 192, 207–209
Schott, Winn 15, 41n22, 46–47, 52–53, 58–60, 70, 74, 89, 123, 129, 134, 182, 185–186, 192, 202–203, 207–208
sexism 2, 6, 12, 16, 20, 22, 25n65, 37–38, 134, 143, 153, 189
Silver Banshee 1, 21, 46, 93–95, 112
Sinclair, Vernonia see Roulette
Smythe, Siobhan see Silver Banshee
stereotype 12, 18, 21, 90, 107, 114, 153
Strayd, Lyra 46–47, 52–53, 58, 182
Superman 31, 39, 47, 49, 91, 102, 126, 161, 164, 167, 169, 174, 193–195, 203–204; comparisons 7, 12, 15–17, 20–21, 27–28, 37, 65, 69–74, 103–114, 119–121, 132–135, 180–189

toxic masculinity 2, 87, 191–192
Toyman see Tycho, Simon
Trans* 119, 123–127, 129
Trump, Donald 3, 8n7, 22, 124, 155n17
Tumblr 140–146, 151, 153–154
Tycho, Simon 41n22, 106, 110, 192

Warren, Elizabeth 3, 8n7, 135, 188
Wayne, Bruce see Batman
Willis, Leslie see Livewire
Wonder Woman 8n10, 88, 119–120, 132–133; in media 4, 23, 121, 135–136, 188

Xena: Warrior Princess (series) 119, 154

Zor-El, Alura 184–185, 193, 195, 203–205, 211

www.ingramcontent.com/pod-product-compliance
Lightning Source LLC
Chambersburg PA
CBHW032041300426
44117CB00009B/1143